Life

As A

Passenger

How Driverless Cars Will Change the World

by David Kerrigan

Preface

In the Fall of 2015 while on a business trip to California, I persuaded my colleagues to take a slight detour with me to Mountain View. We were returning south to Menlo Park after meetings in San Francisco and continuing past our exit on Highway 101 didn't immediately make any sense to them. "Just drive around", I said; "I want to try to see something very important that you can only see in Mountain View", knowing I probably sounded a little crazy.

Mountain View is a small town of about 75,000 thousand people that is home to many of Silicon Valley's most famous companies, but I was there to see its most famous non-human inhabitants. After my increasingly exasperated colleagues drove around seemingly aimlessly for about 15 minutes, I suddenly spotted what I had come to see - a Lexus SUV with a spinning dome on the roof. A car that could drive itself. There, on the public streets, mixing with "normal" traffic. And by normal, I mean cars driven by humans.

It turns out there's an easy way to spot tourists in Mountain View - they are the ones who point at the Google Self Driving Cars being tested there and reach for their phones to take a photo. The locals are so used to these automated marvels that they barely look at them anymore than they would a "regular" human-driven SUV. At some point in the distant future, it may be the other way around - people might take photos of humans crazy enough to be driving a car themselves, if that's even still legal on public roads. Should we return to Mountain View in just 10 years' time, the definition of what's normal may have changed dramatically.

As we contemplated the self-driving car in front of us, I urged my colleagues to think what this could eventually mean. For safety, for pollution, for time, for employment, for shopping, for where people live. The implications are so profound, I decided to write a book to explore the pros and cons of this powerful emerging technology, perhaps the technology with the biggest potential to change society in centuries. How we react will determine how ready we are for the next wave of revolutionary technologies.

Acknowledgements

My thanks firstly to my family, and my friends who bought my first book, encouraged me to finish this one, and put up with me talking incessantly about robocars for the last few years....especially Aideen, David, Caroline, Lorraine, Simon, Kim, Johanna, Susan, Sylvia, Fergal, Gregg, Sinead, Gabrielle B., Adam, Ian, Abhi, Andy, Peter, Trish and Rob. Special thanks to Ken Johnstone for the cover design.

Dedication

This book is dedicated to all those who have lost their lives in, and those whose lives have been changed by, car crashes.

Also by The Author

Your Phone Can Save Your Life (2015)

Web Site

Please visit the web site for this book at
http://www.lifeasapassenger.com for color versions of all illustrations/photos, to contact the author and for quick links to reference materials.

Copyright

Contents

Glossary of Terms

AAA - American Automobile Association
ABS - Anti-Lock Brakes
AEB - Automatic Emergency Braking
AI - Artificial Intelligence
AV - Autonomous Vehicle
BJS - Bureau of Justice Statistics
BLS - Bureau of Labor Statistics
BMJ - British Medical Journal
CDC – Centers for Disease Control & Prevention
DARPA - Defense Advanced Research Projects Agency
DMV - Department of Motor Vehicles
DOT - Department of Transportation
EV - Electric Vehicle
FHWA - Federal Highway Administration
IIHS - Institute for Highway Safety
ICE - Internal Combustion Engine
LDW - Lane Departure Warning
MTBF - Mean Time between Failures
NHTSA - National Highway Traffic Safety Administration
UN - United Nations
WHO - World Health Organisation
V2V - Vehicle to Vehicle
VMT - Vehicle Miles Travelled
VR - Virtual Reality

Chapter 1: Introduction

"Difficult to See. Always in motion is the future"

Yoda

If someone were to tell you of an invention that could save you thousands of dollars per year, reduce taxes for everyone, give you more space in your home and your neighborhood, reduce air pollution, reduce noise pollution, negate the concept of drink-driving, allow you to sleep or work while you commute, enable the young, elderly and disabled to get around, save you hours on commuting <u>and</u> eliminate about 90% of the millions of road deaths and injuries each year, would it seem a bit too good to be true?

The positive news is that it's not necessarily too good to be true. It's very real and it's firmly within our grasp over the coming years. The catch? It comes with a steep price, and not a direct financial one. It disturbs many facets of life we've come to take for granted, challenges many powerful vested interests, and may cause significant unemployment or, at the very least, upheaval on a scale akin to the agricultural and industrial revolutions. For some, this price may seem too high. For others, this may seem like one of the greatest advancements in our civilisation for centuries.

The technologies required to create fully autonomous, self-driving cars and trucks are coming soon. Though daunting barriers to widespread availability remain, it's already clear from a quick look at the test vehicles competently navigating themselves around the streets of Mountain View and several other test locations around the world that it's only a matter of time until they are ready to take over our streets and highways. Regardless of whether it's 5, 10 or even 20 or more years away from daily reality, we can be confident it's no longer purely the stuff of science fiction.

These vehicles will be able to undertake journeys with no human control, signifying the first time in history that we have the chance to cede control to machines on the open road regardless of distance or destination. This is not another one of the over-hyped Silicon Valley solutions to first world problems like having your laundry delivered to you in less than an hour; this is a very definite (and many might say overdue) example of technology that will have a measurable, positive impact on improving human existence far greater than the plethora of apps vying to deliver luxury goods ever more rapidly.

Although it represents one of the most impressive advances in the history of technology, and harnesses decades of technological advances across multiple areas of sensors, processors and algorithms, the primary purpose of driverless cars is not to prove how clever technology is; it's to reduce death and injury, as well as to reduce pollution and free up time and money. This is actually a profound, challenging technology that deserves the buzzwords like transformative and disruptive that are used with such scant restraint by commentators and journalists when typically reviewing incremental advances. The emergence of driverless cars deserves massive amounts of genuine debate, analysis and planning. This book is intended to help that debate, whether you are new to the topic or already have a view on it.

Many of the people I've spoken to about driverless cars weren't aware of how close they are to reality and were frankly incredulous. To convince some people, I had to produce my photos of self-driving cars on the streets of Mountain View. Those who have heard of driverless cars and their impending arrival, are frequently quick to dismiss them as impractical, "they'll never work" or "I love driving". And those who say they will never work may well be correct; at least that's quite likely the outcome if we continue to apply today's thinking to what is tomorrow's technology. But to do so focuses on the challenges and the negatives only to overlook the potential benefits on offer without really considering the significance of what will happen if driverless cars can and do work as promised. It also represents a narrow way of thinking, applying current paradigms to what is a topic better thought of without such constraints. Applying 100-year-old thinking to some of the most technologically advanced machines yet created is hardly likely to yield an optimal result. But whichever side of the fence you're on, there are many pros and cons that merit careful consideration.

Outline

Evaluating the potential impact of driverless cars is not as simple a topic as it might first seem where you can quickly take a binary position on their benefits or otherwise. Though many initial simplistic responses may be along the lines of "it'll never work", "it'll save lives" or "I don't want a robot driving me", it actually is a much more complex proposition and crosses disciplinary divides including economics, geography, urban planning, technology and even philosophy. As such though, it is a fascinating journey that raises questions fundamental to the very evolution of our society. It's hard to find any area of daily life that escapes the scope of this seemingly innocuous new arrival. To enable an accessible and comprehensive look at the topic, I've chosen to structure this book as follows:

In Chapter 2, I'll begin our journey into the world of driverless cars by taking a step back and looking at how the car has come to dominate so much of modern society and how significant any change to that position would prove. It's worth examining the origins of this dominance of the automobile, and reminding ourselves of the deep impact it has had on our lives over the last century. This will help frame the debate about the revolution we now face. Whether you own a car or not, it has, more than any other factor, dictated the evolution of our modern society. Now, after some 100 years where little has challenged its dominance, technology is threatening to rapidly change the face of driving as we know it, and alongside that offering life-changing alterations to our lifestyles. This section will chart the rise of the car, highlight a few key moments in its history and summarize an acknowledgement of its impact. It'll examine the relationship we have with cars, as it has evolved over the last 100 years but primarily to serve as a preface, a context and a reminder; an empirical foundation for the discussions ahead.

Next, Chapter 3 examines the technologies we're talking about, to give a basic understanding of what makes driverless cars possible, along with a look at the mixture of firms, old and new, leading their development. Given the importance of this topic to society, it's worth considering the players determining the agenda so this section examines both the new entrants and the incumbents in the transportation space. That will help frame the discussion about their strengths and weaknesses, what areas remain to be developed and the steps along the way to a fully autonomous future for vehicles.

For Chapter 4, I've extracted one specific topic to review in more detail and that's the topic of safety. I'm not alone in focusing on this area. The World Health Organisation has declared a whole *decade* of global action to address the issue of the vast numbers of people killed and injured each year in car crashes.

Having discussed safety, Chapters 5 and 6 move on to look at the myriad sectors facing unprecedented changes, both good and bad. These two chapters will look at the changes to be encountered and the challenges to making driverless cars a reality across technical, economic, social, philosophical and legal paradigms. After reviewing the progress to date and the human context, Chapter 7 looks at the unique regulatory challenges posed by this technology, along with the inevitable public perception debates and how we might come to trust these machines. "Far-reaching" doesn't do the scope of change justice - but I'll review both the obvious and less obvious questions posed. This technology unleashes existential challenges to market leaders across numerous industries. While its impacts include those on government (local and federal), car makers, insurers, police forces, health services and many others, driverless cars may ultimately stand or fall based on public acceptance.

Finally, in Chapter 8, I'll wrap up the discussion and hopefully provide you with a framework of final thoughts to decide where you stand on driverless cars. For now, I ask that you put aside initial reactions for or against driverless cars and consider the pros and cons with an open mind, giving due consideration to the scale of changes - social, political and economic - that lie ahead.

Trillions of Dollars and Millions of Lives are at Stake

Cars are a big deal. In their May 2013 report, "Disruptive Technologies: Advances that will transform life, business and the global economy",[1] McKinsey estimates total worldwide automotive industry revenues at $4 trillion. The combined 2013 annual revenues of the 10 largest international car manufacturers was $1.3 trillion and collectively they provided 2.3 million jobs. Let's be clear from the start: a trillion dollars is a huge amount of money, too much for most people to even imagine, let alone fully comprehend. I'm not using the term lightly - it really is a staggering amount of money and I want to be as clear as I can about the significance and scale of the disruption we're discussing. One trillion is a million times a million. If you spent a million dollars every day, it would take 2,730 years to spend just one trillion dollars. Cars, and all that surround them, are worth several trillions to the world economy.

---

[1]

http://www.mckinsey.com/~/media/McKinsey/Business%20Functions/ McKinsey%20Digital/Our%20Insights/Disruptive%20technologies/MGI _Disruptive_technologies_Full_report_May2013.ashx

The stakes involved in this discussion run to many trillions. Devastating wars have been fought over amounts a fraction of what is in play here. Individual motorised transport is one of the pillars of modern economics and the historically unprecedented economic growth of the last century is no mere coincidence with the concomitant rise of the car - the two are materially intertwined. The scope of the changes and economic upheaval that driverless vehicles could unleash over the coming decades is unparalleled in modern times.

According to a comprehensive report from Morgan Stanley,[2] autonomous vehicles can contribute $1.3 trillion annually to the U.S. economy in a base case scenario.

Autonomous cars will generate huge economic benefits U.S. market, non-exhaustive

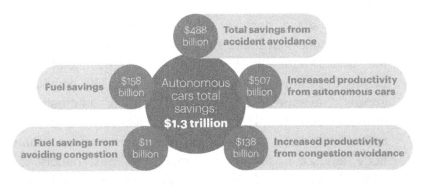

Source: Predictions for U.S. market, Morgan Stanley research, 2014

Anything which has that much potential influence is surely worthy of some of our time to consider. But although such huge financial impact is worthy of a book in its own right, it is only part of the scale of what we are talking about - the social impact is at least equally as massive. Driverless cars are the first of a coming series of seismic changes that our species faces as we reach a point in evolution where technology challenges

[2] http://www.morganstanley.com/articles/autonomous-cars-the-future-is-now

fundamental social norms in ways that may at first seem deeply threatening to our established and familiar way of life.

Driverless cars have the potential to fundamentally alter transportation systems by averting deadly crashes, providing unprecedented mobility to the elderly and disabled, increasing road capacity, saving fuel, and lowering polluting emissions. Complementary trends in shared rides may lead us from vehicles as primarily a personally owned product to an on-demand service. Infrastructure investments, travel choices, parking needs, land use patterns, trucking and other activities may be massively affected. Additionally, the design of cars may be transformed: former "drivers" may soon be working on their laptops, eating meals, reading books, watching movies, and/or calling friends from the comfort of a car– safely.

Yet, the imminent proliferation of autonomous vehicles is far from guaranteed. High costs of some of the technologies required will, initially at least, hamper large-scale production and mass consumer availability. Complex questions remain relating to legal liability, privacy, licensing, security, and insurance regulation. That's before you talk about the loss of revenues from traffic offenses and other motor-related taxes that form a crucial income for many cities. And then there's the question of consumer acceptance, which is unlikely to be straightforward.

These changes will save money for some. But one person's savings are another's lost income. People will likely need Netflix (the world's largest streaming video subscription service) more than they'll need insurance providers, or Minecraft (the world's most popular computer game) more than they'll need car repairs. Historically, technological advances have largely offset the job losses they've displaced in traditional industries with new opportunities. The change from artisanal to mass production brought a precipitous decline in the need for skilled workers, but at the same time gave rise to the importance of highly trained engineers and technicians, who would take growing responsibility for planning and managing the production process. This may not be the case for self-driving cars, particularly as their emergence is not an isolated technology - in fact driverless cars are an example or an embodiment of another big-picture trend - the emergence of machines that are intelligent enough to replace not just manual labour but also complex and variable tasks that were previously reserved for more skilled humans.

The Hard Wave

The history of technological developments has seen an increasing number of tasks becoming automated; human inputs being reduced as processes become mechanised or computerised. So far, this has largely related to repetitive tasks in controlled environments that have little variation; e.g. robots on assembly lines in factories, or trains on closed circuits. To date, implementing these technologies as fast as possible when they become available has been the default and obvious response due to the clear benefits they offered in terms of productivity, reliability and/or cost reduction. Thus far, most technology deployment decisions have actually been fairly easy. Replacing back-breaking work in fields with mechanisation and intensification of agriculture may have destroyed jobs but it was clearly more efficient, and arguably required in order to meet growing demand. Over time we managed to create new jobs to replace those lost in agriculture. Despite the costs involved, most people don't view motoring today as intolerably inefficient, and they've built their lives and settled their families frequently based on the availability of personal transport.

That easy era is now coming to an end as technology encroaches into new realms. We're now entering a new era of technology. The coming decades will see repeated examples posing one of the most fundamental questions facing the developed world...how much of our lives and traditional activities do we delegate to technology as automation readies a move from a supporting role to a leading role. Technology has so far been quite consumer friendly, innocuously growing into our lives in a gradual way. But the scope of change now ahead requires awareness and management - we need both new public policy decisions and new personal decisions as the range and capabilities of technology fundamentally shift, changing the equilibrium of society. Technology is approaching (or may already have reached) a point where laissez-faire and "hope it works out" is no longer enough. We now have, or are about to have, capabilities that challenge fundamental assumptions across society not just in distinct industrial silos. Make no mistake, it's going to be hard for many people.

Driverless cars are one example of this accelerating torrent of disruptions that will shape our future - what I call the "Hard Wave". These are the advances that present challenges we are scarcely equipped to deal with. The era of easy adoption is over, and we now should prepare for an era of adaption; ready to adapt to new realities and ready to reconsider previously immutable assumptions. And while these approaching changes are driven by technology, it's not really about technology - but more about how society chooses to harness technology; who makes those decisions and for whose benefit.

What's it to You?

Words like revolutionary, disruptive and game-changing are thrown around all too frequently as new technologies emerge. And while the glut of new technologies in recent decades undoubtedly includes many interesting ones, in general most are evolutionary or incremental rather than being truly epoch-level. It's important when examining this level of change to reset your expectations and to focus on the big picture - thinking with a timeframe measured in decades rather than the more immediate, more certain challenges we're used to, that make for easier understanding, analysis and commentary.

Change on this scale is bound to be highly complex and contentious, even if it doesn't seem massively urgent. Such has been the pace of change in recent decades that we can be slightly blasé about it all - putting us at risk of missing a truly significant change. When you're in the midst of daily life, this may all seem abstract, hypothetical or irrelevant (for now at least). But if you just dropped your kids to school driving your own car and then continued to your workplace in your car before parking it for the rest of the day, remember that according to the World Economic Forum in 2016,[3] some 65 percent of those kids will leave school to a job that doesn't yet exist. But that may not be the whole story: Instead of facing their classmates or off shoring facilities for jobs, they may find a robot or an algorithm where they expected to sit.

So why should you care about changes in transportation? Transportation forms the basis of much of our civilization. Even if you don't care about cars—even if you don't own a car, even if you never summon an Uber or Taxi from your phone or you never step into an autonomous vehicle—these changes are going to transform your life. Because transportation doesn't just impact how we individually get from place to place. It shapes what those places look like, and the lives of the people who live there. Busy people living busy lives don't tend to think much about big issues they perceive to be far in the future. But the kinds of issues we face in the coming decades really need thought and debate on a wider societal level, or we may end up with a result we don't much like. Is technology creating the kind of future you want? Have you thought about it? Technology is almost always double-edged. The day stone tools were invented we could chop wood but axe murder also became possible. There is often a sense that as an individual you have no influence on the future of these technologies and elated policies. But of course, if everyone thinks that way it very quickly becomes a self-fulfilling prophecy. There is still time to influence

---

[3] http://www3.weforum.org/docs/Media/WEF_FutureofJobs.pdf

the shape of future transportation, but as discussed in Chapter 7, regulations are being put in place right now that will have a long-term impact.

In a world of sound bites, quick wins and instant gratification, we rarely stop to consider complex issues in any depth. The purpose of this book is to examine the potential impact of the development of driverless cars in more depth than is possible in a blog or article. Although at first glance, driverless cars may seem like just another cool technology, they may in fact be one of the most profound change-enablers in human history, with far-reaching implications for employment, mobility, the built environment and beyond. Much of the commentary on this topic to date has been quite extreme - from advocates saying it's nearly ready to doubters claiming it's more like 30 years away to opponents saying it'll never work or shouldn't be allowed. There are many players in this drama - technology companies, auto companies, regulators, professional drivers and ordinary citizens. I believe it's important to look rationally at the challenges and opportunities facing us - there aren't always simple facts to base our decisions on yet, with much speculation or extrapolation. But if we don't at least start to think about it, start to ask questions and consider consequences, we risk either delaying benefits or arriving unaware at undesirable outcomes.

Modern politics has created a culture of short termism that's ill-equipped to tackle big issues proactively. And on an international scale, challenges like peace, health, poverty and global warming may seem of more immediate import than robot cars but I think it's important to extend the driverless cars debate to a wide audience. The issues in this book, though largely specific to driverless cars, raise larger questions about how we as a society deal with massive change. Who are the leaders - the politicians, the technologists, the regulators? Who is involved or even aware? Who sets the agenda? Can regulators keep up? Who are the lobby groups and how transparent is lobbying activity? Will there be a disconnect between consumers and governments? There is a very real risk that governments will hesitate to push for autonomous cars, thus saving lives and money, in the face of opposition from car, oil and other traditional industries. Governments are also likely to be wary of the potential for unpopular job losses in traditional car-related sectors. This is not the time or the place for knee-jerk reactions that driverless cars are the solution to all transport and urban problems or that driving is an inalienable right. This book aims to suggest a more thoughtful assessment of the issues that will shape the world for us and for our children.

Back to the Future

"The only constant is change"

Heraclitus

Just because things have been a certain way for 100 years doesn't mean they should stay that way; nor does the possibility of a new approach mean it's necessarily the correct and immediate way forward. There probably needs to be a balance between the opposite views of "always been this way" vs techno-utopianism.

History tells us that all large transportation and communication innovations—whether cars, carriages, canals or cables—have involved great uncertainty. Innovation invites speculation. But our individual ability to influence its direction is interesting. The only certainty is that these technologies will continue to develop - how we choose to use them, and when, is the only open question. The automation genie cannot be put back in the bottle but some of its course can still be controlled and regulated.

For those who are skeptical, who feel that cars cannot be replaced and that things never turn out as hoped or hyped, the one thing I can guarantee is: change happens, even if it takes longer or surprising detours along the way. The mighty can and do fall. 20 years ago, there was no Facebook, or Amazon, and Apple was nearly bankrupt. Now they are three of the most valuable companies in the world. It's not easy to look at a 20-30 year timeframe but so much can change in that kind of time - smartphones and Google didn't exist either, just 20 years ago. It's sobering to look at this graph showing the virtual disappearance of "big oil" from the top 5 companies in just the last 10 years as an example of unthinkable change that happened with little fanfare:

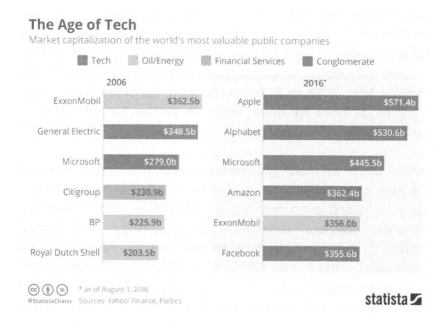

The Age of Tech

Market capitalization of the world's most valuable public companies

■ Tech   ■ Oil/Energy   ■ Financial Services   ■ Conglomerate

2006		2016*	
ExxonMobil	$362.5b	Apple	$571.4b
General Electric	$348.5b	Alphabet	$530.6b
Microsoft	$279.0b	Microsoft	$445.5b
Citigroup	$230.9b	Amazon	$362.4b
BP	$225.9b	ExxonMobil	$356.0b
Royal Dutch Shell	$203.5b	Facebook	$355.6b

* as of August 1, 2016
@StatistaCharts   Sources: Yahoo! Finance, Forbes

statista

How Soon?

Depending on who you listen to, a driverless world has already started, could start to happen in as soon as 3 to 4 years (2020/21), or be as far out as 20 or 30 years away, if ever. Generally, when discussing emerging technologies, we tend to overestimate the effect of a technology in the short run and underestimate the effect in the long run - this is known as

Amara's Law.[4] For example, just 10 years ago, an assertion that 2 billion people would have a computer in their pocket with more power than a supercomputer and access to millions of apps would have seemed ludicrous. But it's only taken 10 years for the smartphone to reach this prevalence and now it seems perfectly normal.

Driverless technology is not an area where there is a clear consensus on the way forward or the path to it. A partner at leading Silicon Valley investment house Andreessen Horowitz, Ben Evans, recently noted the "Huge variance in informed opinion as to how long fully-autonomous driving will take and what it needs."[5] Each of the major car companies and new entrant technology companies have announced expected dates ranging from 2018 to 2025 and beyond - a pretty wide target. Chapter 3 looks in more detail in at the current state of technology for driverless cars.

While there is much optimism around the future potential benefits of self-driving cars, there's a mixture of uncertainty, pessimism and even fear around the timing of the transition. Sceptics compare driverless car technology with Zeno's dichotomy paradox:[6] every leap will take us halfway to our destination without ever reaching it. Some pundits believe we are nearing the infamous "Peak of Inflated Expectations" in the Gartner Hype Cycle (see below), and a long let-down is ahead before the technology eventually meets our expectations. I believe we are entering a foreseeable phase of negativity for driverless cars as people look beyond their initial allure, identify the problems and then set about proposing and implementing solutions for these problems, both real and imagined.

---

[4] https://en.wikipedia.org/wiki/Roy_Amara
[5] https://twitter.com/BenedictEvans/status/763209924302090240
[6] https://en.wikipedia.org/wiki/Zeno%27s_paradoxes#Dichotomy_paradox

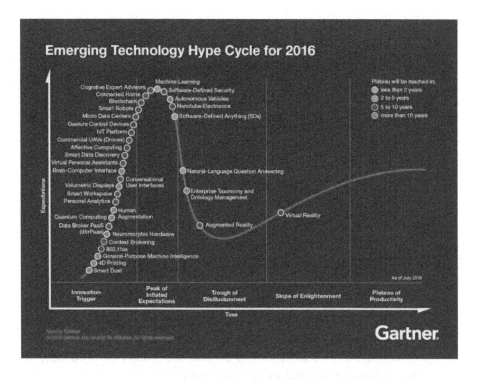

While there are certainly technology, infrastructure, political and social challenges to face, the sheer weight of investment in the space is overwhelming. Many of the brightest minds in academia and industry, backed by almost unlimited quantities of capital, are pushing autonomous vehicle technologies forward with great haste, but against an uncertain timetable. Traditional automakers GM and Ford have partnered with technology companies investing billions in partnerships and acquisitions with an eye toward an autonomous future. The US government has gotten involved, with the Obama administration earmarking $4 billion to prepare the way for autonomous cars, though it remains to be seen if the Trump administration will have a less supportive view.

It's hard to assess driverless cars in light of the uncertainty, but one thing that is certain is that basing our opinion on driverless cars purely in terms of the compromises we've lived with for a century makes no sense, however ingrained it may be as our referential framework. As Evans[7] comments, *"there is a point in the cycle of all technologies where pointing out where it will inevitably lead is a route to certain ridicule. For close to a decade, suggesting that essentially everyone on earth would have a mobile was lunacy. Now, with 5 billion phones, it's boring and obvious. Plotting out what effects fully autonomous cars would have, one should assume they'll change things as much as *cars* changed things. The really big innovations don't get x% of y, they change what y is. You couldn't (wouldn't/shouldn't) model cars from horses, jets from liners, PCs from typewriters, mobiles from landlines, ride-share from cabs or AV from cars."*

We must challenge ourselves to think bigger if we genuinely want to see progress from the current situation regarding transportation and all its costs to society. As we will discuss in upcoming Chapters, there remains much to be done to address technological and social challenges. For those millions of people that will die in the intervening period, we surely have a duty to make it happen as fast as is practicable.

It is also worth pointing out that these driverless cars do not operate in isolation and the parallel development of many other technologies will also shape our future landscape - for example, many commentators believe that 3D printing may see the term "factory" redefined and lead to mass layoffs in manufacturing. There are also many more anticipated developments in communications, materials sciences and energy production, not to mention healthcare and even other forms of transport up to and including the mythical flying car (which has recently started to seem less mythical with demonstrations from companies such as Lilium[8] and Uber,[9] among others).

---

[7] https://twitter.com/BenedictEvans/status/771115479393906688

[8] https://lilium.com/

[9] https://www.uber.com/info/elevate/

Predicting Perils

"Your intuition about things you don't know much about isn't very good. I don't think we're doing a good job as a society deciding what things are really important to do."

Larry Page, co-founder Google

Nothing in society beyond the most trivial can be precisely predicted. Technology is at a point of sophistication where its impacts on society are significantly beyond isolated improvements or even predictable improvements. On the other hand, it is not the case that it is hopeless to try to anticipate things to come, or that anyone's guess is as good as anyone else's. Intuition, research and debate can help to identify possible and likely futures. Even though the future cannot be predicted (and certainly no prediction of the future, no matter how eminent the source, should be uncritically "believed"), there are theories and methods that futurists have developed, tested, and applied in recent years which have proven useful. Some time spent carefully considering the future logically will enable individuals and groups to anticipate the possible futures more usefully, and to shape it appreciably more to their own preferences. "Preferred futures" can and should be envisioned, invented, implemented, continuously evaluated, revised, and re-envisioned. It is also important to remember that any radical idea about the future may appear at first to be ridiculous, but it's important not to let that initial response become our definite opinion. Because new technologies permit new behaviors and values, challenging old beliefs and values which are based on prior technologies, much that will be characteristic of the future is initially novel and challenging. It typically seems at first impossible, stupid, "science fiction", or ridiculous. And then it becomes familiar and, eventually, "normal."

A Complex Future

Regardless of how exactly and when driverless cars impact the world, we know for sure we won't continue to exist for long in the "normality" we know today. Lots of parallel technological developments such as Augmented and Virtual Reality, voice interfaces, smart homes, robots and intelligent assistants will compete for our time and our money, offering to save us both. Many of the "low hanging fruit" technological wins have been taken. As I've said, the next ones will be harder, competing to displace deeply entrenched behaviours. The future may involve bigger wins and losses, making planning harder as interests fight to protect or grab huge wealth. Two of the biggest dangers of trying to imagine the future are 1. assuming linear progression and 2. assuming too much too soon or too little too long. And of course, your own starting point and prejudices are crucial to the future you will imagine: attitudes to the future vary. As Douglas Adams said, *"anything invented after you're 35 is against the natural order of things, anything invented between when you're 15 and 35 is new and exciting and anything that is in the world when you're born is just a natural part of the way the world works"*.[10]

In researching the topic, I found a perhaps predictable amount of debate and disagreement among experts and commentators. Regardless of the conclusions, for me the important thing is to think about and create the future we want, mindful of the consequences, compromises and end-game along the way. It's so important we don't rush to judgement, good or bad but afford it some learning, exploration, thought and debate. How we approach this discussion is important. Assessing it only against what we know in a world built on current capabilities, we may miss something important. Using existing thinking to assess new developments is notoriously fallible. The IBM President in 1943 suggested a worldwide market of 5 computers, and even the

---

[10] The Salmon of Doubt, Douglas Adams, 2002

bicycle faced resistance when it was invented as a "dangerous contraption".

My previous book, Your Phone Can Save Your Life, explored the emerging mobile-related technologies that could help you lead a healthier and possibly even longer life. One of its key conclusions was that technology increasingly presents us with the capability to take more responsibility for our own well-being but poses a disruptive influence on many existing norms. Similarly, this current volume tackles the question of what sort of future you may find yourself living in thanks to technology. Once again, technology is posing questions that challenge both society and individuals to make difficult decisions that weigh potentially very sizeable benefits against lifestyle and political/socio-economic upheaval. I for one believe it would be a shame not to try to find the best way to harness the potential of driverless cars, but to miss out on its benefits through ignorance would be a tragedy, just as failing to understand and plan for the negative consequences would be too.

When the Tools Take Over

"If you asked people in 1989 what they needed to make their life better, it was unlikely that they would have said a decentralized network of information nodes that are linked using hypertext."

Farmer & Farmer on emergence of the Internet[11]

Although varyingly referred to as Autonomous, Driverless or Self Driving cars, automated cars are essentially what have been referred to more commonly as robots - machines that are capable of carrying out a complex series of actions automatically. These cars may become the first major intrusion of robots into our daily lives and into the consciousness of the public. For people who haven't worked in factories, driverless

---

[11] http://farmerandfarmer.org/mastery/builder.html

cars will likely be their first encounter with robots on their own patch. That will change our world view and the way we think about ourselves and even what is our role. This isn't intended as a doomsday scenario of robots overthrowing humans, but a serious look at the decisions we face.

Historically, humans have a habit of resisting change. From coffee to refrigeration to genetically modified food, our past is littered with innovations that sparked resistance before becoming accepted fixtures in everyday life. Calestous Juma, a professor in Harvard University's Kennedy School of Government, explores this phenomenon in his book, "Innovation and Its Enemies: Why People Resist New Technologies."[12] Among Juma's assertions is that people don't fear innovation simply because the technology is new, but because innovation often means losing a piece of their identity or lifestyle.

Many people are somewhere along a continuum from nervous to reluctant to hostile about new technology, but the simple fact is that the planet is not capable of sustaining either the number of people who now occupy it, nor the lifestyles we have chosen to aspire towards, without massive systematic use of technology. We mostly take technology for granted, and are generally neutral about it when we're unaware of it. The technological marvel that is the modern jet liner is seen as normal, as are the immensely complex computerised systems that support air traffic control to safely manage 237 flights every hour at Atlanta airport. And while we accept the wholesale computerisation of much of our lives as long as it's invisible, we can choose to react differently to visible technology that changes how we like to do things that we personally control. We only drive ourselves as there has never really been an affordable alternative and we have grown used to it, and it is a behaviour that is subtly and not

---

[12] https://global.oup.com/academic/product/innovation-and-its-enemies-9780190467036?cc=us&lang=en&

so subtly reinforced by the powers than benefit from our choices. If we are offered an alternative, will we want to take it?

Deciding What We Want

"Nobody knows the future. The future is not set. There is no fate but what we make for ourselves"

John Connor, Terminator T2

Just because we can automate something, should we? So far, it's been fairly easy to decide but as the value of the activity being replaced increases, it needs more consideration. People will need time to get used to driverless cars - just like any technology, it will face a hype curve and an adoption curve as it matures. It will face incident, accident and attack from vested interests as it tries to find its place in our world. As Henry Ford once said, if you'd asked people what they wanted, they would have asked for faster horses. You can't reliably predict reaction to a completely different technology than you're familiar with. Asking people their views about self-driving cars in simplistic surveys at this point does a disservice to the complexity of the issue, and sidesteps the fact that much remains to be determined to make the technology practical, let alone viable. We'll come back to question of public acceptance in Chapter 8.

But before we move on to look in more detail at the practicalities of driverless cars, let's take a chapter to look at the importance of the car and how it has come to define so much of our lives, whether we realise it or not.

Chapter 2 - The Machine That Changed the World

"The car is an incredible device,
which no sane society would tolerate"

Arthur C Clarke[13]

According to Time Magazine,[14] the car is undoubtedly one of the most revolutionary developments of the 20th century. In terms of impact on daily life, the now ubiquitous car is arguably the most impactful, even alongside such inventions as television, computers, the internet and the airplane. Somewhat subtly, it has come to dominate numerous aspects of our existence. More than any other technological artifact of the modern age, whether we realise it or not, the car has shaped the evolution of our physical environment, our domestic choices, economy, culture and even social relationships.

Nobody who is alive today remembers a world without cars, though older people will remember a time when they were less numerous and less sophisticated than today's models. They are so ingrained in modern life that we don't even realise just how significant a force they have been. The car has come to underpin virtually all the urban development of the 20th century yet it remains a very 20th century device - and on current estimates, it is likely to undergo the largest change in its history before the 1st quarter of the 21st century is complete.

Before we look at the future of the car, let's review how it has come to occupy its dominant position and reflect on the changes it has wrought on our world during its journey. Such has been the influence of the car on geography that it has pretty much

---

[13] Profiles of the Future, 1962
[14] http://content.time.com/time/photogallery/0,29307,2026224_2200963,00.html

single handedly led to the defining features of modern urban life - the creation of suburbs, shopping malls and commuter belts, as well as determined the planning and building of the dominant infrastructure of most countries.

The benefits of the car are pretty obvious - with relatively little expertise or skill you can get to where you want, leaving when you want (if not always arriving when you expect), in most weather conditions. Cars are unbound by timetables or connections that define and confine much public transport. Compared to other personal modes of transport such as bicycles, motorcycles or horses, cars offer levels of range, comfort and convenience that are highly attractive. Ironically, this personal independence comes with significant dependence on public roads and fuel supply, as well adverse environmental impacts.

Although the car provides an individualistic and privatized approach to transportation, it also has required collective efforts on a massive scale. Cars are of little value if they do not have adequate roads to travel on, and road construction has been an activity best done by some level of government. It was the work of the 20th century, funding, planning and building the nearly 4 million miles of paved public roads that criss cross the US. For many decades roads and the enforcement of traffic regulations were the chief areas of government involvement in automotive matters, but this began to change in the 1960s when the dangerous and destructive consequences of widespread automobile ownership became impossible to ignore. Concerns about safety, air pollution and energy use have since been reflected in a larger role for government regulation of the automobile. These shifts in the balance of power, between public and private interests, will continue as technology plays an increasing role in the future of our mobility.

From Zero to Everywhere in 100 Years

"What's past is prologue"

William Shakespeare[15]

The early days of cars saw very tentative introduction of this emerging technology into the then horse-centric world. In 1865, Britain enacted the Locomotives on Highways Act which required a self-propelled road vehicle to be preceded by an individual waving a red flag during the day and a red lantern at night. The act also restricted these vehicles to 4mph in the countryside and 2 mph in towns. This inhibiting ordinance also required a minimum of two people in the vehicle and a third on foot carrying the red flag or lantern to give warning and help control frightened horses. A revised Act in 1896 eliminated the red flag and lantern and elevated the speed limit to 14 mph.

The automobile revolution started for real around 1890 when car production started rising. Thus began the transition from centuries of horse dominance to car. Revolutions usually do not announce themselves at their first manifestations; the automobile was initially a marriage of existing parallel technologies of engines and carriages. At first, there was some optimism about the benefits of these new contraptions:

"The general introduction of the automobile in cities also carries with it numerous advantages to the general public. When the horse has become a rarity in city streets the wear of pavements will be enormously decreased, the dust nuisance will have been largely done away with, and it will be possible to keep the streets almost perfectly clean with very much less labor; the sanitary conditions of the cities will be improved and the noise and traffic lessened; owing to the greater speed and shorter length of the vehicles, there will be room for more traffic with less crowding,

---

[15] The Tempest, Act I, Scene I

and finally owing to the greatly superior control of motor vehicles, the streets will be safer for the pedestrian."

Some Advantages of the Automobile, 1902

Despite such early optimism, the growth in car numbers and speeds rapidly made the streets a more dangerous place. At the time cars were introduced, pedestrians and horses ruled our city streets and had done so for as long as anyone could remember. There were no traffic lights, no motorways and no service stations. Streets were a primarily social place, a meeting place, a place where goods were sold and where children played.

At first, widespread consumer car ownership seemed impossible — roads weren't paved and no one knew how to drive cars. But the product was a consumer hit, and everything changed to make way for them. Not only did industries spring up to sell them, maintain them and scrap them, the very layout of our towns and cities changed to accommodate them. We'll revisit this point repeatedly as we examine driverless cars - the world changed massively in response to cars in ways that were dauntingly unthinkable at the time but Governments, local administrations and corporations combined to facilitate unprecedented physical and social change over just a few decades. So, if we do face a transition from the dominant form of transport today (cars) to self-driving cars that requires large scale change, there is a historical lesson and precedent.

Peak Horse

In 1902, there were 175,000 horses on the streets of Manhattan and Brooklyn. As the Times reported, the new arrivals "cars" were scaring the horses. By 1920, there were already 8 million cars in the US, the year horses were at their peak in the US, before they began a rapid decline.

1920 was Peak Horse

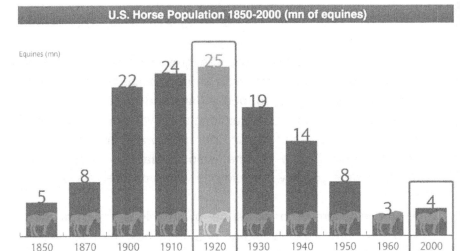

Source: Barclays[16]

The Rise of the Car

In 1900, 28% of American cars were electric (as opposed to about 1% in 2016[17]). The first World War saw the focus turn away from the electric car towards the internal combustion engine (ICE) - where speed, durability and power on a battlefield were critical requirements. The state began to fund paved roads out of general taxation. The first cars evolved from steam-powered machines to primarily use ICE, with the front-mounted configuration still common today. The Oldsmobile of 1901 had a single cylinder 7 HP engine offering a 7-mph top speed. In 1903, it took a Packard 53 days to drive across America from San Francisco to New York. In 1901, New York became the first

---

[16] Disruptive Mobility: AV Deployment Risks and Possibilities, Barclays Research, Jul 2015

[17] https://cleantechnica.com/2017/02/04/us-electric-car-sales-59-january-2017/

state to require the registration of automobiles. The first drive in gas station opened in St Louis in 1905. In 1914, Detroit was the first city to erect a stop sign and in August the same year, Cleveland installed the first electric traffic signals.

Only 4,000 cars were sold in the U.S in 1900, representing approximately one car for every 20,000 residents. At this time, it's fairly safe to say the car was still a niche product. Henry Ford released the iconic Model T in 1908, but there was still less than one car for every 400 residents. It wasn't until 1914, one year after Ford's moving assembly line had been in full swing, that the car became part of the average American experience. By 1914, the U.S. boasted 1.7 million cars, or about one car for every 60 residents. Fast-forward to 1925, and there were more than 20 million automobiles registered — enough for the vast majority of urban households to own a car of their own. Although the human population of major cities grew a combined 19.9% between 1910 and 1920, the number of horses fell 57%. The rural transition from horse to car took a little longer than cities, but was still largely complete by the end of the 1920s.

As cars surged in popularity in the late 1920s (only mildly slowed by the Great Depression), an urban lifestyle and travel revolution unfolded. To help put in context how important the car has been in determining modern life: it is a fact that where we live and work and shop are all hugely influenced by individual motorized transport. The operating radius of a horse and buggy was no more than twenty miles and this distance effectively had defined the world that people regularly inhabited. Truly, the car could be said to have broadened horizons for more people as no other prior invention had done. Cars also created the new pastime of leisure travel - visits to national parks sextupled as car ownership grew.

Cars encouraged the development of residential suburbs, poorly served by transit (public transportation) because the routes were unprofitable. Cars also created the concept of the shopping mall which virtually required a car. By 1929, the first 3 shopping centres existed in the U.S. According to Encyclopaedia.com[18] of nearly 47,000 shopping centers in the United States, about 1,100 are categorized as enclosed malls, Regional malls contain at least two department stores or "anchor stores" and, depending on population density, attract consumers from within a 20-mi (32 km) radius. Super-regional malls, of which about 350 exist, include at least five department stores and 300 shops and may serve an area of up to a 100-mi (160-km) radius. Without the car, these malls would not have existed.

Early Conflict in the Streets

Cars and their drivers were initially reviled by many. As Woodrow Wilson, then President of Princeton University, said in 1906, "Automobilists are a picture of arrogance and wealth". Cars met with particular hostility in densely settled cities, where people living in crowded tenements routinely used the streets for games, socializing, buying and selling, and other activities that had nothing to do with transportation. In this environment, the appearance of an automobile represented a threat to an accustomed way of life, while at the same time it posed a very real safety hazard.

The transition from a horse-led street to a car-filled one wasn't immediate or straight forward. People were used to sharing streets with horses, but streets were also widely used by children playing and vendors selling goods. That's not to say that horses and humans were never in conflict - in the New York of 1867, horses were killing an average of 4 pedestrians a week.

A Chicago Tribune headline asked: "Is the Automobile Mania a Form of Insanity?" Chicagoans called automobiles "buzz wagons" and "devil wagons." Reckless drivers were "scorchers," a word that originally described speeding bicyclists in the 1890s.

---

[18] http://www.encyclopedia.com/literature-and-arts/art-and-architecture/architecture/shopping-center

"Auto Scorchers a Terror," the Tribune declared in 1902 — at a time when about 800 people in a city of 1.7 million had automobile licenses. In those early years, the police didn't have any motor vehicles of their own to chase after speeding cars. And they had no easy way of identifying motorists or automobiles.[19]

As cars became more pervasive in the 1920s, automotive interests proposed that customary social constructions of the street were outdated and that only a revolutionary change in perceptions of the street could ease congestion and prevent accidents. According to the book Fighting Traffic, The Dawn of the Motor Age in the American City[20], *by casting the problem in terms of political freedom and market freedom, motor manufacturers and associated interests ("motordom") found it could sidestep difficult questions of justice, order and efficiency. For example, in acquiring street railways and then scrapping them, automobile Interests acted in concert, secretively and sometimes illegally. The new automobiles were incompatible with old streets, particularly with street uses of long standing legitimacy but motor groups were determined to position the car as progressive, essential and desirable. They could characterise low speed limits as oppressive. They proposed that street uses that impeded automobiles were misuses of the street. As an ally to the rhetoric of freedom, motordom turned to the rhetoric of modernity. Some proposed a more radical social reconstruction of the street as a motor thoroughfare, confining pedestrians to crossings and sidewalks. Cities that failed to adapt were "backward".* Though the actions of the motoring lobby may be long forgotten, it will be interesting to see if the same tactics and arguments now resurface with the first concerted threat to the dominance of the car in a century.

---

[19] http://www.chicagotribune.com/news/ct-chicago-auto-show-early-cars-flashback-0208-jm-20150207-story.html

[20] Peter Norton, 2002

The motorised newcomers to city streets did not get off to a good start as there were frequent pedestrian deaths, yet early outrage over urban pedestrian deaths did not impede the rise of the car. The initial focus was on the interplay of automobiles and pedestrians - so the focus began from the concept of regulating pedestrians; education programmes and the crime of jay-walking were introduced. Later attention would turn more to collisions between automobiles.

"This dreadful slaughter must be stopped. If necessary, regulations severe and searching enough to do it must be adopted and enforced. If reasonable safety of life and limb can only be had by impairing the motor car's efficiency, the motor car will have to pay that price."

"As a result of the accident situation, a reaction against the purchase, use and toleration of motor vehicles has already set in. There is a great danger of large numbers of people beginning to look on the automobile as more of a menace than a blessing"

Charles Price, National Safety Council, 1922[21]

Automobile manufacturers knew that they had to win the battle for public opinion and in cases where there was what they considered overtly negative coverage of "motor-killings", they withdrew their advertising to persuade newspapers (then key influencers of public opinion) to place less blame on motorists. The American Automobile Association (AAA) even tried to find a word to describe menace drivers without overtly blaming speed - the winning suggestion was "flivverboob"[22]. Thankfully, that word never made it into common usage.

---

[21] Proceedings of the National Safety Council, Tenth Annual Safety Congress, Boston 1922

[22] http://www.detroitnews.com/story/news/local/michigan-history/2015/04/26/auto-traffic-history-detroit/26312107/

It would not be surprising if driverless cars are met in some quarters with the same hostility towards early automobiles referenced here. They promise to interfere with long established norms, and force changes in very personal behaviours. For all their proponent's talk of safety and efficiency, those who stand to lose employment, revenues or control are likely to resist vociferously.

Incipient Traffic Planning

Dealing with the growing issue of how to allocate and manage street space quickly become a big political issue and municipalities determined that the limited amount of space available in the city streets and the conflicting views on its proper use justified the regulation of streets. This led to the emergence of a new discipline of traffic engineers. Traffic planning in the 1920s was a nascent profession without its own set of tools - now it features the latest techniques such as deep machine learning and sensors offering millions of real time data points. In the interim, there has been a plethora of attempted solutions to the challenge of balancing the competing demands of road users, landowners, transit users and non-motorists. Cars present a huge challenge for efficiency-minded planners - they occupy space either while in motion or while parked, space that's in inverse proportion to their transportation efficiency compared to other modes of transport.

Those forms of transport which relied most on the continued unchanged use of street space argued for preferential consideration in any new regime. In the mid-1920s, the majority of people in cities travelled on streetcars which led to the President of the American Railway Association to declare, "we must regard ourselves as representing the interests of the masses of the people" in 1926.[23] By the early 1920s, the Federal Government had started to take an interest in motoring.

---

[23] Frank R Coates, American Electric Railway Association, US Chamber of Commerce, Washington, May 1926

Secretary Hoover's National Conference on Street and Highway Safety which met in 1924, 1926 and 1930 had a variety of industry-sponsored attendees. But in an early example of political lobbying, representatives of motoring interests held most of the leading positions on the committees that worked out the new principles of traffic and determined what would become the new normal for our streets.

The Car and Urban Development

"I believe mayors, planners and developers have done untold damage to cities in the name of private automobiles that we'll still be grappling with a century from now"

Anthony Townsend, Author, Smart Cities[24]

By 2020, the UN estimates that 82.5 percent of Americans will live in urban areas.[25] But the human migration to being a predominantly urban species is a relatively recent phenomenon. The cities of today are a far cry from those that first greeted the car. Cities then were much smaller, largely constrained by available modes of transport - horses and walking. Originally, towns and cities were constrained by how far you could walk in about an hour a day. Ancient cities' walled areas reflect this dependence on pedestrian transport. Even in the 1950s, it was rare for a city to be larger than about 3 miles across. The growth of cities has been marked by advances in the ways we have had available to get from one place to another. The city kept growing by roughly the amount proportional to the speed increase of the new commuting technology, but always such that the center of the city was easily reachable for most people. Walking cities were densely occupied with houses, shops, offices, warehouses and industry jostling for space on narrow streets.

---

[24] https://medium.com/@anthonymobile/peak-city-b5457846ce11
[25] https://esa.un.org/unpd/wup/Publications/Files/WUP2014-Report.pdf

With the advent of horse-drawn trams, and then buses, bicycles, metro and suburban trains, cities progressively grew larger. The citizen's daily travel time stayed the same but faster travel meant it was possible to commute further. From the 1950s onwards, growing car ownership made it possible for cities to develop in any direction, regardless of transit availability. Places of employment become spatially separated from housing and housing decoupled from amenities. Increasingly, we shaped our towns and villages around the highways, building vast suburbs miles beyond our gritty urban centers, adding "big-box stores" and mega-malls surrounded by acres and acres of parking lots.

Cars were never really necessary in early cities, nor were they the ideal cohabitant. In many respects, they worked against the founding purpose of cities: to group people together in a space where trade, social and cultural synergies would develop. Ironically, as cars demand so much space for movement and storage (parking), they undermine this urban ideal. In fact, cars have caused cities to expand simply in order to provide the additional land cars need. In recent years, there has been an acknowledgement among many urban planners that cars have damaged the fabric of towns and they have adopted policies discouraging automobile use in favor of walking, cycling and public transport. An example of this is the Norwegian capital Oslo where they have proposed that its downtown centre will soon be made a no car zone[26] in order to reduce pollution and improve air quality, as well as to improve safety and accessibility for pedestrians and cyclists.

The Road Network by Numbers

While cars have changed the layout, size and use of cities, they have also necessitated the creation of massive nationwide road networks to connect urban and rural areas and to facilitate

---

[26] https://www.theguardian.com/environment/2015/oct/19/oslo-moves-to-ban-cars-from-city-centre-within-four-years

longer journeys. Just how big is the road network? The numbers for the US are readily available[27] - since the early 20th century the US has devoted significant resources to the creation of a roadway system that connects every major population center. Over 164,000 miles of highways in the National Highway System form the backbone of the 4-million-mile public road network. Approximately one percent of all public roads are part of the Interstate Highway System. Of these 47,000 miles of Interstates, 65 percent are in rural areas and 35 percent are in urban areas. Seventy-four percent of the remaining public roads are located in rural areas, with 26 percent in urban areas. Since 1980 an additional 183,000 miles of public roads have been constructed, an average of 6,500 miles of new roads each year.

US highways sustained nearly 3 trillion (3,000,000,000,000) vehicle miles traveled (VMT) in 2009. Private vehicles, which include automobiles, light trucks, vans, and motorcycles, are used for 84 percent of all trips nationwide. Most of these trips – 55 percent of total trips – are made by car or van. In 2009, 16.1 billion tons of freight – with a total value of $14.9 trillion (in 2009 dollars) – moved along the US road transportation network. The number of registered privately and commercially owned motor vehicles (which includes cars, commercial and non-commercial trucks, SUVs, and motorcycles) per person in each state vary significantly. States' rates of vehicle ownership range from 0.54 vehicles per person in Nevada to 1.21 vehicles per person in Wyoming.

Almost two-thirds (63%) of daily vehicle trips are between one and nine miles in length, 16 percent of all daily vehicle trips are between 10 and 19 miles in length, while 9 percent are between 20 and 49 miles. Trips less than one mile in length are 10 percent of all trips, while long-distance travel (trips of 50 miles or greater) are three percent of all trips. These findings indicate that most personal vehicle trips are short, with seven of every 10

---

[27] https://www.fhwa.dot.gov/policyinformation/pubs/hf/pl11028/chapter1.cfm

trips less than 10 miles in length. However, trips less than 10 miles in length account for only 23 percent of all VMT, indicating that frequent, shorter trips are prevalent, but those trips greater than 10 miles in length account for a majority of road use. Conversely, long-distance travel (trips of 50 miles or greater) account for three percent of all vehicle trips by number, but represent 31 percent of all household-based VMT. In summary, the road network is a vast and vital infrastructure. Extensive further detail and graphed data are available on the FHWA website here.[28]

Too Successful for Its Own Good?

Those numbers illustrate clearly the impact the car has had on the planet's landscape. The vast majority of populations in the developed world now live in environments that were designed almost entirely around the private car. By encouraging the dispersion of residences to the periphery of cities, by increasing the distances among places of employment, commercial and entertainment centers, and residences, and thereby accentuating the move toward motorization, the automobile has made itself a necessity. It's self-perpetuating and central to the individualist, consumerist culture of contemporary capitalism. The car dictates placement of housing, placement of offices, planning laws, use of domestic space, use of commercial space, policies like congestion management and parking. An estimated 22% of all restaurant meals are ordered through a car window in America.[29] Automobiles enable suburban sprawl, while suburban sprawl creates demand for automobiles. These co-dependencies magnify certain negative impacts of today's automobiles and create some barriers to change, but they also promise to magnify the positive effects of any improvements arising from a change to the dominance of the car.

---

[28] https://www.fhwa.dot.gov/policyinformation/pubs/hf/pl11028/chapter4.cfm
[29] 'Traffic', Tom Vanderbilt (2008)

A huge contributor to the growth of cities and suburbs that are home to most of the people on the planet, the car is becoming a victim of its own success. The growth in the number of cars has become unsustainable considering the space and budgets available for roads and infrastructure. For all its influence in shaping the built environment and unquestionable personal convenience, the rise of the personal automobile is not without several negatives. Most car drivers attest that owning a car is expensive and frequently frustrating - often failing to get you where you want in the timeframe you wish, and then presenting storage challenges when you do reach your destination, either in terms of availability, cost or both.

The Cost of Driving

Anyone who owns a car, whether by necessity, habit or special interest, will tell you that it's an expensive acquisition. We spend more on transport than on food or healthcare or anything other than housing:

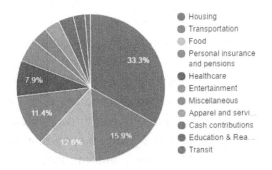

Chart source: 2015 Data - (released April 2017), Bureau of Labor Statistics[30]

---

[30] https://www.bls.gov/opub/reports/consumer-expenditures/2015/home.htm

Each day, average Americans spend about a quarter of their eight hours at work paying off their car, which many purchase on credit primarily to get to that job. With the second largest single capital outlay for most people after their house, the costs don't end with the initial purchase. Maintenance, fuel, tax, and insurance all combine to account for a significant portion of income: and that assumes you don't have any repairs to pay for as the result of a collision. Even then, that litany of recurring personal expenditure is before any attempt to quantify the cost to society at large. There are significant direct costs to society, as well as significant less visible or indirect costs - the very real costs of accidents, noise and air pollution.

While the costs of car ownership and operation are likely to continue to increase for individuals and for society as a whole, in all probability they will continue to be borne with little complaint because few devices have offered as large and varied a package of individual benefits as has the car. The car is an individualising technology, which encourages us to make self-interested choices and adopt self-centred values. The very freedom promised by the automobile has been at least partially offset by a parallel set of restrictions - traffic laws, congestion, massive financial demands in depreciation, maintenance, repairs and insurance and taxes to main and expand roads. But the lack of a compelling alternative that offers comparable flexibility and convenience has led to car ownership reaching levels that outstrip the supply of road space. The resulting traffic congestion that is a crippling feature of most large cities is not pleasant to be in or to observe. It creates time waste, journey uncertainty, and personal stress along with noise and air pollution. There is a clear correlation between economic prosperity and traffic jams so as the economy improves, so too do commute times.

Congestion

Day to day driving experiences are in stark contrast to the advertisers' portrayal of personal freedom on free flowing, expansive roads. The US is the most congested developed country in the world, with 11 cities in the top 25 for most gridlocked.[31] The Texas Transportation Institute[32] estimates that the total traffic delay in the United States went from 0.7 billion hours in 1982 to 3.7 billion hours in 2003 to 4.8 billion hours in 2011 to a whopping 7 billion hours in 2015. That equates to 3 billion gallons of wasted fuel (equivalent to three months' operation of the Alaska Pipeline), and $160 billion in combined delay and fuel costs. That's $960 per year for each commuter.

The average American commuter now spends 250 hours a year behind the wheel of a vehicle; whether the value of that time is measured in lost productivity, lost time for pursuing other interests, or lost serenity, the cost is high. Studies have found that people with commutes longer than 40 minutes are unhappier, more stressed and generally experience more worry than those who only have a 10-minute commute. A study by New York University[33] looking at 21,000 U.S. commuters found that there was a strong correlation between length of commute and hypertension. Another study out of Texas that looked at 4,297 adults found that commuting distance was associated with larger waist circumference and higher blood pressure. And finally, a study from Sweden that looked at 21,088 Swedes confirmed previous research that commuting contributed to poor sleep quality and everyday stress. But bad as congestion may be for our health, it is far outweighed by the costs of crashes - we'll return to that subject in Chapter 4.

---

[31] http://inrix.com/scorecard/

[32] https://mobility.tamu.edu/ums/report/

[33] http://www.ncbi.nlm.nih.gov/pubmed/10505818

Although traffic and the tension between urban life and transport may seem like a relatively new problem, it isn't. Roman law and tradition forbade the use of vehicles in urban areas, except in certain cases. As far as we know, Rome's narrow streets were not marked "One Way" but in effect they were one way, because each driver sent a runner ahead to hold up traffic at the other end of the street or alley until their chariot had passed through. In an effort to keep the city more habitable, Caesar even outlawed vehicles in the city for the first 10 hours of each day, unless they were involved in the building of a temple.

Mitigating congestion is not easy. With the exception of congestion charging in cities like London, Singapore and Stockholm, most road owners/policy makers have chosen not to apply the concept of scarce resource pricing to most peak time travel. For road users, the cost of using the road typically remains the same regardless of the time - unlike the peak models applied to numerous sectors such as airlines, hotel rooms, holidays and telephone calls. Congestion charging works because it forces people to make a conscious decision if the trip is "worth it" with indisputable benchmark pricing, but is not politically popular, and can be seen as a harsh tax. On the other hand, the negative impacts of traffic are vast: lost time, increased pollution, people having to get up earlier, lost time with family, stress. In the middle of the last century, the preferred solution to "the traffic problem" was more cement: new highways, bridges, and lanes. More recently as costs rise, environmental opposition grows and space runs out, many cities have been trying to divert trips or move journeys to alternative forms of transport. Today, the proposed solutions include smarter roadways - more sensors and better computers: leading to hopes of highly automated vehicles that use existing roadways and roadway networks much more efficiently. An evaluation of the last 58 major road construction schemes implemented by the Highways Agency in the UK found time savings to road users at peak times on average of just 3 minutes.[34] Building more roads is not the solution - 90% of our roads are uncongested 90% of the time. With such uneven demand, you can't practically build your way out of congestion, so efforts should turn to congestion management and more efficient use of vehicles. In 2010, 94% of all US commuters drove alone. Even when vehicle usage is at its peak, fewer than 12 percent of all personal vehicles are on the road, which means, of course, that 88 percent are not in use.[35]

Gaming Traffic

Trying to outsmart traffic is almost a pastime for many commuters but numerous studies have shown that congestion is a delicate balance - not too far removed from "the butterfly effect" - a small change can have much greater knock-on consequences that would first seem logical. But that is due to the small margins, with many major routes operating perilously close to capacity at peak times. Canceling the trips of 1 percent of drivers from carefully selected neighborhoods would reduce the extra travel time for all other drivers in a metropolitan area by as much as 18 percent.[36] A 2009 Japanese study found that a 2–5% reduction in peak-hour traffic volumes has been shown to lead to a 27%-35% reduction in total traffic delay.[37] Traffic simulations of the city of Berlin[38] suggest that at around 20 per-cent of vehicles fitted with traffic-aware navigation, everyone's journey times might be cut by up to 30 per-cent. The presence of just a few autonomous vehicles can eliminate the stop-and-go driving of the human drivers in traffic, along with the accident

---

[34] http://assets.highways.gov.uk/our-road-network/pope/major-schemes/POPE_meta_2011_main_report_final.pdf

[35] https://www.rita.dot.gov/bts/sites/rita.dot.gov.bts/files/subject_areas/national_household_travel_survey/daily_travel.html

[36] http://cityminded.org/daily-commute-need-talk-99-12436

[37] http://ieeexplore.ieee.org/document/5409622/?reload=true&tp=&arnumber=5409622&url=http:%2F%2Fieeexplore.ieee.org%2Fiel5%2F4149681%2F5409610%2F05409622.pdf%3Farnumber%3D5409622

[38] http://360.here.com/2014/04/30/jams-game-theory-equations-science-of-traffic/

risk and fuel inefficiency it causes, according to research from the University of Illinois.[39] Their experiments show that with as few as 5 percent of vehicles being automated and carefully controlled, it can eliminate stop-and-go waves caused by human driving behavior.

Many people think that they can outwit others and improve their lot in a congested environment by making changes to their route. However, applying the Nash Equilibrium from Game Theory, (no one player can make himself better off by his own action alone), one person cannot solve congestion. In fact, individual attempts to circumvent congestion can have the opposite to the intended outcome - this is known as Selfish Routing - each person is moving through the network in the way that seems best to them, but everyone's total behaviour may be the least efficient for the traffic network. Ironically enough, opening new roads can even actually increase traffic jams; and closing existing roads can make it smoother. You can thank a concept known as Braess's Paradox[40] for that: everyone thinks the new road will make their trip faster, so they use it, but then it simply creates new bottlenecks somewhere else. Traffic can be counter-intuitive: sometimes it's actually sensible to sit in a tailback - like on the access road to a fast highway, for example, which leads to an overall faster journey even if it feels slow as you queue for access to the highway.

Parking

*"A pedestrian in America is someone who
has just parked their car"*

Unknown

Given how hard it always seems to be to find parking when you're looking for it, it might come as quite a shock to many

---

[39] http://engineering.illinois.edu/news/article/21938
[40] http://en.wikipedia.org/wiki/Braess%27s_paradox

people to learn that there are approximately 4 spaces for every car - according to a 2011 study[41] by the University of California-Berkeley, there are as many as a billion parking spaces in the US. Another study in the Journal of the American Planning Association[42] estimates that in 2010 there were approximately 18.6 million parking spaces in Los Angeles County alone. That's about 3.3 spaces, or 1,000 square feet, per vehicle—literally more space for each car than for each person in the county. The authors also note that the amount of parking has continued to grow over the years, from around 2.5 million spaces in 1930, to 12 million in 1970, to 18.6 million in 2010. Disney's Epcot center in Orlando, Florida is an example of one of the biggest parking lots in America. With room for 12,000 cars, it sprawls out over 7 million square feet—about the size of 122 football fields.

Despite the fact that people ostensibly buy cars because they need to move around, the amount of time they actually do move around is relatively tiny. A car spends most of its time waiting, parked, for us to need it again for what is usually another short burst of activity. Often there can be 12 hours between each of those bursts. So cars are more often than not immobile, but they require multiple spaces in different locations: a car owner needs a spot in or near their home, but also spots near the other places he or she might go, whether frequently or infrequently—the office, a shopping mall, or a leisure destination such as Disneyland.

In his book Rethinking a Lot,[43] Eran Ben-Joseph notes, *"In some U.S. cities, parking lots cover more than a third of the land area, becoming the single most salient landscape feature of our built environment."* Parking lots and garages form urban dead zones, draining vitality and activity from city streets. It can be hard to grasp the scale of parking when it's distributed throughout the

---

[41] http://chester.faculty.asu.edu/library/access39_parking.pdf
[42] http://www.transportationlca.org/losangelesparking/
[43] Rethinking a Lot (2012), Eran Ben-Joseph

entire region in the form of residential one- and two-space garages, on-street parking, and underground, podium, and surface parking lots. It's there, though. When we look at it all put together, side by side, it's clear how much we've given up to make space for cars—to say nothing of the roads and highways that complement these parking spaces. The totality of parking spaces is widely distributed, so the effects can be difficult to perceive at a macro level; putting all those spaces side-by-side really helps to illustrate just how much space is devoted to the temporary storage of vehicles. If you totaled up all the area devoted to parking in the US, it would be roughly 6,500 square miles - bigger than the state of Connecticut. Just as a thought exercise, if this space could be repurposed, covering this area with solar panels could generate 11 billion KWH of electricity per day - enough to power 11 million households or 10% of the households in the US, with zero emissions.

Because of the focus on cars and co-located parking (where the car is stored close to its owner) as a solution in urban planning in recent decades, the distance between people and their destinations is typically greater than before, so they spend more time in traffic or on the bus; parking is baked into the price of most housing, goods, and services, so we pay more for all of them (hundreds of dollars per month, at least); and since we've built our city around the assumption that most people will drive, most people do—because all the incentives point in that direction.

Parking & Congestion

According to Donald Shoup,[44] Professor of Urban Planning at the University of California, Los Angeles, a surprising amount of traffic congestion isn't caused by people who are on their way somewhere. Rather it is caused by people who have already arrived. Our streets are congested, in part, by people who have gotten where they want to be but are cruising around looking for

---

[44] http://shoup.bol.ucla.edu/CruisingForParkingAccess.pdf

a place to park. Sixteen studies of cruising behavior were conducted between 1997 and 2001 in the central business districts of eleven cities on four continents. The average time it took to find a curb space was eight minutes, and about thirty percent of the cars in the traffic flow were cruising for parking. In congested urban areas, about 40 percent of total gasoline use is in cars looking for parking. Even a small search time per car can create a surprising amount of traffic. Consider a congested downtown where it takes three minutes to find a curb space and the parking turnover is ten cars per space per day. For each curb space, cruising thus results in thirty extra minutes of vehicle travel per day (3 minutes x 10 cars). If the average cruising speed is ten miles an hour, cruising creates five vehicle miles traveled per space per day (10 mph x 0.5 hour). Over a year, this driving in circles amounts to 1,825 VMT for each curb space (5 miles x 365 days), greater than half the distance across the United States. Over a year, cruising in Westwood Village (near UCLA) creates 950,000 excess VMT—equivalent to 38 trips around the earth, or four trips to the moon. The obvious waste of time and fuel is even more appalling when we consider the low speed and fuel efficiency of cruising cars. Because drivers average about ten miles an hour in the Village, cruising 950,000 miles a year wastes about 95,000 hours (eleven years) of drivers' time every year.

As well as parking lots and multi storey garages, the other primary parking location is on the side of the roadway itself. After 1935, when they were first introduced, parking meters changed parking radically by making the parking space a commodity to trade and a source of income for municipalities. While often very convenient for the intended destination of the driver, kerbside parking is an appropriation of public space for private use. Streets should really be for moving vehicles, not storing them. Parking is not just a case of assigning space for one purpose (temporary storage of vehicles) over another (domestic or leisure). There is an opportunity cost of using a space for parking instead of a use with a higher value. Given the time spent looking for it, and the relative uncertainty of availability compared to dedicated multi-storey car parks, why is curb parking still so popular? Because the average price of curb parking is only twenty percent of the price of parking in a garage. And here's another inconvenient truth about under-priced curb parking: cruising 950,000 miles wastes 47,000 gallons of gasoline and produces 730 tons of CO_2 emissions in a small business district.

Congestion caused by cars looking for curbside parking is by no means a US only problem. According to a survey,[45] the average UK motorist spends a shocking 106 days of their life looking for a parking spot, and it takes 20 minutes to find a spot in London alone, thanks to restrictions like resident-only parking and yellow lines. Since parking space is limited in cities, private parking spots can sell for more than houses. Recently, a parking spot near Hyde Park in central London was put on the market at £350,000[46] – more than the average house price in the UK. In New York, according to appraisers Miller Samuel, the average parking space costs $165,019, or $1,100 per square foot, close to the average apartment price of $1,107 per square foot.[47]

Regulation & Parking

As with congestion we discussed earlier, parking is an age-old problem. Assyrian King Sennacherib who ruled from 705 to 681 BC, had signs posted along the main highway of his capital city to ensure the route was kept clear of parked chariots. In a rather extreme position on parking, he declared that anyone parking a chariot so as to obstruct a royal road should be put to death with his head impaled on a pole outside his house.[48] Julius Caesar introduced the first off-street parking laws. A further example of

---

[45] http://www.telegraph.co.uk/motoring/news/10082461/Motorists-spend-106-days-looking-for-parking-spots.html

[46] http://www.telegraph.co.uk/cars/news/london-parking-space-goes-on-sale-for-350000/

[47] http://www.nytimes.com/2007/07/12/us/12parking.html

[48] Edge City: Life on the New Frontier, Joel Garreau, 2011

the impact that the private car has had on urban development is the fact that the provision of parking is a key parameter in planning permission decisions for both domestic and commercial properties, showing just how car-centric our society has become. Regulation continues to play a big part in determining parking assignments. At its flagship new headquarters building Apple (the world's most valuable company, and widely believed to be researching driverless cars technologies itself) is building 11,000 parking spaces not because it wants to but because local planning regulations in Cupertino, the city where the new headquarters is located, require it. In all, the new headquarters will contain 318,000 square metres of offices, facilities and laboratories. The car parks will occupy 325,000 square metres.[49]

The impact of regulation on parking was highlighted in a 2016 White House report[50] which identified parking as one of the "local policies acting as barriers to housing supply. Parking requirements generally impose an undue burden on housing development, particularly for transit-oriented or affordable housing. When transit-oriented developments are intended to help reduce automobile dependence, parking requirements can undermine that goal by inducing new residents to drive, thereby counteracting city goals for increased use of public transit, walking and biking. Such requirements can also waste developable land, and reduce the potential for other amenities to be included; a recent Urban Land Institute study found that minimum parking requirements were the most noted barrier to housing development in the course of their research."[51]

---

[49] http://www.economist.com/news/briefing/21720269-dont-let-people-park-free-how-not-create-traffic-jams-pollution-and-urban-sprawl
[50]
https://www.whitehouse.gov/sites/whitehouse.gov/files/images/Housing_Development_Toolkit%20f.2.pdf
[51] Bending the Cost Curve – Solutions to Expand the Supply of Affordable Rentals." Urban Land Institute Terwilliger Center for Housing: 19. 2014

If given the opportunity to reducing parking and by designing more connected, walkable developments, cities can reduce pollution, traffic congestion and improve economic development. Minimum domestic parking space requirements have a disproportionate impact on housing for low-income households because these families tend to own fewer vehicles but are nonetheless burdened by the extra cost of parking's inclusion in the development. The significant cost of developing parking – from $5,000 per surface parking spot to $60,000 underground – is incorporated at the start of the project, which can impede the viability and affordability of the construction. The deep irony is that cities rarely require developers to construct enough affordable housing, but they pass strict laws making sure vehicles can be adequately housed. "We don't force [developers] to build the right number of bedrooms for people! We just force them to build the right number of bedrooms for cars," according to Jeffrey Tumlin, Director of Strategy for Nelson Nygaard, a parking consultancy.[52]

Millennials, On-Demand & Peak Car

After almost a century of virtually uninterrupted growth, there are signs that the dominance of the car may be waning in some circles, before the arrival of any self-driving cars. This may signal the beginning of an opportunity for change, or may simply be a temporary change in attitudes and priorities.

Losing Licenses

As a proxy for popular demand for cars, the rate and timing of applications for driving licenses is a good indicator. In the US, for the baby boomer generation especially, turning 16 and getting a driver's license was a rite of passage. But demographics are changing, as are attitudes towards driving. The percentage of Americans holding driver's licenses has fallen

---

sharply over the past several decades, especially among the young. In 1983, more than 91 percent of 20-to-24-year-olds held a license. By 2014, that number had dropped to approximately 77 percent and shows little sign of recovering. *"Young Americans drive less than older Americans and use public transportation more, and often use multiple modes of travel during a typical day or week,"* concludes a 2014 U.S. Public Research Interest Group study.[53]

Drivers Wanted

Fewer young Americans are getting driver's licenses. Licensed drivers as a percentage of their age group.

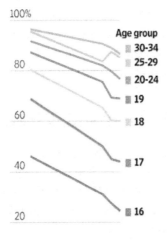

100%

Age group
- 30-34
- 25-29
- 20-24
- 19
- 18
- 17
- 16

80

60

40

20

0

1983   2000   '14

Source: University of Michigan Transportation Research Institute

THE WALL STREET JOURNAL.

---

[53] http://www.uspirg.org/news/usp/new-report-shows-mounting-evidence-millennials%E2%80%99-shift-away-driving

The obligations and costs of transportation are driving them out of automobility altogether. Younger generations, the ones who grew up with game consoles and smartphones, are not so in love with cars. This group—members of the "Millennial" generation—are not rushing to get driver's licenses the way baby boomers did. They live perpetually connected lives, and while they may have the same desire for mobility on demand, some see the act of driving as a distraction from texting, not the other way around.

Writing in the Journal of Transport and Land Use,[54] Glenn Lyons, founder of the Centre for Transport and Society at the University of the West of England noted: *"Young people have stood out particularly. Car licence acquisition has been going down among younger age groups, and there are strong suspicions that the digital age is contributing to why people now have less reliance on physical mobility. We are in the midst of a fundamental regime transition in society. We are increasingly seeing the car as a functional technology to get from A to B, rather than the much more symbolic representation it had in defining society in previous generations. That is not to suggest the car is done and finished with, but I believe it will become a background technology."* There is also a suggestion that the internet has reduced the need to drive so much: no-one actually has to drive to the shops anymore if they don't want to.

Similarly, Richard Wallace, Director of Transportation Systems Analysis at the Center for Automotive Research says *"What we're seeing is a group of millennials who don't want to be behind the wheel. After all, who wants to worry about insurance, oil changes or parking? The car was the cutting-edge technology of its day. For the post-war generation, going through the 1970s, there was nothing else out there you could own that had the technological sophistication - Now it's smartphones and maybe*

---

[54] https://www.jtlu.org/index.php/jtlu/article/view/751

virtual reality. The Internet superhighway is much more the Route 66 of the current generation."[55]

But while some point to the drop in license rates among the young, others point out that may not conclusively indicate an end to interest in cars. *"It's not about desire, it's about how difficult it is,"* says Scott Le Vine, an Urban Planner at Imperial College London.[56] "There's little support for the argument that young people have fallen out of love with the car." Instead, Scott says it is just more expensive and more difficult to pass your test than it used to be. Lessons alone can be £1,000. And pass rates for the practical test are well below the levels of the 1990s. According to the UK's 2014 National Travel Survey[57], more than half of 17 to 29-year-olds without full licences say they are either learning to drive, put off by the test, or put off by the cost, especially the cost of learning. It remains to be seen if the younger generation change their attitude to driving and car ownership as they age.

New Kid on the Block

As the Millennials grow into the largest cohort, meanwhile, big cities are growing faster than the country as a whole. The Pew Research Center found that 48 percent[58] of Americans would choose walkable urban areas over suburbs, a number that is expected to grow. How will these two trends collide? America's love affair with driving seems to be cooling off, while our obsession with urban living is heating up. The new player in the mix of urban life is cars on demand, either on a trip basis with a driver with a service like Uber or Lyft, or on a usage basis - with a service like Zipcar - essentially rental by the hour or by subscription. Taxis have long been a popular way to get around

---

[55] http://www.cnet.com/uk/news/a-future-of-self-driving-cars-were-ready-now/
[56] http://www.bbc.com/news/business-35242514
[57] https://www.gov.uk/government/statistics/national-travel-survey-2014
[58] http://www.people-press.org/2014/06/12/political-polarization-in-the-american-public/

when driving yourself doesn't suit or isn't possible. But the modernisation of taxis via the smartphone has given the concept a new lease of life. As of May 2017, leading on-demand provider Uber operates in over 580 cities and saw over $20 billion of bookings in 12 months. Rival company Lyft provides over 20 million rides per month. Ride sharing is currently responsible for about 4 percent of the miles traveled by car globally and Morgan Stanley believe the number will be nearly 30 percent by the year 2030.[59] We'll look at ownership and its alternatives in more detail in Chapter 5.

Peak Car

Peak car[60] is a term popularised by Phil Goodwin, Professor of Transport Policy, UCL. It is a hypothesis that motor vehicle distance traveled per capita, has peaked and will now reduce. The theory was developed as an alternative to the prevailing market saturation model, which suggested that car use would saturate and then remain reasonably constant, and GDP based theories which predict that traffic will increase again as the economy improves, linking recent traffic reductions to the recent recession. Going against the theory is the UK Department for Transport, which predicts that road traffic in the United Kingdom will grow by between 19 and 55% by 2040.[61]

In a study examining urban car use, Jeff Kenworthy, a professor of sustainability at Curtin University in Australia, found that the pace at which people increase their use of cars has been slowing. It may be explained, at least in part, by a concept known as the "Marchetti Wall."[62] Back in 1994, the Italian physicist Cesare Marchetti observed that throughout history—

---

[59] http://www.morganstanley.com/ideas/car-of-future-is-autonomous-electric-shared-mobility
[60] https://en.wikipedia.org/wiki/Peak_car
[61]

https://www.gov.uk/government/uploads/system/uploads/attachment_data/file/411471/road-traffic-forecasts-2015.pdf
[62] https://en.wikipedia.org/wiki/Marchetti%27s_constant

going back to ancient Rome—the majority of people disliked commuting more than one hour to work. If you're faced with a longer commute, you hit the Wall and rearrange your life, finding a new, more local job or moving closer to the office. In the 1990s and early 2000s, not only did use of public transit grow, but Kenworthy found that cities worldwide were becoming denser, in part because millennials weren't decamping for the suburbs (like their boomer parents did), and because seniors were moving back to urban cores, to enjoy the walkable life.[63] The advent of driverless cars may be the biggest challenge to the strength of the Marchetti wall yet.

How Has the Car Persisted So Long?

[...] Many of them are the size of small houses, with incredible sophistication, yet carry only one person. They can travel at over 100 miles per hour, but usually at no more than 40mph. In one lifetime they have consumed more energy than the whole previous history of mankind [...] the casualties are on the scale of a large war (every year)"

Arthur C Clarke

With so many apparent negatives to the rise of the car, it's perhaps surprising that it has lasted until into the 21st century before the arrival of such a focus from the world's largest companies on replacing it. The car is an example of Metcalfe's law (the concept that a network becomes more valuable the more people use it). There's been a self-fulfilling element to cars - "So things become less convenient for the car-less and thus more people got cars."

More than any obviously popular technology - TV, radio, smartphones or social media, transportation permeates our daily

---

[63] https://www.washingtonpost.com/news/in-theory/wp/2016/02/29/are-americans-leaving-cars-behind/

lives. As Door to Door[64] author Edward Humes put it, *"In ways both glaringly obvious and deeply hidden, thousands, even millions of miles are embedded in everything we do and touch. Americans drive 344 million miles every hour. 4 Americans die every hour and one is injured every 12.6 seconds. Cars have evolved into objects of culture, power, status, desire, image and habit."* Cars are often seen as more of a right than a responsibility. Cars provide status to their owners. They have evolved into literary and visual icons, representing freedom - the on the road liberation of individualism and a means to explore. As we saw earlier, the growth of the car invoked a radical process to restructure streets, cities and society. With widespread car ownership being the norm for most people alive today, it's easy to overlook what a profound impact the arrival of affordable cars has had on our development. The car has dictated a huge amount of urban decision making - from roads to parking lots that sit beneath or around workplaces and shopping destinations. After massive investments in building better roads, attempts to slow cars required planned dis-improvements to the quality of the road via speed bumps or other calming measures.

Something's Got to Change

"While the usual approach has been to focus on fairly ancient technologies of pavement, paint, and colored lights to move cars and trucks around, this report focuses on using today's technologies to deliver services, safety, and convenience"

Peter Marx, the former Chief Technology Officer for Los Angeles[65]

I don't want to seem overly negative about the human driven car. It has delivered much economic prosperity over the last

---

[64] Door to Door: The Magnificent, Maddening, Mysterious World of Transportation, Edward Humes, 2016

[65] http://la.curbed.com/2016/9/9/12824240/self-driving-cars-plan-los-angeles

century and in many ways shaped the world we live in today for the better. And in its defence, there hasn't really been a compelling or even credible alternative. But now it's time to consider the next evolution of transport. How can we keep all the good things about cars - something that's still point to point, on demand, personal and flexible? Something (relatively) affordable and individual. But we need to find ways to tackle the hitherto insoluble: the deaths, the injuries, the pollution, the spiralling costs. The delays. The wasted capacity. We need to reinvent mobility.

Today, about a century after Ford introduced the Model T and mass motorisation, nearly a billion cars and trucks move people and goods along the world's roadways and consumers spend trillions of dollars each year on personally owned vehicles (including the costs of fuel, depreciation, financing, insurance, taxes, parking, and time) to experience the resulting mobility benefits of personal transport. While this mobility system undoubtedly provides considerable personal freedom for those who can afford it and enables substantial economic activity, it is also associated with serious side effects in terms of safety, energy, the environment, land use, traffic congestion, time use and equality of access. If we want to truly make progress as transportation evolves, the aim for any improved system of transport must be to maintain or even enhance current levels of mobility whilst reducing deaths, injuries, cost, pollution and wasted time.

Fifty years of car-first infrastructure has created a vocal constituency of drivers both as individuals and lobby groups. If you've sunk all that money into buying a car, and if you can't really get out of your neighbourhood without it, you're going to want to be able to use it everywhere, with as few restrictions as possible. Any street reconfiguration to de-prioritize cars or parking space removal is going to be seen as a direct affront to you and makes it difficult for local politicians to implement such policies. This is what economic theory calls "uninternalized externalities", where we are not feeling the pain we are causing others and not willing to give up familiar comforts for the greater, if somewhat abstract, good.

As the move towards more urban living continues, car ownership in the traditional sense is not feasible. In the 20th century, the car was king. Henry Ford's vision that every individual would own their own vehicle and travel as they pleased has certainly come true, but along with it has come congested roads, air pollution and safety concerns. This century, we will see those trends reverse. Collectively we have paid a substantial price for the personal freedoms and mobility that the car affords us, and for the most part we have done so willingly (perhaps even blindly), if not always intelligently or completely rationally. Until now, we have never really had a choice as there has never been a compelling or even close alternative to the convenience of the automobile. Technology, if not society, is now at a point where a viable alternative is emerging, as we'll see in the next Chapter what's changed to make this even possible to talk about.

Reinventing the Automobile

"The automobile is a complex cultural artifact. For each of the values it carries with it, it also spreads the opposite value. While fostering individualism, it gives rise to anonymity. The apotheosis of individual freedom, but dependent on the state to provide roads and oil companies to provide gasoline. [66]

It's coming time to reassess our relationship with the automobile. It's a world that most of us have been born into and probably never really questioned. And until now, there hasn't been a huge number of alternatives for personal transport. Attempts at alternatives have met with limited success - the Sinclair C5[67] or

---

[66] http://sustainablemobility.ei.columbia.edu/files/2012/12/Transforming-Personal-Mobility-Jan-27-20132.pdf
[67] https://en.wikipedia.org/wiki/Sinclair_C5

the Segway[68] personal transport promised short range individual mobility but never caught on. While public transit has seen large investments in most countries to provide services and alternatives, the car has been the bringer of freedom to many for decades.

Our attitudes to cars and the way we will be travelling in the future has huge implications for the present. For decades, transport policies in most countries has been based on the assumption that car use would carry on growing, even if many believed that it had gone beyond the point of sustainability. Such an apparently illogical position was based largely on the lack of viable alternatives, a reluctance to invest in expensive transit projects, and a tacit acceptance of longer commute times as a modern fact of life. So, if individual car use has indeed peaked for whatever reason, or if there are genuinely practical alternatives available or imminent, any policy plans to build new roads and supporting infrastructure should be carefully considered.

It took several decades to fully transition from the horse to the car, and more to become so dependent on the car. Surely few could have imagined the impact the car would have as it tore through cities, countries, and economies worldwide. Its dominance has been unchallenged for a lifetime. In the last few decades, owning and driving the personal car has become the normal, largely expected means of transport to the virtual exclusion of most alternatives. In a short period of time, the car has become integral to the way most people commute, shop and spend leisure time. It's hard to avoid the impact of cars - even non-car owners live in a world largely designed around the needs of cars. Changing from this reality that has held firm for decades will require dramatic developments - developments that have until recently seemed the stuff of science fiction. But in the

---

[68] http://www.segway.com/

next Chapter, we'll see what's on the horizon and who is leading the charge to remove the driver.

Parked end to end, the vehicles currently in use on the planet would circle the globe nearly 100 times. Americans drive three trillion miles a year on four million miles of roads. Over the last hundred years successive technological breakthroughs have made our vehicles more powerful, easier to drive and control, safer, more energy efficient and more environmentally friendly (or at least less hostile - they still contribute significant chemical and noise pollution). While the improvements have been dramatic, they have been largely evolutionary and may have plateaued. The average urban speeds can be below 10 mph due to congestion but cars have delivered significant societal benefits and been a key catalyst in economic prosperity for millions. Bemoaning the rise of the car and its ills is rather pointless without positive alternatives. In an urban area designed for cars, the current alternatives of walking, ridesharing, biking or transit each have challenges. If we are unwilling to make changes, the only thing that can replace the car, is well, the car. But the car that drives itself. Let's explore how and when that might be possible.

Chapter 3 - Self Driving Cars: Really?

*"Mastery of self-driving under real-world conditions
is not going to be easy"*

Raj Rajkumar[69]
Director of Autonomous Driving Research, Carnegie-Mellon
University

Had the technologies required for self-driving cars existed when cars were first invented, it's unlikely many people would have thought that individual human control of potentially fatal vehicles was a good idea. If it had it been possible, I'm sure we would have skipped straight from the horse drawn carriage to driverless cars, instead of the "horseless carriages" phase we have been in for the last century.

Although undoubtedly a very advanced and dexterous species, humans don't always display their best characteristics when in charge of two-ton vehicles travelling at high velocities and in situations where a momentary lapse in concentration can easily kill or maim themselves or others. Humans introduce uncertainty, estimation and emotion. The relative safety of car travel on a daily basis lulls them into a false sense of security, leading to an ongoing complacency that prematurely ends up to a million lives each year worldwide.

Before we spend the rest of this book looking at the problems that driverless cars might solve and the challenges they will likely create, I want to first explore how we've gotten to this point - how are we even able to talk about self-driving cars? What has

[69] https://www.wired.com/2016/10/teslas-self-driving-car-plan-seems-insane-just-might-work/

changed in the world of technology to make it even plausible, and who is at the forefront of this new era?

In this chapter, I will explain at a high level how driverless cars work, and identify some of the key players behind this technology. Actually, it's more accurate to refer to it as a combination of technologies rather than one - the parallel massive advancement of sensors and computing power are both required in various combinations to begin to make this possible. The developments have been pushed primarily by high tech companies and their rapid progress has driven the auto industry to wake up. Drawing the attention and investment of both Alphabet[70] and Apple, the world's two most valuable companies, the depth of the changes now sweeping the transport sector begins to become apparent.

Just as many drivers today don't know much about the operation of their car's engine, future car "users" (the replacement term for "drivers") won't need to know much about how their robotic chauffeurs work. For those interested in understanding, I'll provide a brief high-level overview of the technologies involved. Perhaps a slightly better understanding of how it works on some level will aid in "trusting" driverless cars, a key factor in uptake that we'll discuss in more detail later. I think it's important to have at least a basic understanding of the technologies involved in driverless cars to enable an informed debate about their arrival on our roads.

Slow Progress?

"We wanted flying cars, instead we got 140 characters."

What Happened to the Future - Founders Fund[71]

---

[70] Alphabet is Google's parent company and owner of Waymo, formerly known as Google Self Driving Car project.

[71] http://foundersfund.com/the-future/

"Great as have been the engineering advances since 1920, we have today basically the same kind of machine as created in the first twenty years of the century" wrote Alfred Sloan,[72] President of General Motors (GM) over 50 years ago in 1964. Cars now are definitely much safer in the event of a crash, quieter and pollute less, but development has in many ways been incremental. The modern automobile is in fact one of the most sophisticated pieces of technology in the world - it has around 30,000 individual parts. About 40% of the cost of a luxury vehicle is for electronics, computers and software. Yet they remain very much creations of the 20th century. If Sloan were still alive, he would see the car on the brink of an entirely new generation of technology: the first fundamental change in 100 years. And indeed, his successor is heavily involved in trying to figure out the brave new world, having recently spent over $1 billion of GM's money acquiring new companies to gain an urgent foothold in the forthcoming revolution.

Moore's Law (the doubling of computer processor power every 18 months) is well known in the technology sector, but it has been said that if it were true of automobiles, it would have seen cars develop at a different pace and we now would be driving $25 cars that got 1,000 miles to the gallon. Although slightly facetious, the underlying point that cars have not advanced at the breakneck speed of other technologies has been somewhat valid. As Edward Humes[73] notes, more than 80 cents of each dollar spent on gasoline is squandered by the inherent inefficiencies of the modern ICE. Airliners are 74 times more efficient in terms of fuel per passenger than they were in the

---

[72] Alfred P. Sloan, My Years with General Motors, 1964
[73] Door to Door: The Magnificent, Maddening, Mysterious World of Transportation, Edward Humes, 2016

1970s.[74] It appears that the car has not kept pace with the efficiencies seen in other industries.

In some ways, progress towards self-driving cars has seemed quite slow since they were first widely touted, but that is to underestimate the sheer complexity of automating driving on a mixed-use open roadway. TV show Knight Rider in the 1980s made self-driving cars seem perfectly reasonable to a generation of children and it is this generation that will see it come to fruition, but more in time for their children. Those like me, who grew up watching Knight Rider, have wondered why it's taken so long. So many future-set Hollywood blockbusters (I, Robot, Demolition Man, Total Recall and Minority Report to name a few) have also featured driverless cars that you might think it's a foregone conclusion that the future will not require humans to acquire driving skills. In fact, it's hard to find a science fiction movie that doesn't feature self-driving cars, however dystopian the future involved may be. Unfortunately, all those movies skip over the details and practicalities of how we get to a world of driverless cars, presenting it as a fait accompli.

From Science Fiction to (Almost) Fact

"The car just drove around the truck, it steered itself.
I hate it! I like to make my own decisions"

Michael Knight drives KITT for the first time in Knight Rider

The dream of a self-driving car first appeared in the pages of science fiction and then in the General Motors (GM) Futurama display at the 1939 New York World's Fair.[75] Both RCA and GM experimented in the early 1960s with road-based systems to

---

74

http://www.slate.com/articles/business/the_juice/2014/07/driving_vs_flying_which_is_more_harmful_to_the_environment.html

[75] http://www.computerhistory.org/atchm/where-to-a-history-of-autonomous-vehicles/

maintain vehicles a safe distance apart. Computing power didn't catch up with our imaginations until the 1980s, when Carnegie Mellon University came up with a robot Chevy van and Bundeswehr University Munich developed an autonomous Mercedes van.[76] But these prototypes were unable to function in anything but the most limited circumstances and received little public attention.

"But isn't it still science fiction", you may be thinking? It seems that is still quite a widely held perception. Many consumers are not yet aware of the recent rapid progress. Since 2009, Internet giant Google has taken the lead in publicly developing and talking about the sector. Yet outside of tech circles, many people are unaware of the extent of driverless cars today and label it as still purely being in the realms of science fiction. But as of May 2017, there are trials of the technology by 30 different companies authorized in California alone.[77]

Driven by DARPA

Although not a household name, the US Department of Defence agency, DARPA, has touched billions of lives. Its best-known project? The creation of ARPANET, the basis for the future Internet. So when DARPA turned its attention to autonomous cars in 2002, the tech community took notice. It announced a challenge[78] - create an autonomous car that could navigate a 150-mile (240 km) route in the Mojave Desert region of the United States. On a March morning in 2004, 15 teams assembled take part in this first DARPA challenge for autonomous cars. All failed. And failed badly. None of the robot vehicles finished the route or even came close to finishing it. The vehicle of Carnegie Mellon University's Red Team traveled the farthest distance, completing 11.78 km (7.32 mi) of the course, or

---

[76] https://www.theatlantic.com/magazine/archive/2014/11/the-secret-history-of-the-robot-car/380791/

[77] https://www.dmv.ca.gov/portal/dmv/detail/vr/autonomous/testing

[78] http://archive.darpa.mil/grandchallenge/

just 5% of the target. The assembled minds from the leading institutions in the world were literally miles off. There seemed to be little hope. Yet just a few years later, Google announced it had made major progress. And as I said in the foreword, a Google-powered Lexus drove itself past me less than 10 years later on a public street in California. How has this come to pass?

The first DARPA challenge in 2004 is now a footnote in transport history. Just over 10 years ago, a robotic car couldn't make it more than a few miles on a dedicated course. Now, it can mix it with regular traffic in downtown streets. The DARPA event 2004 was a failure for those who took part, but it was an unqualified success in that it spurred a period of intense development that has seen dramatic progress and the realization of capabilities that were considered impossible. In 2005, five driverless cars successfully navigated the route that had proven so baffling just a year earlier. And just two years later, in 2007, six teams finished the new DARPA Urban Challenge, with the participating Autonomous Vehicles (AV) required to obey traffic rules, deal with blocked routes and manoeuvre around fixed and moving obstacles, together providing realistic, everyday urban driving scenarios.

Learning to Drive

Driving is probably the most complex everyday thing that most of us do (unless you are a surgeon or rocket scientist driving to work). It is a skill that consists of at least fifteen hundred sub skills. Many of us seem to take driving a car fairly lightly but it is actually a hugely complex and demanding task: we are processing a bewildering amount of information, we are constantly making predictions and calculations, and on-the fly judgements of risk and reward, and we're engaging in a huge amount of sensory and cognitive activity. Perhaps most importantly, we are not in control of our own destiny - we must operate within the confines of agreed rules of the road, and trust that others will do likewise, which is true to varying degrees.

Although we may struggle to learn at first, most humans take to the mechanics of driving reasonably well given some tuition and practice. Learning to drive is a normal activity for large numbers of people and has traditionally been a rite of passage for teenagers in developed countries. Although it can take a while to get the hang of, most people find it quickly becomes routine, despite the huge number of mental calculations and coordinated physical movements required. While we may not do as good a job on the rules of the road at all times, we generally get the basics of turning, stopping and starting to move. But humans are not very good at calculations - we make judgements that are quite imprecise, often relying on the reactions and/or accommodations of other drivers to avoid incident.

We make our driving decisions not with some kind of mathematical probability in the back of our heads but with a complicated set of human tools. We don't typically assess an overtaking manoeuvre as "I have a 97.5% chance of passing this car successfully"...we make a judgement call that we think we'll be able to get past safely based on the road space, their speed, our speed and our car's acceleration abilities. Different drivers will have different risk profiles and judge each situation differently. Imagine if we did make such decisions mathematically - what would an acceptable probability be? Would we make a manoeuvre that had a less than 100% likelihood of safe completion? 80%? 60%? And of course, robocars will make astonishingly accurate and rational decisions. Whether or not that is always a good thing will be discussed in more detail in Chapter 6.

You can't of course categorise all (human) drivers as being the same. Most driving schools teach how to drive in normal conditions to avoid creating adversity, but not how to react in adversity. Different people drive differently - consider the careful driver vs the impatient driver who considers an amber light a challenge to "get through" rather than an instruction to stop unless unsafe to do so. The stereotypes of cautious older vs impatient younger drivers have an element of truth. And not all driving situations are comparable - The more controlled the environment, the easier it is to drive and to automate driving. So a highway with clearly marked lines is easier for a driverless car than a twisty road with no markings, just as it is for a human.

Levels of Driverless

Just as most human strategies for learning to drive start slowly and preclude learners from certain environments (such as motorways), teaching computers to drive can be thought of in stages. A variety of capabilities and technologies can be labelled as self-driving cars, so it is important to be clear about terminology as the phrase "driverless car" can be interpreted in different ways. Truly driverless, or fully autonomous, vehicles would mean that a driver does not need to be present and there may be no human controls (such as a steering wheel, pedals) present in the car. However, most commentators do not expect vehicles capable of such fully autonomous operation on all manner of public roads in all circumstances to become available until at least the early to mid-2020s and likely sometime beyond that. Before the technology reaches this stage, vehicles will become available which can undertake increasingly large proportions of journeys autonomously, while still requiring that a driver takes manual control some of the time, in certain situations or is at least available to take control.

The nomenclature around autonomous vehicles and self-driving cars can be confusing - not least because (and not without precedent for new technologies), there are two different scales being widely used to discuss this area. I'm opting for the terminology issued by SAE International.[79] They have outlined six levels, numbered 0-5:

---

[79] http://www.sae.org/misc/pdfs/automated_driving.pdf

- Level 0: Automated system has no vehicle control, but may issue warnings.

- Level 1: Driver must be ready to take control at any time. Automated system may include features such as Adaptive Cruise Control (ACC), Parking Assistance with automated steering, and Lane Keeping Assistance (LKA) Type II in any combination.

- Level 2: The driver is obliged to detect objects and events and respond if the automated system fails to respond properly. The automated system executes accelerating, braking, and steering. The automated system can deactivate immediately upon takeover by the driver.

- Level 3: Within known, limited environments (such as freeways), the driver can safely turn their attention away from driving tasks.

- Level 4: The automated system can control the vehicle in all but a few environments such as severe weather. The driver must enable the automated system only when it is safe to do so. When enabled, driver attention is not required.

- Level 5: Other than setting the destination and starting the system, no human intervention is required. The automatic system can drive to any location where it is legal to drive.

Note: The SAE model takes no account of the ownership of the technology and commentator Ben Evans has suggested the need for a 6th level: city-wide dynamically optimised shared fleet.[80] We'll revisit the topic of ownership in Chapter 5.

---

[80] https://twitter.com/benedictevans/status/771233171518005248

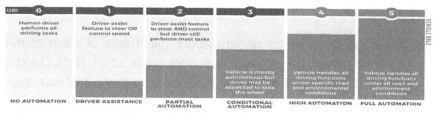

LEVEL	0	1	2	3	4	5
	Human driver performs all driving tasks	Driver-assist feature to steer OR control speed	Driver-assist feature to steer AND control but driver still performs most tasks	Vehicle is mostly autonomous but driver may be expected to take the wheel	Vehicle handles all driving functions under specific road and environmental conditions	Vehicle handles all driving functions under all road and environment conditions
	NO AUTOMATION	DRIVER ASSISTANCE	PARTIAL AUTOMATION	CONDITIONAL AUTOMATION	HIGH AUTOMATION	FULL AUTOMATION

Image courtesy of Driverless Cars Coalition for Safer Streets

Who Is In control?

So why are the levels important? They serve as general guidelines for how technologically advanced a vehicle is. In terms of what consumers need to know, the important distinction is whether or not the human is required to be alert and available to take over control. In Levels 0 to 3, there must always be a human driver in the driver's seat, and there must be traditional controls available for them. For Level 4, the car should be able to complete all tasks without human intervention, but only in a defined area, such as a designated region for the use of driverless cars. In this case, a human should be able to engage in other activities in the car while it's within this zone. Outside of the zone, the human will be required to remain attentive. Level 5 refers to truly autonomous cars - there may be no steering wheel present as the car is designed to operate itself in all conditions and in all regions where car traffic is legal. While drivers themselves may be less concerned with the distinctions, the subtleties could be significant when it comes to issues like car insurance, which is expected to change radically in the era of self-driving cars, as we'll discuss later. Perhaps the most useful role for the levels is understanding the handoff between human and machine. Remember too, that any form of system that relies on returning control to a human present in the vehicle takes away from certain use cases such a blind, elderly or underage passengers.

Skill Atrophy

There has been much debate about the merits of each of the levels, and the differing risks associated with each. Both Google and Ford have said, following their own research findings, that they believe it is important to skip to Level 4, rather than bringing Level 3 cars to market earlier. In Level 4, the car is full autonomous, within certain designated areas. There are still likely locations where a human will be required to re-take manual control. However, this is intended to occur in a planned manner rather than intending to have the driver on standby at all times, as is required with Level 3. The reason both of these vendors propose moving to Level 4? - the inability to rely on humans to retake control quickly enough. By sharing control between the human and computer, Level 3 (and below) risks nobody really being in charge and probably a situation where the human is not ready when required. High levels of automation, without full autonomy capability, could provide a false sense of security.

NASA has been studying the psychological effects of automation in cockpits for decades. Stephen Casner, a research psychologist in NASA's Human Systems Integration Division explains: *"If you're sitting there watching the system and it's doing great, it's very tiring."* In fact, it's extremely difficult for humans to accurately monitor a repetitive process for long periods of time. The better things work, the more they may encourage us to zone out—but in order to ensure their safe operation they require continuous attention. This so-called "vigilance decrement" was first identified and measured in 1948 by psychologist Robert Mackworth. *"No one is going to buy a partially-automated car [like Tesla's Model S] just so they can monitor the automation,"* says Edwin Hutchins, a MacArthur Fellow and cognitive scientist.[81]

---

[81] https://www.scientificamerican.com/article/what-nasa-could-teach-tesla-about-autopilot-s-limits/

An experienced driver today is probably competent enough to monitor a self-driving car and likely able to take over control (though potentially not in time) but what about a driver twenty years from today who will likely not have spent any meaningful amount of time driving a manual car? In his book "Human Error"[82] James Reason cautions that *"Manual control is a highly skilled activity, and skills need to be practiced continuously in order to maintain them. Yet an automatic control system that fails only rarely denies operators the opportunity for practicing these basic control skills. One of the consequences of automation, therefore, is that operators become de-skilled in precisely those activities that justify their marginalized existence. But when manual takeover is necessary something has usually gone wrong; this means that operators need to be more rather than less skilled in order to cope with these atypical conditions".*

Building a Driverless Car

The first time a car pulls up beside you in traffic with nobody in the driver's seat will probably be quite a shock. Just picture it. Then try to imagine the technology required to achieve this feat. You may notice some visual clues in the form of sensors popping out from various points on the car. But other than that, the first generation of driverless cars will look quite like today's cars. Together with the sensors, your robot fellow-traveller will be replete with massive amounts of computing power, and likely significant amounts of pre-provided data about its environment in the form of highly detailed maps. It is this combination of inputs, processing and interpretation capabilities that will enable it to move through traffic alongside you. A self-driving car is a phenomenal technological achievement - it is orders of magnitude more complex than building a flying car, even if that's counter-intuitive. It is hard to overstate the complexity involved, from collision detection to discerning the difference between

---

[82] Human Error, James Reason, 1990, Cambridge University Press

objects, and even divining the intention of other drivers and passers-by in as varied an environment as our roadways.

A key challenge for automating driving is that very little of learning to drive is actually about the control of the car. It's primarily about how to interact with the road and other road users. To achieve the awareness required to even contemplate creating a self-driving car, it requires the ability to "see" and interpret the world around it. The actual mechanics of accelerating, braking and steering are relatively simple actions that pose little challenge to modern control systems. As I've mentioned, there is no one technology that is making it possible to develop driverless cars. Unlike say, the steam engine, which was a relatively stand-alone system, driverless cars require radical developments in several fields - sensors, image recognition and Artificial Intelligence. These need to be combined to achieve a solution that can begin to be credible as a substitute for human control.

Sensor Fusion

As human drivers, we rely primarily on our eyes for inputs, while our brains analyse the situation and direct the muscles in our legs and arms to control the car via the steering wheel and pedals. For automation, sending the commands to the steering, braking and acceleration controls is technically very easy. The hard part is "seeing" the world around it, interpreting it correctly and then proceeding safely. There is no one type of electronic sensor that provides all the inputs needed to drive as efficiently as the human eye, so most driverless cars rely on an approach of adding multiple types of sensor to vehicles and combining their inputs using a technique called Sensor Fusion.

The following illustration shows a prototype driverless car, and the position of the various sensors that contribute to the overall ability of the car to "see".

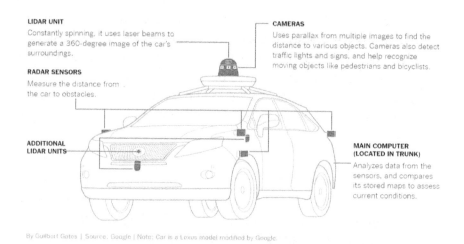

LIDAR UNIT
Constantly spinning, it uses laser beams to generate a 360-degree image of the car's surroundings.

RADAR SENSORS
Measure the distance from the car to obstacles.

CAMERAS
Uses parallax from multiple images to find the distance to various objects. Cameras also detect traffic lights and signs, and help recognize moving objects like pedestrians and bicyclists.

ADDITIONAL LIDAR UNITS

MAIN COMPUTER (LOCATED IN TRUNK)
Analyzes data from the sensors, and compares its stored maps to assess current conditions.

By Guilbert Gates | Source: Google | Note: Car is a Lexus model modified by Google

Image courtesy Guilbert Gates/New York Times[83]

With their combination of sensors, these cars can also sense far more than humans can. The image below shows how a prototype car "sees" the road with its laser, radar, and camera vision:

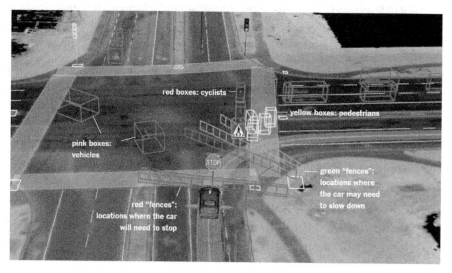

red boxes: cyclists

yellow boxes: pedestrians

pink boxes: vehicles

green "fences": locations where the car may need to slow down

red "fences": locations where the car will need to stop

---

[83] http://www.nytimes.com/interactive/2016/12/14/technology/how-self-driving-cars-work.html

The screen shows the wireframe created in real time by combining the sensor inputs, with yellow boxes for pedestrians, red boxes for cyclists, and pink ones for other vehicles. The car can see not just what is ahead of it, but fully 360 degrees around the car. If you're interested in additional examples of images of what a driverless car sees, refer to this article.[84]

LiDAR

The developments behind enabling fully autonomous cars are hugely complex and among the most advanced technological challenges undertaken to date in any field. Technologies are still being tested and refined and will undoubtedly change in the coming years, but for now, the majority of driverless cars rely on a technology called Light Detection and Ranging (LiDAR) as their primary sensor, supplemented by additional technologies which in combination create a reliable and actionable 360-degree view of the vehicle's environment.

LiDAR-based systems can provide 360-degree images in real time but have been relatively expensive to date. The LiDAR system first used in the test Google car, for example, cost about $70,000, with newer iterations said to cost about 10% of that price. LiDAR, a kind of 3D laser scanning, was conceived in the 1960s for submarine detection from aircraft. Although commonly used as an acronym of Light Detection And Ranging, the term lidar was actually created as a portmanteau of "light" and "radar".[85] The LiDAR instrument fires rapid pulses of laser light at its surroundings. A sensor on the instrument measures the amount of time it takes for each pulse to bounce back. Light moves at a constant and known speed so the LiDAR instrument can calculate the distance between

---

[84] http://uk.businessinsider.com/how-googles-self-driving-cars-see-the-world-2015-10/#while-googles-cars-can-anticipate-a-lot-of-things-by-using-this-collected-data-there-are-still-going-to-be-situations-that-arise-that-have-never-happened-before-9
[85] Oxford English Dictionary, LiDAR

itself and the target with high accuracy, allowing the creation of a 3-dimensional map. The latest LiDAR returns 6.4 million points per second, compared to 2.2 million from the earlier (and more expensive) systems.

Most implementations for driverless cars work using a spinning "lidar", coupled with further information from sensors elsewhere in the car, feeding into the on-board processor. This allows the software to choose a safe speed and trajectory for the vehicle. Although the cost of LiDAR still sounds prohibitive for most vehicles (compared to the average cost of a car in the US of approximately $33,000), we know that, like all electronics, over time, the cost and size will fall dramatically and the performance will increase. In late 2016, Velodyne, a leading maker of laser-based LiDAR sensors and supplier of the original modules to Google before the latter designed its own, announced[86] a new solid-state version of its technology that will cost less than $50 per unit when manufactured at high volume. That's a fraction of the c. $8,000 cost of its current mechanical spinning LiDAR devices used in prototype robotic cars.

Not everyone is relying on LiDAR. Tesla's self-driving hardware doesn't include it, using radar as the cornerstone of the system instead, supplemented with camera technology - the company has opted to develop its own vision processing tools used for helping cars perceive the world around them. This choice could help keep costs lower in the short term, but LiDAR is expected to drop in price thanks to heavy investment from automakers and companies developing the tech. Alongside Tesla, Udacity founder Sebastian Thrun, who also started Google's self-driving car project, said he believes a fully photographic sensor system should be able to handle autonomous driving without LiDAR.[87]

---

[86] http://www.forbes.com/sites/alanohnsman/2016/12/13/velodyne-unveils-lower-cost-lidar-in-race-for-robo-car-vision-leadship/#5d5997903970

[87] https://techcrunch.com/video/udacitys-sebastian-thrun-is-democratizing-education-and-self-driving-cars/57d82caca6237819a6341ff2/

Still, as costs decrease and investment goes into refining the LiDAR manufacturing process, it's hard to see any reason why future autonomous driving systems might not include LiDAR alongside radar and photographic sensors, too, just to produce the most comprehensive possible picture of driving conditions to onboard image processing hardware. Although LiDAR can build up detailed maps of its surroundings in milliseconds, it does have limitations: it can't, for example, read the writing on a sign - all it can show is that there's a sign-shaped object. And it struggles to work accurately in limited visibility such as snow or fog. This is part of the reason that multiple sensor types are required to complement LiDAR.

Radar

While LiDAR is great for accurately mapping surroundings, one of its flaws is in its ability to accurately monitor speed of surrounding vehicles in real time. Radar is very adept at motion measurement, using radio waves to determine the velocity, range and angle of objects. While less accurate than LiDAR at measuring distance, radar can work in virtually every condition and is ideal for driverless cars to "cross validate" with LiDAR data to identify what they're seeing and to predict motion. Most driverless car designs include front-mounted radar units - in fact many current cars already use the same technology for adaptive cruise control systems to maintain a specified distance between cars when cruising.

Cameras

While LiDAR and radar are great technologies for building up a picture of the environment, driverless cars need an actual picture too in order to help identify the objects that other sensors are seeing, and to read street signs and to "see" traffic lights. Driverless cars typically use multiple cameras, both for redundancy and to create an overlapping view of the car's surroundings, not unlike human eyes which provide overlapping images to the brain before determining things like depth of field, peripheral movement, and dimensionality of objects.

Camera technology will continue to advance as it has rapidly in recent years. The additional investment and demand generated by driverless cars is already creating breakthroughs: Panasonic recently demonstrated a camera sensor technology in development that can see in virtual darkness[88], while Sony has announced a new sensor[89] for cameras that combines an anti-flicker function (that means images of LED road signs come out clearly) with a HDR (high dynamic range) function enabling it to see more detail in scenes with high contrast, such as when a car is entering and exiting a tunnel on a sunny day - just as human eyes need to adapt to the sudden change in contrast in the same situation.

Putting it together

Google's driverless car prototype comes equipped with eight different types of sensor - a combination of LiDAR, radar and cameras as discussed, as well as short range sonar, GPS, altimeters, gyroscopes, and tachymeters. The multi-sensor approach compensates for the limitations of each type of sensor. And most driverless cars methodologies compare the sensor inputs with very detailed maps (much more detailed than Google Maps or Apple Maps that humans use) that include street signs, billboards and even the height of curbs.[90]

The following diagram from Hyundai shows how different sensor technologies (Radar, LiDAR and Camera) combine to create a complete picture:

---

[88] https://www.engadget.com/2017/02/09/panasonics-new-image-sensor-could-help-cars-see-in-the-dark/

[89] http://www.pcworld.com/article/3195256/components/sonys-clever-image-sensor-helps-autonomous-cars-see-better.html

[90] https://medium.com/waymo/building-maps-for-a-self-driving-car-723b4d9cd3f4

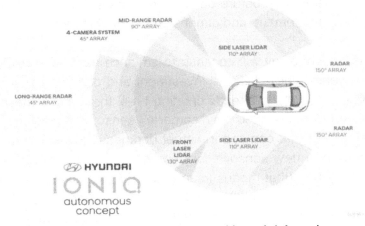

MID-RANGE RADAR
90° ARRAY

4-CAMERA SYSTEM
45° ARRAY

SIDE LASER LIDAR
110° ARRAY

RADAR
150° ARRAY

LONG-RANGE RADAR
45° ARRAY

RADAR
150° ARRAY

FRONT
LASER
LIDAR
130° ARRAY

SIDE LASER LIDAR
110° ARRAY

HYUNDAI
IONIQ
autonomous
concept

<- Direction of Travel. Image courtesy Hyundai America

While this next diagram shows the Tesla sensor suite's combined coverage:

Rearward Looking Side Cameras
Max distance 100m

Wide Forward Camera
Max distance 60m

Main Forward Camera
Max distance 150m

Narrow Forward Camera
Max distance 250m

Rear View Camera
Max distance 50m

Ultrasonics
Max distance 8m

Forward Looking Side Cameras
Max distance 80m

Radar
Max distance 160m

Direction of Travel ->

Making Sense of it all

A plethora of the world's most advanced sensors isn't of any use if you don't know what to do with all the information. As sensor technologies have improved and been combined to create highly accurate depictions of the world in real-time, which can be compared to stored maps for additional validation, there remains the challenge of making sense of all that data and interpreting potential hazards or obstacles that are changing by the second. Humans use a combination of stored memories and sensory input to interpret events as they occur and anticipate likely scenarios. For example, if a ball were to roll onto a road, a human might expect that a child could follow. Artificial intelligence cannot yet provide that level of inferential thinking.

Just collecting all the combined sensor data is no small feat. The sensors on a Ford Fusion driverless car prototype collect 600 gigabytes of data in an hour to help it create 3D renderings of each location it passes through. For context, the average American broadband household[91] uses nearly 200 gigabytes per month. According to Ford, its 3D mapping system is considerably more accurate than using GPS (which is only accurate to within 10 yards) - it says these tools can accurately sense its environment to within a single centimetre. The photo below shows what the trunk of a Ford Fusion prototype car looks like, showing there's still much work to do on reducing it to production size in the next 4 years if Ford stick to their stated schedule of launching in 2021.

---

[91] http://www.telecompetitor.com/igr-average-monthly-broadband-usage-is-190-gigabytes-monthly-per-household/

Image credit: Sam Abuelsamid[92]

Learning to Drive - Machine Intelligence

Making sense of 600 gigabytes of data an hour is a massive computing challenge. Luckily, the pace of progress in computing power remains astonishing. What took 1 year of computer time 25 years ago, now takes about five seconds for today's computers - that's some 6.8 million times faster. And it's advances of that magnitude that are making driverless cars possible as it requires enormous computing power to make sense of all the data generated by the myriad sensors, as well as cross referencing it with that provided by maps. For example, the nVidia Drive PX2 computer designed for self-driving cars has the equivalent computational power of about 150 MacBook Pros. And with rapid development in this space, their next generation of chip is said to offer some 20 trillion operations per second (TOPS) of performance while consuming only 20 watts of power.[93] For context, the most powerful gaming console on the

---

92 https://photos.google.com/share/AF1QipMohX-8qyL-jKD1gOOHffaG_3M2zzMVDTnBKm8rpZW_VZZHgLrWrhK_uNwabU0AKQ?key=ZmNvaGdkSmM2RE5WVW5Pcnl0S003bXhKU1hOY3R3

93 https://blogs.nvidia.com/blog/2016/09/28/xavier/

market at the time of writing, the Sony PlayStation 4 Pro, offers just over 4 TOPs[94] while consuming about 70 watts.

Group Learning

While the individual sensor and computing power available to a driverless car is huge, it has another potentially decisive learning advantage over humans. While we only learn from our own quite limited experience, driverless cars can learn from every other driverless car out there. They can have the accumulated situational knowledge of every mile ever driven by another autonomous car. Google tells of the time one of its test cars encountered a person in the middle of the road, in a wheelchair, chasing a duck, with a broom.[95] I think it's safe to safe that most human drivers have never, and will never, encounter this situation. But once a single Google car does, they all do. Driverless car intelligence can therefore accumulate much faster. If one driverless car makes a mistake once, it can be fixed for all driverless cars. While humans can't automatically download driving experience from a more experienced driver, robot cars learn new skills as soon as one car learns it.

Few people have completed advanced driving courses. Designed for professional drivers such as emergency services, these courses teach techniques such as controlling skids. Many of these techniques are counter intuitive and for anyone who hasn't been on one of these courses, they are highly likely to make bad choices. But autonomous cars can be trained to react as well or better than a highly trained professional driver would. And they will respond consistently every time, devoid of any delayed reactions or fears that inhibit accurate assessment of the situation and the best course of action.

---

[94] http://www.gamesradar.com/do-xbox-scorpios-6-teraflops-really-make-it-the-most-powerful-console-ever-lets-look-closer/

[95] https://www.ted.com/talks/chris_urmson_how_a_driverless_car_sees_the_road?language=en

I've spent many hours watching driverless cars being tested in Mountain View, Singapore and San Francisco, and to date they remind me most of a competent but incomplete learner driver. They have pretty much mastered the basics of stopping, starting and manoeuvring smoothly, but are not at ease in unfamiliar or unexpected situations - remaining noticeably cautious and tentative. The companies building them are eager to learn and are doubtless well on the road to giving them full proficiency, but without the risk of picking up the negative traits, misplaced confidence or complacency that afflicts humans. For now, the driverless prototypes remain under the watchful eye of an experienced advisor who is human, but probably not for much longer, as we approach Level 4 systems capable of autonomous operation in constrained conditions.

To get a sense of driverless cars in operation, it's worth watching this one minute Waymo promotional video demonstrating their progress in dealing with driving scenarios - showing the camera and lidar views as it encounters construction, obstruction, railroad and cyclist scenarios: https://youtu.be/fbWeKhAPMig

Want to Know More?

To keep the subject as accessible as possible, I don't want to turn this book into a deep technology debate. But if you're interested in understanding some of the technology advances, I've included some additional sources in the References section at the end of the book. And if you're really interested, Udacity offers a nano-degree programme[96] for driverless cars, which was created by Sebastian Thrun, the former head of Google's driverless cars project.

---

[96] https://www.udacity.com/course/self-driving-car-engineer-nanodegree--nd013

Testing Times

As the sensor and processing technologies evolve, the key to advancing driverless car tech now lies in testing the systems and iterating until sufficient machine learning has been achieved to create systems that are deemed to be safe. Google first tested its cars primarily on highways, where they interacted mostly with other cars. Highways are relatively easy testing grounds - by design they are simple compared with city streets - with minimal intersections, clearly demarcated lanes and good visibility. In 2014 the company rolled them out on city streets, where they had to fight for space with cyclists, pedestrians, and freight trains, among other obstacles. In May 2017, Waymo (the new name for Google's Self Driving Car project) announced it had now reached 3 million test miles or about 450 years of driving. After initial testing around its Mountain View campus, it had expanded testing to Kirkland Washington specifically as it's wetter there than in San Francisco, and on to Arizona to test in more arid conditions. One of the harshest conditions for a driverless car is snow, because of the effects of deep cold and snow not only on traction and vehicle handling, but also on sensors and optics. Here you can see Waymo expanding their testing to Tahoe in search of harsher conditions.

Snow Testing: Image Courtesy Waymo.

To help car companies work through the challenges of city driving in a safe environment, the University of Michigan has created a $10 million mock 32-acre simulated urban and suburban environment, called Mcity,[97] located on their Ann Arbor campus, about 40 minutes outside of Detroit.

---

[97] https://www.cnet.com/roadshow/news/mcity-americas-true-nexus-of-self-driving-research/

Image courtesy, University of Michigan.

Including a roundabout, a railroad crossing, a tree-lined street that blocks GPS line of sight, or a high-speed freeway merge, Mcity's four-plus miles of roadway allows testers to repeatedly test, observe and shape the behavior of connected and autonomous vehicles in a way that can't safely be carried out with real-world driving. The test roads, fixtures and buildings have been expressly designed to replicate as wide a variety of road environments as possible, including various road surfaces and lane markings, streetlights, even differing curb heights and styles. And the building facades themselves (which are made of real brick and glass) can be moved to be closer to the sidewalk or farther away to simulate different city environments.

Learning to Fail

Every electronic device experiences glitches from time to time, whether it's a cell phone, a computer, or even a simple toaster. Naturally, people monitoring the development of driverless cars technology are concerned about what happens if something goes awry with the equipment operating a self-driving car? The firms working on it are coming from a starting point that the systems that power our self-driving cars need to be more robust than your average household or office computing device. Cars are a harsh environment for electronics, with vibrations and changes in temperature that are a far cry from the calm environment electronics normally find themselves in.

Driverless cars researchers must design for safety, starting with practical measures such as strengthening the most basic components — things like connectors and wiring harnesses that enable the hardware and software to communicate. Testing includes contingencies for all manner of potential faults: a loose cable in the hardware, a shorted wire, loss of power, and the inevitable bugs in the software. As they move, driverless cars perform thousands of hardware and software checks every second to ensure that key components are working as intended. The cars can be designed to detect an issue and determine whether it's small enough to continue driving for a short time (e.g. the tire pressure is lower than expected but not critical) or big enough to stop or pull over (e.g. a key sensor stops working). With the complementary sensors, the cars can still safely pull over if one sensor fails. For critical driving functions, driverless cars makers build in fully redundant systems, equipping each car with a secondary computer to act as a backup in the rare event that the primary computer goes offline. It can even provide for things like not trying not to stop in the middle of an intersection in the event of a failure.

Despite all the emphasis on testing and safety, incidents will inevitably occur. The laws of physics can't be changed and moving objects will collide from time to time due to system or component failures. Just as they have with air travel, regulators will ensure that the highest possible standards are required, and lessons will need to be learned from any incidents. The history of human progress and innovation is built upon pushing new frontiers and as we'll see in Chapter 4, there is a very real imperative to make this technology work as soon as we can, despite the risks involved.

Already in Our Midst

Although cars have seemingly not changed dramatically in form since their introduction, the last decade or so has seen a massive increase in the amount of technology in a car, with varying degrees of visibility. Increasingly, that technology is there to help the driver whether they are aware of it or not. The average new car now carries about 100 million lines of software code. All that code is required to operate various systems throughout the vehicle, including engine and transmission management, traction and stability controls, and more. About 20 million lines of code are required just to run a standard navigation, infotainment, and connectivity system in a modern car.

When I first heard the term "Trip Computer" in cars, it referred to about a 1 inch screen that could show distance and temperature. By contrast, the main display in a Tesla is now a 17" screen with near endless information.

A "Trip Computer" of old

A 17" Tesla display

You can even go into a gadget store and add smart technology to your existing car. Devices such as the Automatic (see below), that plug into a port in your car and report to an app, can offer smart features such as trip logging, engine light diagnostics, fill-up logging, crash alert, parking tracking and live vehicle tracking to virtually any car.

Automatic Connected Car Adaptor and smartphone app.

Ford announced a partnership[98] with Amazon to allow you to ask your Amazon Echo to start your car or tell you the remaining range, just with a voice query.

Owner: "Alexa, ask my Ford for my scheduled car start time."

Alexa: "Here is the list of your current go times. You have a start time set for Monday at 7 a.m., with a cabin temperature set to 85 degrees Fahrenheit. Tuesday at 5:45 a.m., with a cabin temperature set to 75 degrees Fahrenheit."

Owner: "Alexa, ask my Ford for my car's driving range."

Alexa: "You have an available range of 56 miles."

Sample Amazon Alexa conversation via Ford SYNC

But in a sobering note for those rushing to add more technology to cars, there is evidence that cars which are already becoming bastions of technology are proving too much for some people. An MIT study in 2016[99] found that less than half of car dealers gave complete briefings on advanced safety features. There's also dedicated website called MyCarDoesWhat.org to educate people about the features they may already have but not even realise! As more assistive features are added to cars, those not watching may find the takeover akin to a coup. The spread of driver-assistance technology will be gradual over the next few years, but then the emergence of fully autonomous vehicles could suddenly make existing cars look as outmoded as steam engines and landline telephones. We will discuss in Chapters 5 and 6 what will the world look like if/when they become commonplace.

---

[98] https://media.ford.com/content/fordmedia/fna/us/en/news/2017/01/04/alexa-car-ford-amazon-shop-search-home.html

[99] https://www.wired.com/2017/01/car-dealers-dangerously-uneducated-new-safety-features/

The New Gold Rush

"It's not often that in a business as big as the business we're in and a company as big as ours, that you stand at a point where the whole foundation of how your business has operated for the last 100 years is up for discussion"

Dan Ammann, President, General Motors[100]

In 2014, the world's car manufacturers produced 67.7 million cars, all identical in one way - they all boasted a steering wheel and a design assumption of a competent human operator at all times. Internet firm Google produced 25 that were different. These prototypes (codenamed 'Firefly'), were designed to be controlled exclusively by computer. Gone were steering wheels, pedals and controls found in every other car. Gone were even windscreen wipers, whose sole purpose is to ensure visibility for human controllers. This symbol of the future came not from a car maker but from a company known for its search engine.

The car industry is not known for frequent new entrants. Building cars at scale is really hard. According to Toyota,[101] an average car is made up of about 30,000 pieces. The challenge of managing that supply chain, making one come off the production line every two minutes and run for 15 years is not to be underestimated. In the US, before Tesla, the last successful auto industry start-up was Chrysler in 1925. Google were not the first to dream of autonomous cars but they have been the first to demonstrate the technology working in a PR friendly way that the Detroit and Tokyo giants have scrambled to catch up. Their current biggest rivals in the PR battle? Fellow Silicon Valley residents, Tesla & Uber. But as we'll see, the car firms are desperate to get in on the action.

---

[100] https://www.buzzfeed.com/matthewzeitlin/gm-president-driverless-cars-coming-sooner-than-you-think?utm_term=.iqj6kR5OLb#.wdbxPdjWyk
[101] https://www.toyota.co.jp/en/kids/faq/d/01/04/

A 2016 article from CBInsights.com[102] details the self-driving projects currently underway at 33 of the world's largest automotive and technology firms. That gives an indication of the momentum and also something of a scramble as the traditional automakers respond to the incursion from the tech firms. With so many players, I'm not going to detail all their plans or seek to explore their comparative progress. Instead, I've chosen to highlight activities by a selection of some of the highest profile players to help establish a sense of how the market is evolving and where their priorities lie.

The established motor industry has displayed a preference to date for augmenting existing cars (to SAE level 2 and 3) rather than focusing on a more human-independent car (levels 4 and 5). Whether this is an example of a prudent step-by-step approach or a self-serving reluctance to create a future that might see them suffer is a matter of debate. What do they have to fear? Car manufacturers sales rely on you requiring personal car ownership to have your desired level of personal independence - something that there is currently no choice about - you can't yet tell your car to come back and pick you up later. If you could, as we'll explore in Chapter 5, perhaps you won't be inclined to buy a new car. Regardless of the ownership question, car manufacturers know that their future margins depend on not being relegated to the function of assembling other peoples' technologies so they must ensure they are involved in the future design and development of cars, not just their manufacture. Car companies must be careful to avoid falling victim to "iPhone syndrome". In that case, an "outsider" (as in not a recognised phone manufacturer) launched a device that established players spent their first year rubbishing. By the time they had seen its significance, it was too late to recover. Industry titans Nokia and Blackberry were rapidly destroyed. And so the giants of Detroit, Germany and Japan are watching

---

[102] https://www.cbinsights.com/blog/autonomous-driverless-vehicles-corporations-list/

and acting to counter the emergence of Google, Tesla and Uber, and perhaps even Apple.

This real estate map of Silicon Valley shows the mix of new and old companies working on driverless cars and related technologies. It's full of household names from the Internet and Automobile worlds, and upstarts hoping to be the next household name.

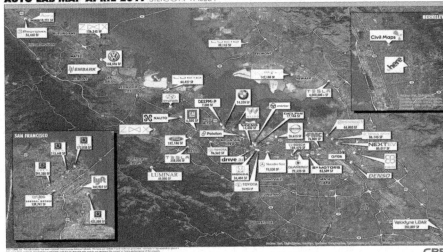

Waymo (Google)

"We're serious about creating full self-driving cars that can help millions of people, to do that, we have to oversee both the self-driving software and self-driving hardware"

John Krafcik, CEO Waymo

Although it has grown to become one of the world's largest companies in less than 20 years on the strength of Internet search and advertising, Google's founders have always also been interested in backing other "big bets". They have disclosed interests in human longevity (Calico Inc.) balloons to distribute Internet signals (Project Loon), smart contact lenses to track glucose levels and in 2010 they revealed their interest in self driving cars.

Google's objectives in 2010 were defined as three-fold:

- To help prevent traffic accidents
- Free up people's time
- Reduce carbon emissions by fundamentally changing car use

Since it broke cover, the team (which included several veterans of the DARPA challenges) have iterated, updated, tested and even crashed. In November 2016, the Google driverless cars project was unveiled as a standalone company within the Alphabet[103] umbrella, named Waymo.

A Waymo FCA Pacifica Minivan. Image courtesy Waymo.

Becoming Human

Google were the first company to embark on a major programme of testing on public roads. Having first tested on their own custom test track at the former Castle Air Force

---

[103] Alphabet (http://abc.xyz) is Google's parent company

base,[104] they graduated to the more demanding, realistic streets of Mountain View. As they learn on public roads, the Waymo cars are currently never unmanned, always having a trained safety driver who can take over if required. A trained software operator in the passenger seat monitors the software (called Google Chauffeur) and notes any disengagements for deeper investigation. The Waymo cars rely on precise mapping of an area before it's handed over to a driverless car - test routes are first mapped by sending out a driver in a conventionally driven car. Waymo cars started from a position of slavishly following the rules of the road. But the company is also teaching them to drive more like people, by cutting corners, edging into intersections and crossing double-yellow lines when safe and necessary to do so. It is working to make the vehicles more "aggressive" like humans -- law-abiding, safe humans -- so they "can naturally fit into the traffic flow, and other people understand what we're doing and why we're doing it," according to Head of Self Driving Technology, Dmitri Dolgov.[105] But autonomous models still surprise human drivers with their quick reflexes, coming to an abrupt halt, for example, when they sense a pedestrian near the edge of a sidewalk who might step into traffic. In 2016, the drivers in Waymo's cars took over control for safety reasons only once per 5,000 miles on average, marking a fourfold improvement from the previous year, according to the company's publicly available disengagement reports.[106]

---

[104] https://backchannel.com/license-to-not-drive-6dbea84b9c45
[105] https://medium.com/waymo/two-million-miles-closer-to-a-fully-autonomous-future-14eb74064e7
[106] https://www.dmv.ca.gov/portal/wcm/connect/946b3502-c959-4e3b-b119-91319c27788f/GoogleAutoWaymo_disengage_report_2016.pdf?MOD=AJPERES

All Aboard

In April 2017, Waymo announced that members of the public in Phoenix could sign up[107] for early free access to a driverless minivan service, boasting a fleet of 600 Chrysler Pacifica vehicles equipped with the latest Waymo technology. All the sensors on these vehicles have been engineered and manufactured in-house by Waymo,[108] and include three types of LiDAR that operate at short, medium and long ranges, and the upgraded system on the Pacifica features eight enhanced camera modules and an additional high-resolution forward-looking multi-sensor module designed to be able to detect smaller objects like traffic cones at longer distances. Much like Apple carefully controls its customer experience because it builds both the software and the hardware for its product suite, Waymo can claim tighter integration between its sensor hardware, sensor fusion software, image recognition and other aspects of its self-driving system. Waymo also claims individual performance benefits in each of its new sensors, including vision cameras, radars and LiDAR, saying each provides better resolution, sensing distance and accuracy than the hardware it has been using on prior vehicles.[109]

Show Me the Money

Some idea of the scope of change we're talking regarding the advent of driverless cars is evident given the investment that one of the world's smartest companies have chosen to put into it. The cost of a 10-year project staffed by hundreds of the world's leading engineers designing and building cutting edge technology is likely enough to make a small country recoil in budgetary horror. Building your own car to test technology is something that nobody outside the car industry has ever done.

---

[107] https://waymo.com/apply/

[108] https://medium.com/waymo/introducing-waymos-suite-of-custom-built-self-driving-hardware-c47d1714563

[109] https://techcrunch.com/2017/01/08/waymo-reveals-completely-homegrown-sensor-suite-for-pacifica-autonomous-test-car/

Driving 3 million test miles, (over 100 times around the earth at the equator) is an undertaking greater than the same company's Street View initiative that documented every single street in the world. Google's move to setup Waymo as a separate company under the Alphabet umbrella shows their plan to turn it from a research project into a viable commercial entity. What motivates a company like Google to invest so much in this venture? I'd love to believe it's born of a genuine desire to improve safety and I do believe that many of the original proponents of the technology were motivated by such altruistic sentiments. However, this is the beginning of a new and unprecedentedly large gold rush. Driverless cars are time machines. They produce that most elusive of resources - new time for people to consume and time is money. In a speculative article[110] discussing the revenue potential of a Google Car, former Googler and now Venture Capitalist, Christian Hernandez concluded that if just 1% of the US car fleet used Google-powered software, the revenue from the additional use of Google services created by driverless cars could amount to $140 billion per annum. It's not hard to understand why Google would invest in that opportunity, nor why other companies want to make sure they don't miss out.

Tesla

"I should add a note here to explain why Tesla is deploying partial autonomy now, rather than waiting until some point in the future. The most important reason is that, when used correctly, it is already significantly safer than a person driving by themselves and it would therefore be morally reprehensible to delay release simply for fear of bad press or some mercantile calculation of legal liability"

Elon Musk, CEO Tesla, Master Plan, Part Deux[111]

---

[110] https://medium.com/@christianhern/self-driving-cars-as-the-new-toolbar-8c8a47a3c598
[111] https://www.tesla.com/blog/master-plan-part-deux

Founded by maverick entrepreneur Elon Musk, Tesla has built its reputation on all electric vehicles that challenged the established automakers and their reliance on gasoline. Although small by car manufacturer standards (25,000 cars produced in Q1, 2017 is a little over 10% of the volume Ford produces in a quarter), Tesla is growing fast. Tesla grabbed headlines when it announced its Autopilot Beta feature in October 2015.[112] This was a software update for its vehicles enabling them to automatically steer down the highway, change lanes, and adjust speed in response to traffic, but is not a full driverless cars solution. Tesla Autopilot was a $2,500 option at purchase time or a $3,000 upgrade, bringing the novel concept of upgrading your car. Tesla cautioned that users adopting the software should exercise caution while using it. Though labelled as "beta" software, Tesla claim every release goes through extensive internal validation before it reaches any customers and say it is called beta to decrease complacency and indicate that it will continue to improve. Tesla have also stated that once Autopilot is approximately 10 times safer than the US vehicle average, the beta label will be removed.

Tesla Autopilot Dashboard. Image courtesy Tesla.

---

[112] https://www.tesla.com/blog/your-autopilot-has-arrived

From Autopilot to Autonomy

"When true self-driving is approved by regulators, it will mean that you will be able to summon your Tesla from pretty much anywhere. Once it picks you up, you will be able to sleep, read or do anything else enroute to your destination."

In October 2016, Tesla announced that all new cars it sells will have an upgraded camera, ultrasonic and radar package that it thinks will enable fully autonomous driving, if and when the software techniques for doing this arrive, at which point it will sell you a software upgrade. It also predicted that it will be able to demo a car driving with full autonomy from coast to coast across the USA before the end of 2017. The proper regulatory approvals remain to be sorted out, so it's unclear when customers will be able to experience fully autonomous driving. Loading cars with hardware that might not be used for years—and requires a software download to unlock the features—is unprecedented in the industry and represents quite a gamble that the hardware is the right hardware and will in fact be somewhat future-proof. The new hardware "suite"[113] includes eight cameras integrated around vehicles for a 360-degree imaging, 12 ultrasonic sensors, forward-facing radar and Nvidia's Drive PX[114] automotive supercomputer to assess the vast amount of sensory data. Tesla claims to have collected 1.3 billion miles of data covered by its vehicles - even when Autopilot isn't switched on it operates in "shadow mode," with sensors tracking real-world data to help train Tesla's software.

Master Plan

Tesla's CEO took the unusual step of publishing his plans for his company on his web site for everyone to see.[115] Rather than the standard corporate approach of not unveiling future plans, Elon

---

[113] https://www.tesla.com/blog/all-tesla-cars-being-produced-now-have-full-self-driving-hardware
[114] http://www.nvidia.com/object/drive-px.html
[115] https://www.tesla.com/blog/master-plan-part-deux

Musk once again eschewed normal behaviour. His somewhat grandiosely titled "Tesla Master Plan Part Deux" was published in July 2016, ten years after his first Master Plan, which was largely achieved. Two of the four pillars of the plan relate to self-driving cars and Tesla's plans to be a leader in this emerging space:

- Develop a self-driving capability that is 10X safer than manual via massive fleet learning
- Enable your car to make money for you when you aren't using it

More generally, Musk reiterated his vision for the future: *"All cars will be fully autonomous in the long term. I think it will be quite unusual to see new cars that don't have full autonomy in the 15-to-20-year time frame. For Tesla, it will be a lot sooner than that. Any cars that are being made that don't have autonomy will have negative value."*

Sharing

A key part of Tesla's plans for self-driving cars is that you will also be able to add your car to the Tesla shared fleet just by tapping a button on the Tesla phone app and have it generate income for you while you're at work or on vacation, significantly offsetting and at times potentially exceeding the monthly loan or lease cost. Since most cars are only in use by their owner for 5% to 10% of the day, a self-driving car could change from a household cost to a source of revenue. In cities where demand exceeds the supply of customer-owned cars, Tesla has said it will operate its own fleet. Tesla owners however won't be permitted to use their self-driving Tesla to pick up people using a competitive ride-hailing app such as Uber. Rather, they Tesla documentation states they can only do so as part of what is now being called the Tesla Network.

Uber

"If we are not tied for first, then the person who is in first, or the entity that's in first, then rolls out a ride-sharing network that is far cheaper or far higher-quality than Uber's, then Uber is no longer a thing"

Travis Kalanick, Uber CEO[116]

San Francisco-based ride-hailing company Uber is also a high-profile member of the race for driverless car technology. It signalled its intent in the space launching a test vehicle on the streets of Pittsburgh, in partnership with Carnegie Mellon University. Its Advanced Technology Group (ATG) had worked to outfit a Ford Fusion with a combination of radar, LiDAR and cameras, as well as developing the software required to interpret the sensor data. I've seen these Uber test rigs on the streets of San Francisco and they are by far the largest most obvious adornments of any of the current batch of tests vehicles.

An early Uber Self Driving Car Prototype. Image courtesy Uber.

---

[116] http://uk.businessinsider.com/travis-kalanick-interview-on-self-driving-cars-future-driver-jobs-2016-8?r=US&IR=T

Their next generation test vehicles, built in collaboration with Volvo, show a more streamlined set of sensors. Uber also grabbed headlines when they purchased Otto, a start-up team working on self-driving trucks for over $600m, but we'll return to the topic of commercial vehicles in Chapter 5.

Image Courtesy Uber.

Uber CEO Travis Kalanick believes that driverless cars pose an existential risk to Uber,[117] and they are working hard to catch up with others in the area. Their big fear is that if someone else develops driverless cars first and launches a fleet of vehicles, they would be able to offer rides at a fraction of the cost that Uber charge, where the bulk of the ride cost is the cost of the driver. In May 2017, Uber's biggest rival in the US, Lyft, announced a partnership with Waymo, just as Waymo and Uber

---

[117] http://uk.businessinsider.com/travis-kalanick-interview-on-self-driving-cars-future-driver-jobs-2016-8?r=DE&IR=T

were embroiled in a legal battle over Intellectual Property concerning LiDAR.[118]

Baidu

China's top online search firm Baidu said in 2015 it aims to put self-driving vehicles on the road in three years and mass produce them within five years, after it set up a business unit to oversee all its efforts related to automobiles.[119] In a surprise follow up announcement, Baidu revealed it would make its driverless cars technology, including its vehicle platform, hardware platform, software platform and cloud data services, freely available to others, particularly car manufacturers, to develop autonomous vehicles.[120]

A Baidu driverless car prototype. Photo courtesy Baidu.

---

[118] https://www.nytimes.com/2017/05/14/technology/lyft-waymo-self-driving-cars.html?_r=0

[119] http://mobile.reuters.com/article/idUSKBN0TX0VB20151214#PUdiIB2o4QBfK5m5.97

[120] https://techcrunch.com/2017/04/18/baidu-project-apollo/

Disruption?

While the interest of technology companies in driverless cars has grabbed the headlines, it's worth considering if these new entrants into the car market are genuinely disruptive? The theory of disruptive innovation published in the Harvard Business Review in 1995 has been frequently misquoted. In its truest form, it refers to a smaller company with fewer resources challenging an incumbent business. They usually service segments overlooked in terms of functional or price needs by established players chasing profits. It is when customers start opting in volume for the entrants' products that disruption has occurred. So Uber is transformative, but not technically disruptive[121] according to the original theory. And the likes of Google and Apple can hardly be cast as having limited resources. Indeed Apple, the world's most valuable company and notoriously secretive, has indicated it is closely monitoring the driverless cars space. In November 2016, Apple responded to an NHTSA request for comment, expressing its interest in the field of autonomy and the testing of self-driving cars, pointing to the safety potential:

"Executed properly under NHTSA's guidance, automated vehicles have the potential to greatly enhance the human experience—to prevent millions of car crashes and thousands of fatalities each year and to give mobility to those without. It is vital that those developing and deploying automated vehicles follow rigorous safety principles in design and production."

Steve Kenner, Director of Product Integrity, Apple[122]

Apple subsequently was granted permission to test vehicles with autonomous technology on California roads and continued its lobbying of the DMV regarding testing processes.[123]

---

[121] http://fortune.com/2015/11/17/uber-disruption-christensen/
[122] https://www.regulations.gov/document?D=NHTSA-2016-0090-1115
[123] https://www.regulations.gov/document?D=NHTSA-2016-0090-1115

The Car Makers

As the Silicon Valley giants rush to find "the next big thing", what are the established pillars of the world's largest traditional industry doing? None of the major car manufacturers turned up for the DARPA challenge in 2004. The car industry has been slow to innovate in a direction that may ultimately radically alter its role. So it's hardly surprising that innovation is now being driven from other sectors, even non-adjacent ones. But the progress of the tech players has forced the car companies to reconsider, which they have done at great cost over the last 12 months. The prize of future mobility is lucrative, and the carmakers want to ensure that software players don't win the lion's share of it. McKinsey estimates[124] that rideshare and onboard-data services could generate an additional $1.5 trillion of annual automotive revenue by 2030, adding to the $5.2 trillion from traditional car sales and services, though much of the latter amount may be under threat if ownership models change as we'll discuss in Chapter 5. In the meantime, traditional car makers want to avoid becoming commodity producers of undifferentiated 'boxes' largely assembled from other peoples' technologies.

As discussed above, Google, Tesla and more recently Uber, have been grabbing the tech headlines with their driverless cars efforts but the incumbents are urgently trying to join the fray. Although wary of eating their own lunch, that's more attractive than the thoughts of becoming the next Nokia, talked about in sad business school case studies of dominance turned to destruction (Nokia had 50% of the global phone market when the iPhone was launched by a non-phone manufacturer). Imagine being in GM or Chrysler facing the prospect that Google or Apple are planning to utterly undermine your established business, that's just returned from bankruptcy. Plenty of

---

124

https://www.mckinsey.de/files/automotive_revolution_perspective_towards_20 30.pdf

"unassailable" market leaders have missed cusps and fallen away. Think Kodak, Borders, Blockbuster, music companies, newspapers. The major car manufacturers don't want to be the "horse" of a new "horseless carriage" era.

The line between the agile technology sector and the lumbering powerhouse automotive industries is blurring. The rise of rideshare and ride hailing companies such as Uber and Lyft means that transportation is being tied ever more closely to your cell phone, while autonomous driving technology will require turning your car into a supercomputer. But these developments are expensive: Carmakers' R&D budgets jumped 61 percent, to $137 billion from 2010 to 2014. Fiat Chrysler America CEO, Sergio Marchionne, has said he believes it makes no sense for carmakers to spend billions of dollars developing competing, yet largely identical systems. Much like the car industry has already seen consolidation, mergers and common chassis/platforms underlying externally different styles, there may be little to gain from attempting to develop driverless cars technology independently. To share some of the risk—and the cost—the incumbent automotive giants and their would-be disruptors are teaming up in an ever-growing, ever more complex series of alliances. Both Reuters[125] and Bloomberg[126] (shown below) have created elaborate interactive guides to these interactions that are instructive if you're interested in learning more.

[125] http://fingfx.thomsonreuters.com/gfx/rngs/SELFDRIVING-SUPPLIERS/010040KW194/index.html
[126] https://www.bloomberg.com/graphics/2016-merging-tech-and-cars/

Bloomberg ▼   The Merging Worlds of Technology and Cars

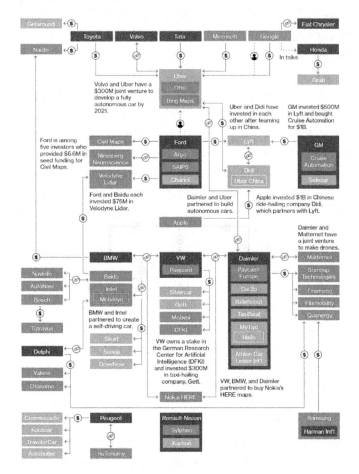

Source: Data compiled by Bloomberg
Additional work: John Lippert, Keith Naughton, Cedric Sam and Kevin Tynan

Ford

Recently departed Ford CEO Mark Fields was committed to shipping a self-driving Ford as early as 2021. Fields expected it to have as big of an impact as the assembly line did. The Ford driverless cars will lack steering wheels, brake or gas pedals, offering full Level 4 self-driving features which don't require a human driver at all.[127] Ford has invested $1 billion in a months-old start up founded by two pioneers in the nascent autonomous vehicle Artificial Intelligence (AI) sector. The Pittsburgh-based AI company Argo AI[128] will develop the brains -- specifically, a virtual driver system -- for the fully autonomous vehicles Ford has promised.

Shown below, Ford's latest test autonomous vehicle[129] has new smaller LiDAR sensors with a sleeker design and more targeted field of vision, which now enables the car to use just two sensors rather than four, while still gathering just as much data.

Image Courtesy Ford Inc.

---

[127] http://www.cnbc.com/2017/01/09/ford-aims-for-self-driving-car-with-no-gas-pedal-no-steering-wheel-in-5-years-ceo-says.html

[128] https://www.bloomberg.com/news/articles/2017-02-10/ford-investing-1-billion-in-ex-google-uber-engineers-startup

[129] https://medium.com/@ford/building-fords-next-generation-autonomous-development-vehicle-82a6160a7965#.uojw6ib99

Ford is not alone in moving into the driverless cars space. The entire automotive industry is in the midst of a radical transformation that is reshaping the very definition of what it means to be a car company. General Motors spent $581 million to purchase of self-driving technology company Cruise Automation, invested $500 million investment in ride-hailing service Lyft, and has launched its own car-sharing service called Maven. According to Fortune, "*there is hype, hope, fear, and insecurity—and at the center of it all is the self-driving car. Thanks to cheap sensors, powerful machine-learning technology, and a kick in the butt from the likes of Google and Tesla Motors, driverless vehicles are becoming a sooner-than-you-think reality. General Motors, Toyota, Nissan, Volkswagen, Fiat-Chrysler, BMW, and just about every other auto company are wading—some cautiously and some with big, headline-grabbing moves—into territory that executives in Detroit and elsewhere not long ago considered a science-fiction fantasy*".[130]

For 125 years U.S. auto companies made their money on the manufacture and sale of motor vehicles. Now they find themselves being dragged into the business of ride-hailing apps, shuttle buses, 3D maps, and computers on wheels that drive themselves. They're no longer content being known as automotive companies either—they're now calling themselves "mobility" companies. But for many of them, it's a stark challenge that extends beyond technology to the core of their brands. The concept of driverless vehicles is especially complicated for companies such as Mercedes and BMW which sell cars on the basis that people will love the experience of driving them but who also seek to portray a cutting edge high tech image. Cadillac CEO Johan de Nysschen said in 2015 that "Autonomous driving and driving passion must co-exist" so that

---

[130] http://fortune.com/self-driving-cars-silicon-valley-detroit/

robots don't take "all the fun and joy out of driving."[131] Even Rolls Royce has unveiled a concept car where the traditional chauffeur's place is taken by an automated assistant Eleanor inspired by the original model behind the Flying Angel hood adornment.[132]

Other Names to Note

It's impossible to detail all the driverless cars firms actively working on bringing the technology to market in what sometimes feels like a new arms race. Along with major auto components suppliers such as Delphi and Bosch, there's a seemingly endless stream of new company moves into the driverless car space, including China's Chuxing Didi, Zoox, nuTonomy, Nuro.ai, Drive.ai, Aurora, and Samsung. This is a fast-moving space and relationships between the key players are changing rapidly. For a further review of the key players, check out this resource from analyst Brian Solis.[133]

It's also instructive to compare the intellectual property race among the key players. Protecting their investment in the driverless cars space represents an important part of the strategy to emerge as one of the winners in this category. This chart[134] shows the most active companies seeking patents:

---

[131] http://mashable.com/2015/10/22/cadillac-autonomous-driving/#WKolOgN4hgqS

[132] http://www.cnbc.com/2016/06/16/rolls-royce-ditches-the-chauffeur-in-this-futuristic-concept-car.html

[133] https://www.slideshare.net/Altimeter/the-race-to-2021-the-state-of-autonomous-vehicles-and-a-whos-who-of-industry-drivers

[134] https://www.forbes.com/sites/oliverwyman/2017/05/17/google-racks-up-more-patents-than-most-automakers-on-connected-and-self-driving-cars/#15cf3e8041ef

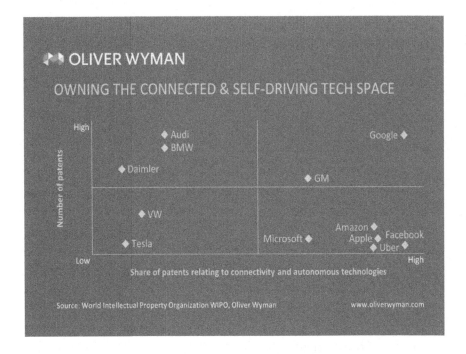

Coming Soon

I do not believe that all the car makers we see on our roads today will survive into the new era of driverless cars, or at least not as independent brands. Those people who will bemoan the end of certain marques need to consider the same fate that befell many custom coach makers as the horse died out - it's similarly unlikely that all the household names of the human driving era will remain. Such a large technological upheaval usually results in the creation of new household names, new empires and new challenges.

Consumers will likely not care about the exact technology used - they will rely on regulation and the desire on the part of the manufacturers to avoid bad publicity to ensure that the overall standard of driverless cars is safe. Just as few drivers know the details of the airbags in their car, they are now accustomed to check that the car has some airbags and then they are generally content, even if the manufacturers glossy marketing materials will try to extol the virtue and differentiation of having more or particular ones. We may yet see some companies try to market their driverless cars based on "more advanced technologies" than their rivals. But will it even be consumers who make the choice? If the first wave of driverless cars is led by fleets, consumers may not be the ultimate arbiters - much as today they don't largely influence fleet purchases - just think how when you rent a car, the providers refer to "equivalent models" where manufacturers would be at pains to differentiate them if selling to a consumer. We'll talk more about the questions posed around ownership changes in Chapter 5.

I'm not going to spend time in this book debating the relative merits of electric vehicles (EV) versus the internal combustion power that has dominated for the last century. While there seems to be a parallel shift towards more widespread electrification of cars as efforts towards self-driving cars intensify, there is no causal link between driverless cars and the system that propels them. A milestone only achieved in 2015, the first million sales of plug-in electric vehicles took 6 years - the second million took only one more year[135] and most forecasts show the penetration of EVs increasing rapidly. It is worth pointing out that the environmentally-motivated emergence of new battery technology, and the associated simplification of car manufacturing and maintenance, represents another facet of pressure on the incumbent and heavily ICE-based car industry.

While there is much work still to be done on the technology front, the sheer scale of effort from so many of the world's leading companies makes it likely that despite the challenges that lie ahead, work will continue apace on developing driverless cars. Much of what is now possible or imminent would have been declared utterly impossible by previous generations - or even seen as demonic. But in the coming years, it seems hard to

---

135 http://www.theicct.org/blogs/staff/second-million-electric-vehicles

imagine a scenario where this type of technology will not be deployed in some form. The main reason being pushed by its supporters? Safety. We'll look at that in detail in the next Chapter.

Chapter 4 - Safety

"And I thought of a girlfriend or a young wife and a State Trooper knocking in the middle of the night to say your baby died in a wreck on the highway".

Bruce Springsteen, Wreck on the Highway

Travelling by car is easily the most deadly form of human transportation. Each year, there are over 1 million deaths worldwide from car crashes, and many millions more that cause serious injuries and yet more that cause property damage. That's 3,287 deaths per day, every day, worldwide.[136] Just one year of motoring deaths and injuries is greater than the combined total of dead and injured in all military conflicts that the US has ever been involved in - combined! Car crashes in the US cause:

- A death every 15 minutes
- A trip to ER every 12.6 seconds
- An injury serious enough for a medical consult every 7.3 seconds
- A crash involving at least property damage every 2.8 seconds[137]

That means that since you started reading this book, 6 people have died, and 740 people have been injured in the US alone in over 2000 crashes. And that's assuming you're so enjoying this book that you've read it non-stop in approximately 90 minutes so far. For every 4 seconds longer than that, add another person to the casualty count from driver-caused collisions somewhere in the world. And as well as the human cost, there's the financial

---

[136] http://asirt.org/initiatives/informing-road-users/road-safety-facts/road-crash-statistics

[137] https://crashstats.nhtsa.dot.gov/Api/Public/ViewPublication/812013

impact - motor vehicle crashes cost society an estimated $7,600 per second.[138] That's about $30,000 in the time it took to read this fact. According to the City of New York, on average, vehicles seriously injure or kill a New Yorker every two hours. Looking at the UK, nearly 10 people are killed in car crashes in Britain every day. Another 250 are seriously injured, and about 1,000 are slightly hurt. Globally that number extends over 1m deaths and 50m injuries. The estimated annual global cost is $518 billion dollars. Even in relatively safe Europe, more than 30 million people have been injured in the last 20 years.

This topic unashamedly gets its own chapter. It is the benefit most frequently mooted by driverless car proponents, and the area that pledges the biggest financial and social impacts - if the technology delivers on its promises. Safety improvement is the primary mission stated by Google behind its massive investments in driverless car technology, and referenced by Apple in their letter to the NHTSA. So it's important to understand the history of crashes, their impacts on society and use that information to decide how valuable the safety gains promised by driverless car are, and what we are willing to sacrifice to achieve those improvements.

Car safety is easy to take for granted until someone you care about dies or is injured in a car crash. It's easy to dismiss based on your own experience that running a red light didn't result in catastrophe, nor does it 999 times out of 1,000. When tragedy does strike, we seem to have come to accept it as the price of mobility. Is it now time to stop accepting the death and destruction as an unavoidable side-effect of personal transport? What if there's a means to retain mobility without the risks? This is the big promise of the driverless car. Let's start by looking at the origins of car safety, the scale, the causes and the downsides - yes there are downsides to improved safety as you'll see later.

---

[138] https://crashstats.nhtsa.dot.gov/Api/Public/ViewPublication/812348

How big is the risk?

"Modern society is impossible to imagine without the automobile, yet it's also one of the biggest destroyers of life. In the United States, crashes claim 1,000 lives every nine days"

"A Public Health Crisis That We Can Fix"
New York Times, 7th March 2017[139]

In 2016, nearly 40,000 Americans died in car crashes.[140] That's more than the number killed by guns (35,763[141]). In another shocking statistic, nearly six million drivers admitted to hitting another car *on purpose* in the past year, in a 2016 AAA survey.[142] If you're interested in statistics on road deaths in other countries, there's a country-by-country list on Wikipedia.[143]

Although the majority of people strive to, and manage to, lead quite safe lives free from regular risk of death, the most obvious and constant threats to our safety actually resides in an activity that many of us engage in on a pretty regular basis: driving. While everyone seems to have an inflated sense of confidence when it comes to their own driving skills, the data say otherwise. In fact, a 2011 car insurance industry estimate[144] suggested that the average driver would be involved in three to four incidents over the course of their lifetimes. Current records show that most American drivers will have a motor vehicle near-incident 1 to 3 times per month and will be in a collision of some type on average every 5 to 8 years.

---

[139] https://www.nytimes.com/2017/03/07/opinion/a-public-health-crisis-that-we-can-fix.html
[140] http://www.nsc.org/NewsDocuments/2017/12-month-estimates.pdf
[141] https://www.cdc.gov/nchs/fastats/injury.htm
[142] http://newsroom.aaa.com/2016/07/nearly-80-percent-of-drivers-express-significant-anger-aggression-or-road-rage/
[143] https://en.m.wikipedia.org/wiki/List_of_countries_by_traffic-related_death_rate
[144] http://www.forbes.com/sites/moneybuilder/2011/07/27/how-many-times-will-you-crash-your-car/

Of course, despite the headline numbers, travelling by car is also statistically quite safe. The sheer number of journeys completed safely each day makes the practice of driving appear and feel very safe. Yet the margin between safety and disaster is extremely narrow. For every 100 million miles driven in the US (thirty thousand times back and forth across the US), there are 1.3 deaths or to frame the same statistic over a lifetime: if you drive 15.5k milers per year for 50 years, there's a 1 in 100 chance you'll die in a fatal car crash.

So on a per trip basis it's incredibly safe and each safe trip reinforces our belief. But yet, on average, every 15 minutes a driver is killed somewhere in the U.S. Highway fatalities spiked 7.2% in 2015 - the highest one-year increase in the tally since 1966. The NHTSA is attributing the increase in deaths on the highways to more driving due to job growth and lower gas prices. Drunk driving, speeding and distraction from phones and other devices are contributing to the alarming increase. "The data tell us that people die when they drive drunk, distracted, or drowsy, or if they are speeding or unbuckled," NHTSA Administrator Mark Rosekind said in a statement announcing the increase in fatalities, reversing recent years of improvements.[145]

"It's an immediate crisis and long-term challenge. Every single death on our roadways is a tragedy. We can prevent them. Our drive toward zero deaths is more than just a worthy goal. It is the only acceptable goal."[146]

Mark Rosekind
Administrator of the NHTSA

---

[145] https://www.nhtsa.gov/press-releases/traffic-fatalities-sharply-2015
[146] http://www.forbes.com/sites/jensen/2016/10/05/going-from-35092-to-zero-a-plan-to-end-roadway-fatalities-auto-makers-are-invited-to-join/#64ed5a294cb8

NHTSA research has shown that 94% of crashes can be tied back to a human choice or error: "decisions like drinking and driving, speeding or distraction behind the wheel." NHTSA research also shows that almost half of passenger vehicle occupants killed were not wearing seat belts[147]. Statistics hide a multitude of detail, especially averages which are frequently quoted. It is worth pointing out that certain types of driving incur greater than average risk - while someone may unfortunately die every 15 minutes on average, more people are killed (one every 7 minutes) on Sat/Sun from midnight to 3am than all those killed during that time on all weekdays. On a Wednesday morning from 3am to 6am, a driver was killed every 32 minutes. In the US, 50% of all road crashes occur at intersections[148]. One study that looked at 24 intersections that had been converted from signals and stop signs to roundabouts found that total crashes dropped nearly 40%, while injury crashes dropped 76% and fatal crashes 90%.

Local News Only

"One death is a tragedy, 10,000 is a statistic"

Josef Stalin

Deaths from car crashes are massive in number but diffuse in nature - they are not visible as a single toll easily reported on the news each day. Yet there have been 1,000 times more deaths in car crashes than plane crashes in the US in the last 15 years (400,000 vs 400) without the same dramatic headlines that surround plane crashes. Deaths as a result of car crashes are usually only reported locally, unless they involve multiple victims or unusual circumstances, so it can be hard to get a sense of the actual scale of incidents on a global or even national scale. As noted above, figures for the US, which is relatively safe

---

[147] https://crashstats.nhtsa.dot.gov/Api/Public/ViewPublication/812319
[148] http://safety.fhwa.dot.gov/intersection/

compared to some countries, put the annual death toll at close to 40,000. To put this in another context, it is the equivalent of a Boeing 737 full of people crashing every single weekday of the year. That would make some significant headlines and the resulting outcry and regulatory oversight would quickly result in systemic changes to address the deaths. Of course, it is not directly comparable, but I think it's a valid paradigm for the discussion. There are many million safe miles driven each day, and the likelihood of death in an air crash is far greater than in a vehicular crash due to the speeds involved. But surely the mere fact that the latter are individual crashes rather than one doesn't diminish the impact of death on the affected families and our resultant social response?

Why do we have such double standard when it comes to safety between aircraft and cars? Or, if we treated road safety as seriously as we treat health and safety at work, would we systematically make it impossible for drivers to behave in such risky ways? Road safety has, of course, improved significantly over the years, but improvements in recent times have been more gradual and there is a persistently high level of death and damage primarily due to the one constant - human control.

A History of (Un)Safety

Car crashes are not a new phenomenon. In 1896 there were only four cars registered in all the United States. Two of them collided with each other in St. Louis. Although the high death toll from widespread car ownership had been the norm decades, it was really the 1960s that saw the first concerted efforts towards improving safety. Ralph Nader's seminal book, "Unsafe at Any Speed", exposed the lack of interest in safety matters among major automobile manufacturers.

Bridget Driscoll (1851–17 August 1896) has the unenviable position in history of being the first pedestrian victim of an automobile collision in Great Britain. Driscoll was struck by an automobile belonging to the Anglo-French Motor Carriage Company that was giving demonstration rides. The inquest returned a verdict of "accidental death". The coroner said he hoped "such a thing would never happen again." However, the Royal Society for the Prevention of Accidents estimate over half a million people had since been killed on UK roads by 2010.

"For over half a century, the automobile has brought death, injury and the most inestimable sorrow and deprivation to millions of people."

Page 1, Unsafe at Any Speed[149]

Published in November 1965, the first sentence of this landmark book from attorney Ralph Nader did not mince words. The rest of the book continued in the same vein decrying the gap between existing design and attainable safety and the auto industry's ignoring of the moral imperative to keep people safer. Some 50 years after the widespread emergence of cars, the spotlight was now placed for the first time on the role of Government in defining safety standards in the automotive industry. 1966 saw the US congress pass the National Traffic and Motor Vehicle Act and created the National Highway Traffic Safety Authority (NHTSA) under the auspices of the Department of Transport (DoT). This created federal vehicle safety standards to set performance criteria for brakes, lights and tires for the first time. Its stated mission is to "Save lives, prevent injuries, reduce vehicle-related crashes."

The NHTSA set about mandating that car manufacturers meet minimum standards - areas that may have been de-prioritised due to cost control or a lack of consumer awareness and thus demand for these features. While the NHTSA has had much success since its inception, not all measures have been embraced by those they are designed to protect. A 1974 attempt

---

[149] Ralph Nader, Unsafe at Any Speed, November 1965

to require all new cars be fitted with seat belt interlock that prevented a car from being started if the occupants' seat belts were not fastened was met with such hostility from car buyers that it was rescinded.

Safety may not be a priority for many people, happy to take the risks and play the odds. They may struggle to afford the additional cost of safety equipment or safer designs. They may place a higher value on thrill-seeking than a more conservative approach to their mobility. The emergence of driverless cars poses many interesting challenges about risk and responsibility. Just because risk can be reduced, should it be? And if it should, who shoulders the cost burden and determines the agenda. Do the industry or the regulators have a moral imperative to make people safer if people don't want to be made safer, or are unwilling to pay the price of such safety?

Cost of Crashes

The highest price we pay for car crashes is in the loss of human lives; however society also bears the brunt of the many costs associated with motor vehicle crashes. According to the NHTSA study[150] released in May 2014, U.S. motor vehicle crashes in 2010 cost almost $1 trillion in loss of productivity and loss of life - a cost of over $900 per person in the US.

The costs of crashes can be assessed based on the Federal Highway Administration's (FHWA) comprehensive costs framework for traffic fatalities and injuries (excluding property damage-only crashes), which place a dollar value on 11 components.[151] These comprehensive cost components include property damage; lost earnings; lost household production (non-

---

[150] https://www.nhtsa.gov/press-releases/new-nhtsa-study-shows-motor-vehicle-crashes-have-871-billion-economic-and-societal

[151] http://newsroom.aaa.com/wp-content/uploads/2011/11/2011_AAA_CrashvCongUpd.pdf

market activities occurring in the home); medical costs; emergency services; travel delay; vocational rehabilitation; workplace costs; administrative costs; legal costs; and pain and lost quality of life. According to FHWA, in 2009 dollars, the cost of a single motor vehicle fatality is $6,000,000. The total value of societal harm from motor vehicle crashes in 2010 was $836 billion. That's 5.6% of US GDP. The United Nations and World Health Organization report that auto crashes cost countries as much as 3 percent of gross national product every year. So the scope of potential benefits is substantial both economically and politically.

What's in A Name?

"Except for highly trained professionals, there are no good drivers - just bad and less bad. The very term accident is a lie we tell ourselves, as almost all crashes result from purposeful negligence, recklessness or law breaking."

Edward Humes, Door to Door [152]

As a society, we make decisions about what's acceptable and what isn't. Whether decided on a personal, local, federal or international level, there are things we believe are ok and others we think aren't. But many of these decisions are not explicit choices - they are "norms" or the established, unquestioned way of things. Most people still refer to traffic collisions as "accidents". However, that implies they were somehow unavoidable or there wasn't contributory negligence. While they may be unintentional, very few are truly accidents. The British Medical Journal (BMJ) stopped using the word in 2001. Similarly, there's a perception gap in reporting where we avoid assigning humanity: 'The car hit the bike' rather than the 'driver hit the cyclist'.

---

[152] Door to Door: The Magnificent, Maddening, Mysterious World of Transportation, Edward Humes, 2016

Our perception of threats influences our response to them. We react to risks such as terrorism or infectious diseases differently than to global warming or car crashes - imminence and motivation are important factors in how we perceive, categorise and respond to threats. But there's also inertia. For some issues, we have a kind of fatalism - a sense that there's nothing we can do or that "things have always been that way". Car crashes have become normal and predictable, even expected. More people are killed on US roads each month than were killed in 9/11 - in polls after those attacks, a majority of citizens thought it was acceptable to curtail civil liberties to help counter the threat of terrorism. Why doesn't the annual road death toll elicit the proportionate amount of concern?

Addressing a driver safety conference in Harvard in May 2016 Mark Rosekind,[153] the head of the NTSA touched on the history of crashes and how they are perceived; *"In the 1920s, when cars were new and unusual, fatal incidents were commonly referred to as 'motor killings', now they are blandly mentioned in media coverage as traffic fatalities or worse 'accidents'. In our society language can be everything."* Almost all crashes stem from driver behavior like drinking, distracted driving and other risky activity. Only about 6 percent are caused by vehicle malfunctions, weather and other factors. The persistence of crashes can be explained in part by widespread apathy toward the issue.

The state of Nevada enacted a law to change "accident" to "crash" in dozens of instances where the word is mentioned in state laws, like those covering police and insurance reports. At least 28 state departments of transportation have moved away from the term "accident" when referring to roadway incidents, according to Jeff Larason, Director of Highway Safety for Massachusetts. The Traffic Safety Administration changed its

---

[153] https://theforum.sph.harvard.edu/events/asleep-at-the-wheel/

own policy in 1997. The Associated Press (AP) news agency also announced a change in policy; "when negligence is claimed or proven in a crash, reporters should "avoid 'accident', which can be read by some as a term exonerating the person responsible."[154] Changing semantics is meant to shake people, particularly policy makers, out of the implicit nobody's-fault attitude that the word "accident" conveys.[155]

Improving Safety

So car-related deaths and injuries are a massive problem, one that somehow has avoided the concerted effort that might have been expected. That's not to say that there haven't been effective initiatives over the years - motoring safety has of course improved over time but there's been a constant struggle between the increasing capabilities of cars versus the technologies being deployed to protect people. Every significant improvement in active safety involves removing human input to counter the shortcomings of human drivers. The total removal of human drivers is the logical end-game for ultimate safety.

Safety is an emotive issue. And not always a rational one. Despite the death figures in this chapter, considering the numbers of safe miles travelled, car transport is unquestionably relatively safe. But it could be safer. Most of us who drive regularly will go through life without any serious consequences. And because most of us suffer no direct consequences from driving, we believe both us and it to be safe. We resent outside interference to the contrary. "It's the other drivers on the road who need to be regulated more than we do" is a typical response.

---

[154] http://bit.ly/1PQM6Gu
[155] http://www.nytimes.com/2016/05/23/science/its-no-accident-advocates-want-to-speak-of-car-crashes-instead.html?_r=0

The Nanny State?

We don't always do what's in our best interests: people don't always choose safety. Fully half of the 33,719 people who died in car crashes in the US in 2013 weren't wearing seat belts that would have saved a great many of them, despite a legal requirement to do so in most jurisdictions. Debates about imposing speed limits more stringently frequently turn to allegations of a nanny state. But for those who oppose "state interference" in their personal lives, it's worth pointing out that the roads are a shared resource - each driver's choices affect others. If we set aside our aversion to being told what to do, the facts speak for themselves. Not wearing seatbelts increases your risk of death. Speed increases your risk of death. But they are a small and unlikely risks, so large numbers of people tend to ignore it for the immediate benefits of faster travel to their destination or a feeling of comfort.

Few people will admit they are bad drivers. Surveys show most people consider themselves to be above average, which is of course quite a significant statistical challenge. We think stricter laws are a good idea for people who need them but overly onerous and unnecessary for us. Illegal behaviour rarely results in a crash or adverse consequence, so people are emboldened to run lights or use cell phones while driving. Even challenges to this reinforcement are ignored or explained - campaigners frequently justify tickets as being down to "quotas for cops" or efforts to raise revenue. Any efforts to impose or even encourage driverless cars must be considered in that context.

Seatbelts

As mentioned earlier regarding the seat belt interlock device in 1973, previous attempts to regulate for increased road safety have met with substantial civic resistance.[156] That's despite evidence of seatbelt effectiveness in saving lives and preventing serious injury. On 31st January 1983 in the UK, seat belts were made compulsory. It wasn't necessarily popular but it saves 300 lives a year. In the US, the national use rate for seatbelts stands at 88.5 percent which means nearly 27.5 million still don't buckle up.[157] In 2015, safety belts prevented 13,941 fatalities and over 325,000 serious injuries. They could have saved an additional 2,804 people. Since 1975 when records began, in total, seat belts have saved 344,448 lives. If every driver and passenger had been wearing a seat belt since, an additional 381,787 lives could have been saved. As campaigns to increase seat belt compliance have failed to further improve their use, the authorities have turned to further technology solutions to improve safety, often favouring solutions that don't require driver compliance for their operation.

Regulated Technology

While some technology is added to cars at the initiative of car makers, keen to demonstrate technological leadership - or merely differentiation - and some technology is added by users, regulators have played a key role to date in mandating the addition of technology to cars, primarily to enhance safety. As of the 2012 model year, all passenger vehicles in the US were required to have electronic stability control as standard equipment.

On 1st November 2015, two new safety systems became standard on new trucks, coaches and buses across Europe. New models must be fitted with autonomous emergency braking (AEB) and lane departure warning (LDW). AEB will detect if the driver is approaching slow-moving traffic ahead too quickly and

---

[156] http://www.thedetroitbureau.com/2009/11/the-great-safety-belt-interlock-fiasco/
[157] https://www.nhtsa.gov/risky-driving/seat-belts

send out a warning. And if the driver doesn't respond, the brakes come on automatically to avoid a collision. LDW monitors the roadway white lines and if an inattentive driver starts to drift out of lane without indicating, it sends out an alert which could be visual, audible, and/or a vibration.

Starting with the 2018 model year, all vehicles sold in the U.S. will be required to have backup (reversing) cameras. According to government statistics, roughly 250 people are killed each year in backover accidents, many of them children. The DOT, NHTSA and Insurance Institute for Highway Safety (IIHS) have mandated that by 2022, all new vehicles made by 20 manufacturers will have automatic emergency braking as standard equipment. The 20 automakers that are part of the agreement cover 99% of the US market for new vehicles.

Largely because of regulation, virtually all cars now feature some combination of airbags, ABS braking and traction control systems. Each of these supposedly life-saving technologies has had serious, even fatal malfunctions, particularly in early roll-out, but also in mature phases of the technology.[158] Despite these edge cases of malfunction, or risks in marginal conditions, both airbags and ABS technologies enjoy a ubiquitous presence in cars. In fact, most consumers would simply not buy a car without these features today. It's recognized that, while not perfect, these systems on balance provide greater safety than otherwise.

In that historical context, as driverless car technologies are considered for regulation, it will be important to consider them through the lens of experience - there will be failures and there will be cases where the technology does not provide the anticipated benefits. But it is also likely that they will do more good than harm and once they can be proven to do so, you can expect to see campaigns to mandate the use of some or all of

---

[158] https://techcrunch.com/2016/11/24/teslas-autopilot-and-the-double-standard-for-automotive-safety-systems/

the technologies involved, even in the face of opposition from those concerned with the (over)reach of the Nanny State.

Risk Compensation

It's not all doom and gloom - there have been significant safety improvements over the last couple of decades but recent trends reveal a stubbornly high level of deaths that current approaches seem unable to remedy.

U.S. Roadway Fatalities per Billion Vehicle Miles Traveled

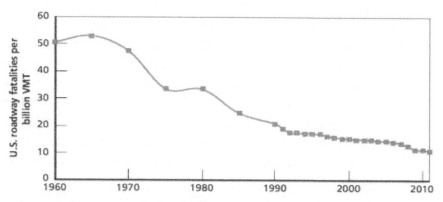

NOTE: Data from BTS (2013) includes all highway transportation modes: passenger car, light truck, motorcycle, large truck, and bus. Fatalities include vehicle occupants for all highway modes, as well as pedestrians and cyclists.
RAND RR443-2.3

As positive as the downward trend in the graph above has been, and especially the improvements compared to the 1960s, the progressive momentum has clearly disappeared. Those investigating this phenomenon believe that a theory called Risk Compensation may play a part. This suggests that people typically adjust their behavior in response to the perceived level of risk, becoming more careful where they sense greater risk and less careful if they feel more protected. The addition of modern safety devices on cars may cause this sense of protection. Although usually having a small impact in comparison to the fundamental benefits of safety interventions, risk compensation may result in a lower net benefit than expected from new initiatives. The reduction of predicted benefit from regulations that intend to increase safety is sometimes referred to as the Peltzman effect in recognition of Sam Peltzman, a professor of economics at the University of Chicago Booth School of Business, who published "The Effects of Automobile Safety Regulation" in the Journal of Political Economy in 1975.[159]

Cars Don't Crash

It's important to point out that currently in almost all cases of car crashes, the car itself is not at fault - a tiny percentage of car crashes are the result of mechanical failure, yet these are more tightly regulated and enforced than the humans that cause over 90% (see table below). Cars in the UK face roadworthiness checks every year once they are 3 years old, while humans face one check when they apply for their license, and can then renew their license every ten years with no further checks, other than one forced by old age or a change in medical or optical conditions.

Table 1. Driver-, Vehicle-, and Environment-Related
Critical Reasons

Critical Reason Attributed to	Estimated	
	Number	Percentage* ± 95% conf. limits
Drivers	2,046,000	94% ±2.2%
Vehicles	44,000	2% ±0.7%
Environment	52,000	2% ±1.3%
Unknown Critical Reasons	47,000	2% ±1.4%
Total	2,189,000	100%

*Percentages are based on unrounded estimated frequencies
(Data Source: NMVCCS 2005–2007)

Source: US National Motor Vehicle Crash Causation Survey[160]

159

http://econpapers.repec.org/article/ucpjpolec/v_3a83_3ay_3a1975_3ai_3a4_3ap_3a677-725.htm

160 https://catalog.data.gov/dataset/national-motor-vehicle-crash-causation-survey-nmvccs-nmvccs-xml-case-viewer

It is human behaviour and decisions that cause the vast majority of crashes. Over 40 percent of fatal crashes involve alcohol, distraction, drug involvement and/or fatigue. Some 10,000 people die each year in crashes where those involved were over the legal blood alcohol limit. Further investigation of the types of human error that cause crashes shows the potential for improvement due to driverless cars:

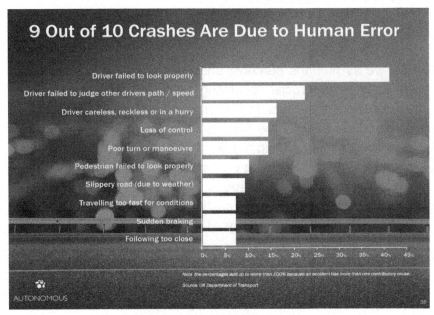

Image courtesy Autonomous

Technology to the Rescue?

The focus of manufacturers' car safety efforts to date has largely and by necessity been on improving survivability, as the technology required to reliably reduce crashes has not existed. Replacing the cause of more than nine out of ten crashes - the human - has not been a practical consideration until recently. Self-driven vehicles would not fall prey to human failings, suggesting the potential for a dramatic fatal crash-rate reduction, assuming automated malfunctions are minimal. And even when the critical reason behind a crash is attributed to the vehicle, roadway or environment, additional human factors such as inattention, distraction, or speeding are regularly found to have contributed to the crash occurrence and/or injury severity, meaning that the eventual improvements could stretch even further. It has been impractical to enforce driving laws in all places at all times where humans can arbitrarily replace the rules of the road with their own judgement, preferences and priorities. That's about to change.

Reactions

How we as humans perceive and react to the world around us as we drive is crucial to driving safely. Modern cars largely isolate us the road outside and create a cocoon where we often disregard the rules of the road in our quest to get where we are going. Legislation relating to speeding may be amongst the most routinely ignored of any statute books. People frequently decide what they deem is a safe speed, while most also overestimate their driving abilities and reaction times, relying largely on chance and other drivers to avoid collisions.

Rapid reactions are crucial to fatality probabilities in crashes - at 20 mph the fatality rate for a pedestrian is less than 10%, at 30 mph it's closer to 50% and at 40 mph, 90% of impacts with cars prove fatal to pedestrian. For drivers too, speed at impact is important. In 3 seconds, two cars travelling at 65 mph will close two football fields of distance. In a crash at 50 miles per hour you're fifteen times more likely to die than in a crash at 25 miles per hour. Applying brakes just half a second earlier in a car travelling at 50km/h can reduce the crash energy by 50%. If driverless cars can offer better reaction times, even in instances where a crash is physically unavoidable, there is a high probability of reduced impact severity.

Human reactions are neither perfect nor constant - drivers tend to be impatient to varying degrees. After 30 seconds, cars waiting to turn will accept smaller gaps as impatience takes hold. We perceived time lost in a car (or transport situation) differently than other time - time we would gladly wait for service in a restaurant but invokes road rage as we sit for 10 seconds longer than we think we should have to at a red light. Drivers encounter red lights 50,000 times per year, often making a judgement call based more on desire to "get through" than on the colour of the signal and safe braking distances. Removing this variable from driving would be a major step forward towards reducing crashes as driverless cars will boast reaction times and speed perception far superior to humans.

Distraction

It is perhaps ironic that another of the largest contributors to the rising deaths in car crashes is technology itself, in the form of the cell phone. During any daylight moment in the United States, some 660,000 drivers are using handheld cell phones while operating a motor vehicle, according to the NHTSA.[161] The AAA says a driver's eyes may leave the road for two or three seconds to check a text or snap a selfie. In 2015 alone, 3,477 people were killed, and 391,000 were injured in motor vehicle crashes involving distracted drivers.

Yet, without waiting for the driverless car, technological solutions for distracted driving have already been proposed. The New York Times reported in September 2016[162] that Apple patented a "lock out" mode back in 2008. In the text of the patent,[163] the company explains that this type of safety feature may be the only way to prevent thousands of needless deaths: *"Texting while driving has become so widespread that it is doubtful that law enforcement will have any significant effect on stopping the practice."* But mobile device manufacturers, perhaps afraid of

---

[161] https://www.nhtsa.gov/risky-driving/distracted-driving
[162] https://www.nytimes.com/2016/09/25/technology/phone-makers-could-cut-off-drivers-so-why-dont-they.html
[163] https://www.google.com/patents/US8706143

losing market share, have largely foregone these fixes — and federal safety regulators have let them. In June 2017, Apple announced[164] that the new version 11 of iOS due in the Fall would finally include a special mode to reduce distractions while driving.

Although we think we can safely drive and still attend to other tasks, humans aren't good at multi-tasking. One study by the University of Sussex[165] involved 20 male and 40 female volunteers who took part in video tests while sitting in a car seat behind a steering wheel. One group of volunteers could "drive" undistracted while another two heard a male voice from a loudspeaker 3ft (0.9m) away. Those who were distracted by the voice engaging them in conversation took just under a second longer to respond to events, such as a pedestrian stepping off the pavement, an oncoming car on the wrong side of the road or an unexpected vehicle parked at a junction. The study showed that asking a simple question - such as, "where did you leave the blue file?"- during phone conversations could mean a driver concentrates on an area four times smaller than normal, because their brain is imagining the room where they left the file, instead of checking for hazards in front of them.

Weight Gain

There are of course two routes to minimise death and injury - (1) reduce the number of impacts and (2) increase the survivability of collisions. The 1970s and 1980s saw most of the effort go into the second of these - crash survivability. Cars gained weight, crumple zones, and air bags. But the increased safety has come at a cost in terms of weight. Average weight has risen steadily, which means that many of the advances in fuel savings have been offset or reduced by additional safety equipment and crash

---

164 https://www.usatoday.com/story/tech/talkingtech/2017/06/05/iphone-get-do-not-disturb-while-driving-mode-ios-11-fall/102524686/

165 http://www.irishtimes.com/life-and-style/motors/hands-free-conversations-dangerously-distracting-for-drivers-study-1.2676864

protection. For model year 2012, U.S. cars averaged 3,482 pounds and light trucks averaged 4,779 pounds, as shown in the graph below, while for comparison, the original Ford Model T only weighed 1,200 pounds.

Average Weight of U.S. Cars and Light Trucks, 1975–2012

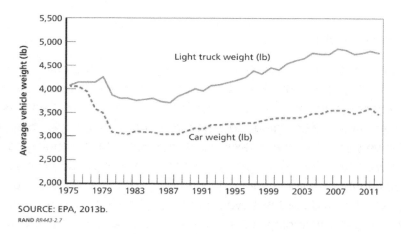

SOURCE: EPA, 2013b.
RAND RR443-2.7

Image Courtesy Rand Corporation

As mentioned already, considering the sheer number of journeys and the variables involved, car travel is remarkably safe. Improved brakes, stability and survivability have contributed perhaps as much as they reasonably can, while the one remaining constant is the controller (human driver). Ultimately, removing this variable will lead to vehicles that should not crash—or at least should not crash under normal operation. Historically, vehicle safety— driver and passenger safety especially—has focused on crashworthiness. This shift means that at some point, self-driving vehicles might no longer require significant amounts of structural steel, roll cages, or air bags, among other safety features. Vehicles could therefore be much lighter. With crashless vehicles, not only can weight be reduced, but cabins can also be redesigned to support activities other than driving and crash survival. If the likelihood of a crash is so reduced as to be negligible, at what point would you remove or reduce crash protection? Although an attractive contributor to reductions in emissions and pollution due to weight reductions, this won't realistically be possible until nearly all human driven cars are removed from the roads - the outcome of a collision between a human-driven 2-ton car and a lightweight driverless car would not be positive for the driverless car occupants.

Why Wait?

The average U.S. vehicle is now 11.6 years old, according to the consulting firm IHS Markit.[166] But that means millions of car owners are missing out on technology that could potentially save their lives. According to research from Carnegie Mellon University,[167] if three existing automobile AI technologies - forward collision warning, lane departure warning, and blind-spot monitoring - were deployed across all U.S. cars, they would prevent or reduce the severity of more than 1 million accidents every year, including more than 10,000 fatal crashes. But the cost of these, coupled with the fact that they remain optional extras on many new cars, means it's unlikely that we will easily see the benefits that would accrue were they standard on all models now. This illustrates that consumers can be slow to adopt optional costly technologies even when they are beneficial, and manufacturers are slow to add them in the absence of regulation.

Other Road Users

I mentioned earlier in the context of Nanny State and resistance to restrictions on personal freedoms, that public roads are in fact shared spaces, and while the major proportion of road use is by cars, there are other categories of road user, many of whom fall

---

[166] http://news.ihsmarkit.com/press-release/automotive/vehicles-getting-older-average-age-light-cars-and-trucks-us-rises-again-201

[167]

http://www.slate.com/articles/technology/future_tense/2016/10/self_driving_cars_effects_on_cities_depend_on_who_owns_them.html

into the 'vulnerable' category. These motorcyclists, cyclists and others often find themselves at the mercy of motorists. Motorcyclists in particular risk their lives on roads – motorcyclists accounted for 27 times more deaths than drivers in cars in 2014[168]. In the UK, the number of cyclists killed or hurt on the roads has climbed since 2003 and now accounts for 14% of all casualties[169], though cycling amounts to only 1% of total distance traveled.[170]

A 2008 Federal Highway Administration Congressional study estimated the total cost of wild-life vehicle collisions at over $8bn per year. Only about ⅓ of large animal collisions are reported. Again, looking at statistics for the UK, since 2010, 38 riders and 222 horses have been killed in incidents on Britain's roads.

And pedestrians could expect to have a better relationship with driverless cars than they have with cars driven by other humans - barring contributory negligence on their part - such as stepping out in front of a car where physics rather than reactions prevent it from stopping - more than 10 pedestrians per day that die now could live. The NHTSA counted 5,376 pedestrian deaths in 2015[171] and more than 70,000 injuries.

The Environment

Leaving aside the human and financial impacts of car crashes, it is also worth noting the relevance of another important issue and its injurious impacts on human health - environmental pollution. The internal combustion engine is a major contributor to air

---

[168] National Highway Traffic Safety Administration. 2016. Traffic safety facts, 2014: motorcycles. Report no. DOT HS-812-292. Washington, DC: US Department of Transportation.
[169]
https://www.gov.uk/government/uploads/system/uploads/attachment_data/file/514912/road-use-statistics.pdf
[170] https://www.gov.uk/government/statistical-data-sets/nts03-modal-comparisons
[171] https://www.nhtsa.gov/road-safety/pedestrian-safety

pollution. The 1965 Motor Vehicle and Air Pollution Act limited hydrocarbon and carbon monoxide emissions from new cars, in an attempt to staunch their environmental impacts. The environmental payback goes beyond the immediately obvious. There would be fewer deaths and lost work days from air pollution - the European Environment Agency[172] (EEA) estimated that air pollution (to which car emissions contribute) caused an estimated 400,000 premature deaths in Europe in 2011.

Safety Conclusions

Very little human endeavour is without risk. Total safety may not be possible, or possible at an acceptable cost and level of convenience. But it's perhaps surprising how accepting we have become of motor vehicle-associated crashes, despite their being an eminently addressable source of injury and death. This doesn't require the speculative investments and research associated with medical enterprise aimed at curing diseases, but deals with much simpler facts - slower cars will kill less people. Vehicles/drivers that obey the rules of the road will result in fewer (if any) crashes. With driverless cars, there will be fewer families grieving over an unnecessary death and fewer people temporarily or permanently disabled.

The stated primary aim of Google's Driverless car project is the reduction of deaths in car crashes. While the more cynical may point to Alphabet and Apples' interests in cars as being commercially motivated, it's hard to argue against a reduction in deaths as a positive outcome, whatever their underlying motivations. The 2nd and 3rd order impacts of improvements in safety are, like all other impacts, difficult to predict. There will be thousands of people saved a life of dependence on, and potentially addiction to, painkillers for injuries sustained in car crashes. But there are downsides too - the people who lived due

---

[172] https://www.eea.europa.eu/

to transplants from car crash victims will need a new source of organs.

Road safety has been identified as a global priority. In 2010 a United Nations General Assembly resolution proclaimed a Decade of Action for Road Safety (2011–2020). This Decade was launched in May 2011 in over 110 countries, with the aim of saving millions of lives by improving the safety of roads and vehicles; enhancing the behaviour of road users; and improving emergency services.

Driverless cars could be the outstanding public-health achievement of the 21st century for preventable deaths. While it is hopeful and even likely that scientists and researchers will make important treatment breakthroughs for other mass killers, it is already clear that technology could be used to address the challenge of road deaths. Driverless cars could, in the coming decades, reduce traffic fatalities dramatically, eventually by up to 90 percent - which means that, using the number of fatalities in 2016 as a baseline, self-driving cars could save over 30,000 lives a year. In the United States alone, that's nearly 300,000 fatalities prevented over the course of a decade, and 1.5 million lives saved in a half-century.

Our societal transition from initial outrage to acceptance of road fatalities shows how attitudes change over time. Some argue that road safety is improving and can continue to do so without driverless cars. There is no denying progress (based on deaths compared to VMT) but for me the total of fatalities and injuries in absolute numbers remains the total to address. We must consider the number of families changed, not just the number of successful miles travelled. The metric of fatalities per vehicle mile travelled has been on a steady, dramatic decline for decades but should that be the key metric and not overall fatalities?

Anyone working on driverless car projects will tell you that the bulk of questions they get relate to "whether self-driving cars are safe". Liam Pedersen, principal researcher at Nissan's research centre in Silicon Valley, sums it up: *"This is perhaps the wrong question; the question should be: 'Are human-driven cars safe? And the answer is no.' An autonomous vehicle is likely to be far safer than a person at all times. It doesn't have to be as good as a good human driver but it just has to be better than a bad human driver. That's where the majority of accidents occur."*[173]

As a society, our aim should surely be to push motor vehicle fatality and injury rates towards those seen in aviation and rail travel as soon as possible - down to about 1% of the current rates. Enhanced technology and reduced human input will be the price required - are we willing to pay? If it were a straightforward question, then perhaps it would be easier. But as we shall explore in the coming Chapters, the advent of driverless cars is not purely a simple matter of safety improvements.

---

[173] https://www.wired.com/2017/01/nissans-self-driving-teleoperation/

Chapter 5 - All Change

"Change is the law of life. And those who look only to the past or present are certain to miss the future"

JFK

Aside from the potential and expected benefits in the area of safety, the eventual ultimate scale and scope of the impacts of driverless cars in the coming decades make it hard to know where to begin efforts to assess them. Some changes are obvious and easier to plan for, but the real difficulty lies in the unanticipated changes, those that happen less visibly or those for which there is no obvious or immediate solution. And of course, driverless cars are not happening in isolation from myriad other technologically-driven changes that in unpredictable combinations will alter our society at an unprecedented rate.

100 years ago, few people would have predicted the changes we discussed in Chapter 2 that were enabled by the widespread use of the personal motor car. With a development so significant as driverless cars, there are far reaching implications which means both far-reaching positives and negatives. You can be sure that those who stand to be negatively impacted will not be quiet. As civilization evolves, long established norms have to change. Previously accepted and expected practices must adapt. There was a time it was perfectly normal for people to gallop through towns on horses with scant regard for anything in the way. But as towns evolved, controls had to be put in place to manage this traffic, to the point where it eventually became unacceptable to consider horse travel through most urban areas.

Although change is hard to predict, I believe it's important to have a plan that considers possible change outcomes, as well as a view of the desired change outcome, so that actions can be taken, in so far as possible to reach the desired outcome. These are big questions, and no certain answers can be given at this stage. The lack of certainty, especially around timing, is no excuse though to delay discussion and decisions to shape the future. How best to use non-incremental new technology isn't always obvious. At first, we tend to use it in existing ways. So when PCs arrived, people used them to write memos instead of on typewriters. Only later did we get to email and then the wide variety of new tasks enabled by PCs that were not envisaged from the outset. Our initial instinct is to fit a new technology to our existing workflows before we work out we can have entirely new workflows. Often, it's easier to imagine how a new invention changes what we're used to before we focus on what new things it enables. It is in the creation of new possibilities that some of the ultimately most positive outcomes may lie.

Cars and the Automobile Ecosystem

Let's start with the most obvious areas for change. However long it actually takes to happen, there are a lot of industries and occupations severely threatened by the advent of driverless cars. Driving schools, crash repairs, valet parking attendants and drivers themselves are all obviously in the firing line and all stand to become largely obsolete. This is change on a massive scale - already more people earn a pay check--or part of one-- from Uber than from any other private "employer" in the world except for Wal-Mart and McDonald's. But what else faces an uncertain future as driverless cars take shape?

I recently saw the sticker below pointing to the exhaust tailpipe on a gasoline car proclaiming - "my next car won't have one of these". That got me thinking that the same could be said of many more features of the owner's conveyance, regardless of their presumed intention to switch to an electric car.

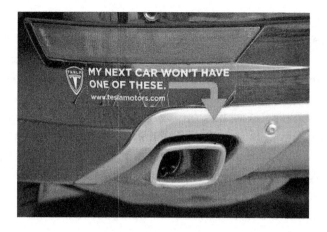

Depending on when they make their next purchase, it may also be devoid of the steering wheel, pedals, gear shift and even the driver's seat. In fact, it may not look anything like what we're used to on the inside or the outside.

Materials & Design

The interior of cars used be a spartan bench seat, with a roof to keep the occupants sheltered and nothing unrelated to the operation of the vehicle. Modern cars are now a fully enclosed steel safety cocoon with climate control, used as a concert hall, a phone booth and often a dining table, along with a storage space. Since its inception, car design has been centred around its controlling force, the human at the controls. Although some countries place the wheel on the left and some on the right owing to the origins of which side of the road they drive on, (with very rare cases such as the McLaren F1 with its central steering position) virtually all car interior designs have one immovable requirement - a front-facing steering wheel, with a surrounding dashboard of controls and information sources. An entire ergonomics discipline has emerged focused on ensuring that all necessary controls are close to hand, while designers have also focused on maximising visibility from the driving seat, though invariably accepting some level of compromise with blind spots an accepted "feature" and warnings etched into mirrors reminding drivers how flawed their perspective is.

On one level, removing the steering wheel would bring a sigh of relief from vehicle manufacturers who incur significant additional cost producing left and right-hand drive variants of their cars to cater for different world markets. But the removal of the steering wheel brings many other design opportunities to consider. In general, you can't get into a car from the front because the engine is there. Even in rear engined cars, the steering wheel still impedes front entry, at least on one side. Entry and exit through the front would have advantages for parking and for safety by not involving stepping out on the street into oncoming traffic. The removal of a fixed steering wheel as the dominant feature could enable designs where passengers enter or exit through a front rather than side door. If we remove the design constraints that have given us the vehicle layouts of the last hundred years, thus given a clean-sheet design, what are some of the questions we might ask? How will design change when relieved of driving controls and a human in pole position? Similarly, for those cars that switch to new forms of propulsion such as electric or hydrogen fuel cell, the front hood is vestigial. Google's prototypes don't have windscreen wipers. In fact, cars of the future may not even have windows. We may choose to have them but we won't need them.

Underneath its exterior styling, the modern car has a huge focus on safety - specifically the survival of impacts with minimum damage to its occupants - massive amounts of engineering effort have gone into safety improvements, both passive and active. This takes the form of strengthened chassis, complex energy absorbing crash structures, devices to pull the engine and controls away from the driver in the event of a collision, as well as numerous restraint and airbag devices. As discussed in Chapter 4, these add significant weight, cost and complexity to the design of a car. Their very construction could change as the compromises made to protect from collisions could become unnecessary if collisions become a statistical anomaly rather than a frequent occurrence. Once collisions reach a certain rarity, cars could arguably forgo some of the emphasis on crash survival and use lighter materials - materials such as aluminum that are not hugely strong but are lightweight (more economical in use) and easily recyclable. Swapping to aluminium could cut a car's weight in half, with corresponding drops in fuel consumption and carbon emissions. The initially higher cost of aluminium (compared to steel) is easily out-weighed over time by the reduced running costs and the higher recyclability. Lighter cars are more fuel efficient so there would be an immediate improvement in fuel consumption/improvement in performance given a better power to weight ratio. Lighter cars also have benefits for reduced road wear and therefore lower highway maintenance costs.

Most cars are actually relatively poorly suited to their core need - the transport of one or two people a short distance, possibly with some cargo. But in today's world of individual car ownership, designs have to be flexible enough to cater for the twice-yearly family road trip as well as the daily lone commute. The size and shape of cars may change significantly as the occupants are free to ignore the road - vehicles may become mobile offices, bedrooms and showrooms. The Mercedes F015 concept car shown here is one of the first automaker explorations of a car design where there is no concern about distracting a driver.

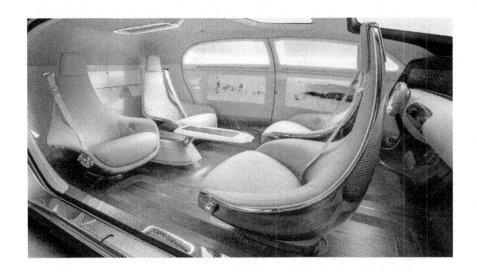

Mercedes-Benz F015 concept car interior.

In contrast, Google's prototype 2-seater car (left) barely had a dashboard at all, while this concept (right) shows alternatives available if there's no steering wheel at the front of the car:

A Sense of Style?

Much commentary from automobile enthusiasts has made a point that driverless car prototypes are ugly. It's true that the prototypes festooned with sensors are not very elegant but that is to ignore where in their development cycle they are. It is not uncommon for technology to start out bulky (or downright ugly) as it is developed before the aesthetics rapidly improve once the mechanics are figured out - the first test 3G phone devices were the size of briefcases and seemed a step backwards from the slim 2G phones that were widely available at the time. Now, even the latest 4G phones are incredibly small and thin and paragons of attractive design. One of the most predictable things in this whole complex, uncertain driverless cars discussion is that the technology involved will quickly get smaller, cheaper and better. Then the designers will be free to add some flair. So far, the prototype cars we've seen have not really tackled the design question. While they show concepts and direction, their creators are, so far, focused on the technical challenges. I have no doubt that aesthetics will be tackled and solved once the core technology is proven.

Perhaps the biggest factor impacting the design of the future car will be the question of who owns it and how it is intended to be used. Consider how a London taxi is designed. The focus is on reliability, ease of maintenance, ease of access, durability and simplicity. Compare this to a luxury car where the focus is on comfort and projecting a prestige image. If people don't own cars, they may be less interested in how they look, coming to view them with a more utilitarian lens.

A Question of Ownership

"But those people and their cars will be considered classics. Rates of ownership will decline, an artifact of an era of hyper prosperity and reckless glut. Twenty-five years from now, the only people still owning cars will be hobbyists, hot-rodders and flat-earth dissenters. Everyone else will be happy to share"[174]

Wall Street Journal

Driverless cars raise new and fundamental questions about car ownership. If cars can drive themselves, do you still need to own one? If a car always shows up when and where you want it and gets you exactly where you want to go, safely, stress-free and at a far lower cost, do you really need to purchase it yourself? The reason we own our own cars is that there is little alternative given that we want them to be available as and when we need them. Paying someone to drive us around is prohibitively expensive for most people on a daily basis. So it has become "normal" to own your own car. Or in the case of families, to own two or more cars. Given the relatively large cost of a car, for most people, this is financed either by a loan from a financial institution or a lease plan, or supplied as part of an employment contract.

But if you use driverless car technology to remove the barriers to non-ownership, what does this mean? If you can be sure that a car will appear outside your house or work whenever you need it, and is affordable because there's no driver to pay, why not be chauffeured wherever you want to go? From an economic perspective, privately owned cars are extremely underutilized assets: They sit idle almost all of the time, aging and wasting space on a parking lot or in a garage. An insightful statistic about our choice to invest tens of thousands of dollars in a car is that

---

[174] https://www.wsj.com/articles/could-self-driving-cars-spell-the-end-of-ownership-1448986572

the average car is static for 95% of the time. Yes, most cars on average are not in use for 23 hours of the day, depreciating heavily as they sit in a parking space at home, work or elsewhere. If there is an alternative, paying so much for something we use so little makes poor sense, even if those times we use it are crucial to our lifestyle.

However, although statistics such as cars sitting unused 95% of the time may seem compelling arguments against ownership, it's important to note that cars are still important to individuals, even when they aren't using them to get from A to B. Consumers in the future may stay attached to private cars — many people like having cars and use them as extended backpacks and purses. Their car is a personal space - where they leave makeup, shoes and gym bags. They leave fitness clothes, files, items to be repaired or returned, purchases, and trash as they go about their daily tasks. They are also status signifiers to neighbours. They are places of privacy. They are vehicles whose sunk costs are turned into travel conveniences, with weekend trips to skiing and annual road trips south made economical by having a car for commuting. So those who want to own their own driverless cars can, should and will continue to do so, but will forgo some of the additional economic benefits that driverless cars on-demand can bring. There are also others though (perhaps the majority?) who want *access* to a car, but don't necessarily feel a need to *own* one, just as they've increasingly adopted streaming services instead of owning vinyl, CDs, or even MP3s. This is a change that takes time but consumer models that don't depend on ownership are clearly not unprecedented, as the popularity of Netflix and Spotify attest.

As we saw in Chapter 2, Americans currently spend about 16% of their after-tax income to purchase and support the use of an asset that sits idle for 95% of the time. Not owning a car would be a significant financial reprieve for many households if driverless cars services are available for less than $9000 per annum (the approximate cost of owning and running your own car).

Car on Demand/Ride Sharing

As we move towards a driverless cars-enabled future, perhaps a pointer to the nature of ownership can be gleaned from the current trend towards ridesharing and on-demand services. Car ownership has, for a long time, been a binary choice. Either you own one or you don't. While car sharing has tried to challenge the private ownership model, the cost of an on-demand approach for individuals has been prohibitive for frequent use to replace commuting. This is because the highest cost for a service provider has always been the driver. If you remove them from the equation, the economics change drastically.

"The idea that autonomous vehicles will be owned and used much as cars are today is a tenuous assumption. Fleets of self-driving vehicles could, he says, replace all car, taxi and bus trips in a city, providing as much mobility with far fewer vehicles" says Luis Martinez of the International Transport Forum, a division of the OECD[175]. A January 2013 Columbia University study[176] suggested that with a fleet of just 9,000 autonomous cars, Uber could replace every taxicab in New York City, and that passengers would wait an average of 36 seconds for a ride that costs about $0.50 per mile. Such convenience and low cost would make car ownership a dubious financial choice. A 2010 report from UC Berkeley's Transportation Sustainability Research Center[177] found that one car-share vehicle could remove 9 to 13 vehicles from the road, either because households decided to ditch their personal automobile or significantly delay the purchase of one. One survey suggests

---

[175] http://worldif.economist.com/article/12123/horseless-driverless

[176] http://sustainablemobility.ei.columbia.edu/files/2012/12/Transforming-Personal-Mobility-Jan-27-20132.pdf

[177]

http://tsrc.berkeley.edu/sites/default/files/Impact%20of%20Carsharing%20on%20Household%20Vehicle%20Holdings%20-%20Martin.pdf that every car added to the fleets of Uber and Lyft leads to 32 fewer car sales, meaning potential "lost sales" by 2020 of over 1 million cars.[178] While that only looks at changes in car purchasing in selected urban areas, and doesn't take account of any changing usage patterns, brought about by driverless cars, that might increase VMT, it is enough to make car manufacturers sit up and take notice.

Local authorities at State level may find themselves in a conundrum. Shared cars might reduce some of their costs (such as in road building and maintenance), but the resulting drop in sales of new cars has a downside: vehicle sales account for 20 percent of state sales tax revenues. They and car manufacturers may yet take some comfort from a McKinsey report that notes: "*However, people aren't willing to ditch their own vehicles just yet. According to data in the report, two thirds of US drivers still prefer driving their own vehicle to using a ride hailing service and 63 per cent wouldn't replace their own vehicle with a ridesharing service, even if it were free*".[179]

From Car-less to Care-less

Self-driving cars will push prices for ride-sharing down to levels that are currently unimaginable. Given that today drivers account for approximately 70% of the cost of Uber or Lyft fares, the advent of self-driving cars could reduce the average ride-sharing fare to well below 50% of current rates. One analyst with ARK Investment Management,[180] is expecting ridesharing firms to drastically lower fares. According to her estimates, the cost for an autonomous taxi would be 35 cents per mile, versus the

178

http://legacy.alixpartners.com/en/MediaCenter/PressReleases/tabid/821/article Type/ArticleView/articleId/950/AlixPartners-Study-Indicates-Greater-Negative-Effect-of-Car-Sharing-on-Vehicle-Purchases.aspx#sthash.q8XdWFRq.dpbs

[179] http://www.mckinsey.com/industries/automotive-and-assembly/our-insights/how-shared-mobility-will-change-the-automotive-industry

[180] http://www.marketwatch.com/story/demand-for-driverless-cars-could-boost-uber-to-2016-09-19?link=sfmw_tw

$2.86 per mile a passenger currently pays in San Francisco, assuming an average gas price of $2.36 per gallon. In another scenario, individuals who buy driverless cars then send them out on the road to work for a taxi service. If those rides are priced at 35 cents per mile, a $30,000 car would be able to pay itself off in about five years, the firm estimates. These kinds of economics would likely make ride/car-sharing vastly more attractive, at least in urban areas. Rural dwellers, where the population density doesn't support ride sharing, will likely still opt for ownership of cars, even if they no longer drive them personally.

In Chapter 2, I noted how Millennials, now the largest demographic group in the United States, seem to be more on board with ditching the car. As a result, ride-sharing, car clubs and other alternatives to ownership are already growing fast. Young city-dwellers are turning their backs on owning a costly asset that sits largely unused and loses value the moment it is first driven. Carmakers insist that such consumers are merely deferring buying a vehicle, pointing to the fact that people continue to drive at an older age than they used to.

The growth of ride hailing/ridesharing (with or without driverless cars) in place of ownership is a grave concern for car manufacturers. People don't tend to pay attention to the brand of vehicles or modes of transport they aren't personally invested in. Who made the last airplane you flew on? Who manufactured the last bus or train you took? Unless you're unusually curious or observant, it's not only that you don't remember—it probably never occurred to you to ask. What brand was the last cab you took? But more likely than not, you do remember the brands of the company that sold you your tickets or operated the service. And that's why major car manufactures are investing in ridesharing services or even turning to providing their own fleets as we'll see a little later in this Chapter. With the advent of fully self-driving cars, it's easy to imagine automobile transport services looking more and more like the airline industry - largely commoditized with little difference between service providers.

And once the price has hit bottom, where will they go next? Will they pay you to take a ride if the marginal cost of providing the service becomes less than the potential revenue to them from advertising or sponsorship?

Ownership Evolution

It's way too early to tell how car ownership will evolve in an era of driverless cars. A lot will depend on what happens in the coming years, what they cost, how they are regulated and on the decisions we make regarding their operation. It's also not necessary that one model or the other will prevail. I suspect that it's like a continuum. We'll see people own their own cars exclusively for their own use and treat them as they do today - a personal, private sanctuary and storage area. Others may continue to own a car to feel a certainty of availability and control, but they may send the car off (via Tesla Network or another similar facility) to provide a service when they aren't using it, much as they might supplement their income by offering themselves and their car today to Uber or Lyft riders. Telsa have said that the majority of revenue will go to owners who provide their car for use in the Tesla network, but that the service will include a margin for the company.[181] And it's likely that others will give up on owning a car and summon a driverless car as and when they need transport.

For those who opt to continue to own their own vehicles and use them to get around, exciting new possibilities will exist for their use if the owner is freed from driving. Individuals could be more productive while in transit. This continuation of the current status quo, barring the actual activity in the car, would have little impact on existing car company business models: individual consumers would still make purchasing decisions and would own and operate their own vehicles, probably through existing financing routes, assuming the incremental cost of driverless cars isn't

---

[181] http://www.cnbc.com/2016/10/26/elon-musk-says-its-not-tesla-vs-uber-it-is-the-people-vs-uber.html

excessive. Just as in today's world, the car would spend most of its time parked, but available at the touch of a button or even available to be sent on an errand to pick up something or for use by a family member.

Others may choose to earn supplemental income by sending their cars, when not in use, to transport other people or goods, using a future version of on-demand services like Uber or Instacart. In this scenario, personal ownership might well blur with more of a fleet ownership model. Cities could also offer incentives to ride-sharing services that augment public transit, feeding people to major subway and rail lines. This is already a trend: Uber reports that in some cities, one-third of its trips begin or end at a public-transit station.

Waymo CEO John Krafcik expects that at least initially, the cost of driverless cars will see more shared use.[182] "Self-driving cars are going to be more expensive physical assets, so we're going to find a way to use them more," he said. This could include your car participating in a service like Uber and potentially earning you some extra money while you're at work or even asleep. Because of this, Krafcik sees average annual car usage skyrocketing to upwards of 100,000 to 150,000 miles. "I think there are going to be positive implications for a lot of dealers," said Krafcik, "And for the OEMs, thinking about that duty cycle is going to be very different." Driverless cars in constant use might wear out much more quickly, offering a lifeline to car manufacturers currently faced with us changing cars maybe every 10 years.

Time Will Tell

The possibilities laid out above are, of course, speculative. As AVs continue to develop in the coming years, there will be many technology, product and business model advances that surprise

---

[182] https://www.cnet.com/roadshow/news/google-self-driving-and-dealerships/

us all. One way or another, autonomous vehicles' impact on the way we live will be nothing short of transformative. It will be an exciting ride.

One need look no further than the current transportation market for an instructive analogy. Today, people get around in their daily lives in many different ways. Some people own their own cars. Some people rent cars when they need them (either through traditional car rental companies or newer models like Zipcar). Some people get everywhere through ride-sharing services like Uber or Lyft. Some people use public transportation or simply walk. People commonly switch from one of these solutions to another over the course of their lives depending on life's changing circumstances. The same will likely be true in the driverless future of tomorrow.

Ultimately, the shape of the automotive future will depend on consumers - their needs, preferences, fears and their pocketbooks. Will they trust these new vehicles, buy them? rent them by the hour or by the trip? Will people still need to own or lease their own vehicles? Will human operated vehicles become as rare as film cameras and record players - the preserve of a passionate niche, and the subject of an occasional passing renaissance? In speculating about these possible AV business and usage models, it is important to keep in mind that this market will not necessarily be "winner take all." It is altogether possible that more than one of these models — and others that have not yet even been imagined — will all coexist profitably in the market. The next big question is: who will be reaping those profits - will it be the incumbents?

Changing the Auto Industry

"Millions of people, directly or indirectly, are reliant on that industry so I don't think it's an option to simply allow it to collapse. We cannot, and must not, and we will not let our auto industry simply vanish"

Barack Obama, 2009

Management guru Peter Drucker dubbed it the 'industry of industries'. Automobile manufacturing was the most significant industry of the 20th century and had a profound impact on world society. Today, automobile manufacturing is still the world's largest manufacturing activity, with nearly 50 million new vehicles produced each year. The auto industry has gained its place at the top of the manufacturing pack on the back of inspiring and harnessing fundamental change in how we make things, twice this century. Centuries of craft production were replaced with the advent, first of mass production on the moving assembly line, and secondly the advent of lean production - concepts that have spread to dominate other industries too. It took just 10 years between 1914 and 1924 for 3 manufacturers to grab 90% of the US car market, at the expense of the hitherto dominant craft producers, of which there were hundreds.

For the century, innovation within the automotive sector has brought major technological advances, leading to safer, cleaner, and more affordable vehicles. But for the most part, since Henry Ford introduced the moving assembly line, the changes have been incremental, evolutionary. Now, in the early decades of the 21st century, the industry appears to be on the cusp of revolutionary change—with potential to dramatically reshape not just the competitive landscape but also the way we interact with vehicles and, indeed, the future design of our roads and our cities. Big Auto has never had to deal with a disruptive technology such as this, and yet much of it has been on its death bed already, culminating in the largest government intervention in industrial America since World War 2.

The importance of the auto industry in the US was evidenced by the events of 2008 and documented in the book 'Overhaul' by Steven Rattner,[183] among others. As their sales tumbled in 2008, the Detroit-based corporations were forced to seek Government injections of cash to the tune of $85bn to stave off collapse and reorganise themselves under Chapter 11 Bankruptcy protection. Their failure would have led to immediate direct job losses in the millions. The choice of top executives to fly initially to Washington cap-in-hand in their separate private jets may remain for many years as a Management School favourite example of how not to act when appealing for public money to save an ailing company.[184] Yet the events that led it to the edge of the precipice in 2008 may yet pale compared to the future the industry now faces.

Facing the Future

"Never has the traditional automotive business model been under constant siege as it is today from multiple fronts. Technology has not only changed the car-buying experience but it is also relentlessly reshaping the entire ecosystem from dealership go-to-market strategies to the automobile product offering itself, all while it creates new, non-traditional competitors based on online, mobile centric utility models."

TechCrunch[185]

---

[183] Overhaul - An Insider's Account of the Obama Administration's Emergency Rescue of the Auto Industry - Steven Rattner, 2010

[184] http://edition.cnn.com/2008/US/11/19/autos.ceo.jets/

[185] https://techcrunch.com/2015/11/29/automotive-disruption-from-the-bay-area-to-atlanta/

As covered earlier, many people probably don't actually want to own cars; they want the ability to get where they want to go in a dependable, predictable, comfortable and personal way. They likely don't want to have to concentrate on avoiding obstacles and not spending time doing enjoyable or productive activities. But until now, they've lacked an alternative to car ownership that met all the criteria. That's the existential fear plaguing automakers today, that an alternative is finally coming. And they're scrambling to do something about it. The explosive growth of Uber, Lyft and Didi, to name only the leaders, shows the latent demand for efficient and affordable transport beyond car ownership. But for car companies, the on-demand ride market is just a first step toward a more radically altered future dominated by autonomous vehicles.

In a report in 2016, investment bank Morgan Stanley said the motor industry was being disrupted *"far sooner, faster and more powerfully than one might expect."* It predicted that conventional carmakers would scramble in the coming years to reinvent themselves.[186] Brian Johnson, Director of Equity Research at Barclays Capital,[187] says that autonomous vehicles shared across family and community lines will displace much of the current fleet of privately owned cars. Annual auto sales in the United States could decline by as much as 40 percent, and there would be a 60-percent drop in the total number of vehicles on the road. Johnson predicts that Ford and GM, which have factories all over North America, will have to cut production by more than half as conventional vehicles cede the roads to autonomous ones. A recent survey of car manufacturing executives by KPMG[188] similarly revealed that 59% of industry bosses believe that more than half of all car owners today will no

[186] http://www.economist.com/news/business/21685459-carmakers-increasingly-fret-their-industry-brink-huge-disruption

[187]
https://www.investmentbank.barclays.com/content/dam/barclayspublic/docs/investment-bank/global-insights/barclays-disruptive-mobility-pdf-120115-459kb.pdf

[188] https://www.theguardian.com/business/2017/jan/09/fewer-car-owners-more-driverless-vehicles-future-survey-reveals

longer want to own a car by 2025. Nikolaus Lang, of the Boston Consulting Group's Centre for Digital in Automotive, points out though that there's a clear difference between a young urban population, for whom owning cars makes little sense, and the millions of suburbanites with families, who will probably still opt to own.

Waking the Giants

"I believe the auto industry will change more in the next five to 10 years than it has in the last 50, and this gives us the opportunity to make cars more capable, more sustainable and more exciting than ever before. Rather than fear disruption, we plan to be lead it by developing cars that don't crash or pollute, that reduce congestion and that keep us connected to the people, places and activities that are most important in our lives."

Mary Barra, CEO GM[189]

Car manufacturers are increasingly dipping their toes into these frightening waters. Their success under their current business models depends on your buying the second most expensive thing you'll ever buy and not using it 95% of the time, and then replacing it after a number of years. Most Car companies have accepted the world has changed, or will change soon, and they're showing their hand by buying, or investing heavily in technology and innovation.

Just like most people, the car giants aren't exactly sure how the future is going to turn out and are therefore making multiple bets against their multiple perceived threats. Taking GM as an example, they have a comprehensive driverless cars development program since acquiring Cruise Automation for

---

[189] http://www.weforum.org/agenda/2016/01/the-next-revolution-in-the-car-industry

over $1 billion[190] and have hired 1,100 staff for a driverless cars R&D center in San Francisco.[191]. They have invested $500 million in Lyft[192] and created their own "personal mobility brand" Maven[193] (car sharing), as well as trying a monthly subscription service[194] for their Cadillac brand.

Left: GM's Maven and Right, Daimler's Croove Apps

The Daimler group has created a strategy for its future called C.A.S.E., which focuses on the topics of Connectivity, Autonomous driving, Sharing and Electrification. The German giant has two ventures exploring new car ownership and usage models Car2Go and Croove,[195] alongside Moovel[196] (an app which compares travel times across modes of transport, including public transportation) and their acquisition of MyTaxi, Europe's largest taxi hailing app. Croove lets car owners rent their car (any brand) to others via an app to earn money, while Car2Go is a free-floating car rental scheme, offering only

---

[190] http://fortune.com/2016/03/11/gm-buying-self-driving-tech-startup-for-more-than-1-billion/

[191] https://www.nytimes.com/2017/04/13/business/gm-expands-self-driving-car-operations-to-silicon-valley.html

[192] http://www.reuters.com/article/us-gm-lyft-investment-idUSKBN0UI1A820160105

[193]
http://media.gm.com/media/us/en/gm/news.detail.html/content/Pages/news/us/en/2016/Jan/0121-maven.html

[194] https://www.wsj.com/articles/gm-tries-a-subscription-plan-for-cadillacsa-netflix-for-cars-at-1-500-a-month-1489928401

[195] https://letscroove.com/

[196] https://www.daimler.com/products/services/mobility-services/

Mercedes group cars. Daimler is also partnering with Bosch, the world's largest auto parts maker, to create driverless taxis. The alliance aims to get a fully automated vehicle ready for use in urban markets in the early 2020s.[197]

The New Urban Environment

"The current American way of life is founded not just on motor transportation but on the religion of the motorcar, and the sacrifices that people are prepared to make for this religion stand outside the realm of rational criticism. Forget the damned motor car and build the cities for lovers and friends."

Lewis Mumford

Chapter 2 set the scene by recalling the dramatic urban changes brought about by the advent and dominance of the private car over the last 100 years. Now, it's time to start thinking about the implications of any move *away* from individual car ownership and/or the ability to separate car storage from your immediate location and the next time you'll need the car. Why dedicate expensive residential space to car storage if the car can find its own way to and from cheaper remote parking? In a world where you can send your car to run errands without you, or summon almost immediate delivery via robots and drones from online retailers, what will become of the out of town malls created and fed by decades of car ownership?

Liberating Space

"The right to have access to every building in the city by private motorcar in an age when everyone possesses such a vehicle is the right to destroy the city."

Lewis Mumford, The Highway and the City, 1957

---

[197] https://www.forbes.com/sites/alanohnsman/2017/04/04/bosch-and-daimler-partner-to-get-driverless-taxis-to-market-by-early-2020s/#1ae1d8b53c4b

As a result of prevalent personal car ownership, the average single-family home in the US includes a two-car garage. These two-car garages are space inefficient, often claiming around 500 square feet of what could otherwise be prime living space. Nationally across the US, that equates to about 40 billion square feet of space, or the equivalent of over 20 years' worth of new domestic residential space construction.

If driverless cars liberate even a fraction of that space for repurposing, we could face a building, DIY and decoration boom. Could the availability of such increased dwelling space alleviate housing shortages and even takes steps to help end homelessness? Will there be an explosion in Airbnb listings as people seek to capitalize on their newly-released-and-converted garage space as a new source of income? As well as the impacts on family homes from garage removal, rental costs in apartments could be reduced - without the need for on-location parking space, more units could be created in the same area as before. Cities could choose also to dedicate more space to storm water management, street trees, and other sustainable features that fall victim to the land demands of parked cars.

Because they can drop passengers off, and then go do other work or park themselves densely in more remote lots, the need for large amounts of parking surrounding commercial buildings should diminish greatly, particularly in suburbs and non-central urban areas. The ability to decoupling parking from destinations is transformative. Garages and driveways will become vestigial and there will be a rush to convert the space for human use. If most of the land devoted to parking can be repurposed, what does that mean for the city and its people?

As we saw earlier, vehicles cruising the street looking for parking spots account for an astounding 30% of city traffic, not to mention that eliminating curbside parking adds two extra lanes of capacity to many city streets. As driverless cars begin to obviate the need for high-value urban real estate to be devoted to parking, these spaces can be reclaimed. This newly liberated land can gradually be transitioned from the less than ideal use of space it currently represents to new housing, urban green space, unique local businesses and the things that make living in an urban environment interesting.

The real estate implications of driverless cars could be enormous. As many cities already grapple with an oversupply of non-residential space due to declining retail demand, what will a torrent of additional space in the form of unrequired parking space do to prices and utilization? Is there sufficient demand to repurpose the land into office or cafe/social space? What about green space, education or fitness facilities? Perhaps the increase in leisure time associated with driverless cars (which we'll talk about soon) will see this space converted to production studios focused on video and gaming content. Of course, not everyone welcomes increased housing supply and the attendant reduction in rental incomes and/or property values. While some locations such as San Francisco have well documented housing shortages and aversion to building additional capacity, driverless cars may change the goalposts.

There will of course still need to be a place to store driverless cars. In a typical parking lot, only ⅓ of the land area is actually covered by cars - the rest of the space is required for cars to turn or to allow people in/out of the vehicle. Since nobody would need to get in or out of them after they parked, they could position themselves as snugly together as Tetris bricks, fitting far more cars into our existing parking lots and garages. Merely not having to open doors to let the driver out when they park provides 20% more parking spaces in the same area. Achieve even this small feat of self-driving, and it could be possible to never build another new parking space. But valet parking attendants will need to look elsewhere for work.

One intriguing possibility: Architects will design parking decks in the future to be convertible to housing, office space and other uses as the need arises. It's not such a strange idea. Cities have long since converted old factories and warehouses to loft housing. But converting parking decks to new uses will mean building them in new ways. For one thing, the slightly sloping floors of most parking decks (allowing rain and snowmelt to flow toward drains) will have to be flat to accommodate potential new uses. Ceilings will have to be higher if we expect people to live there one day. Then, too, office and residential uses tend to carry more weight than parked cars, so the parking structures will have to be designed stronger. And architects will have to think about leaving room for mechanical ductwork and windows, even if a garage may not be converted for many years. [198]

It's not just parking space that may be freed up. If the ownership models discussed above favour on-demand access to driverless cars rather than ownership and therefore car sales fall, auto dealers will be adversely impacted - and as a sector, they own or lease about $130 billion of real estate in the U.S. There are some other less-obvious victims too. Might public storage facilities feel the bite as their largest competitor will become the 40 billion square feet of free garage space opening up over the next couple decades?

---

[198] http://www.freep.com/story/money/business/john-gallagher/2017/05/03/park-downtown-transit-detroit-autonomous-vehicles/100978296/

Urban Planning

"Imagine a city where the street system permits vehicles to move without obstructions, traffic lights or officers with automatic regulation of speed and capacity; where pedestrians can walk continuously through the whole city areas—no matter whether this be in the outskirts or in the center—without any fear and danger of vehicular traffic. Such a city ideal we can make come true."

Fritz Malcher, The steadyflow traffic system, Harvard University Press, 1936[199]

Despite ambitions dating back over 80 years to address the urban impact of cars, the problem has gotten steadily worse. Is it finally time to wrest back control from the car? It's a challenging time for city planners. With such uncertainty about when the technology will be ready, how do they prioritize investments now? Infrastructure projects typically have say a 30-50 year life span but some may be obsolete in half that time if driverless cars arrive. Yet if they don't invest in projects and then driverless cars don't arrive in a timely manner, don't deliver on their promised benefits or a mixture of those outcomes, planners will end up looking very foolish. But although there is much uncertainty about timing and the impacts, in urban planning terms, it is coming very soon even if it's at the outer limits of current estimates.

In fairness, moving to a whole new paradigm is risky for planners. They may be tempted to take a conservative route of sticking with what you know and is proven to work - the old "you'll never be fired for buying IBM" approach. Yet now is the time for vision and strategy. Decisions in this sphere last for decades and cost much to be undone. The uncertainty is

---

199

http://onlinelibrary.wiley.com/doi/10.1002/ncr.4110250227/abstract

currently paralysing many of our planners, and can perhaps be a good excuse for inaction, backed by entrenched interests who may lobby for self-serving conservative choices, aiming to lock in their own well-being for as long as possible. So far it seems that many planners are choosing to ignore developments - despite its notorious traffic congestion issues, Los Angeles' 2015 ten-year vision, "Mobility Plan 2025", doesn't even mention driverless cars. Less than 3% of the transportation plans for the 50 most populous cities in the US even mention the transit impacts of ride-sharing services Uber and Lyft, let alone driverless cars.

Expert opinion on the impact of driverless cars on urban sprawl is divided. On one side, the argument goes that if driverless cars free up parking and garage space, there will be plentiful affordable new residential capacity negating the need for people to move further from city centres for affordable housing. On the other side, the argument goes that if people can be otherwise occupied during even a long commute, they will still be willing to move further from the city centre or their place of employment to have the residence they wish, perhaps with larger gardens than typical closer to the city. Moreover, in the long term, a dramatic expansion in functional roadway capacity that increased commuting distances without, at least initially, increasing commuting times, could also open additional areas to development. It's hard to know if driverless cars will lead to more or less urban living. If you can sleep as you commute, maybe you will opt to live further from the city. That, of course, is on the assumption that city life still exists based on going to work and that the driverless cars or their robotic cousins haven't taken all the jobs.

If more remote and larger houses become more accessible, what will happen cities? Well, they too will see the release of land previously devoted to housing. And if the future holds a fleet rather than ownership mentality, the space devoted to roads can also be somewhat reclaimed. As soon as self-driving cars are readily available, proponents will run into political battles over land use, a challenge familiar to urbanism advocates. These proponents have a compelling vision to reduce traffic-related injuries and lower transportation costs. They also aim to cut car ownership and repurpose parking spaces and garages. That's where the conflict begins.[200]

A Less Idyllic View

Despite the short timelines made possible by some of the world's most advanced logistics systems, when you order a product on Amazon, you are usually prepared to wait a day or two for it to arrive, with it likely coming from a distribution center possibly as far away as another state. But if driverless cars are to become popular, a customer summoning a self-driving car would expect to wait only 5 to 10 minutes for it to arrive and usually less. Indeed, Uber CEO Kalanick has said that the average wait time in major cities for an ordered Uber is about 3 minutes. One way that companies could meet this expectation is by stationing fleets of vehicles within a 5 to 10 minute drive of almost every residential neighborhood in the country. Depots will be required to store driverless cars in large numbers near the demand for them, to enable them to reach people at peak times within the required short timeframes. Mass positioning of driverless cars in or around cities at various times of the day, with perhaps 5,000 leaving their charging stations at the same time of the morning will present an unprecedented new challenge. To neighborhood preservationists, this will represent the biggest threat to community character since the building of the interstate highways in the middle of the 20th century. It's also easy to imagine restrictions being required on unoccupied driverless cars idling on major thoroughfares, both as a way of managing congestion and preventing behaviors like "robot vehicle billboard spam," where companies would operate

---

[200] https://www.bloomberg.com/view/articles/2016-09-21/self-driving-cars-will-create-a-fight-over-zoning-and-land-use

vehicles for the sole purpose of marketing themselves on major roads.

The reality is that some forms of driverless cars could actually make things worse in terms of increasing VMT. The sheer convenience could result in many more miles traveled—up to 35 percent more for personal AVs and an amazing 90 percent more for single-passenger AV taxis, according to Urban Mobility: System Upgrade, a 2014[201] study by the International Transit Forum (ITF) and the Corporate Partnership Board (CPB). This increase is the result of riders acquiring a greater tolerance for long commutes, and vehicles running "deadhead" trips to look for new riders or cheap parking and running errands. Driverless cars will make it less "costly" for people to travel a given geographic distance, partly because they will be free to engage in other activities while travelling, but primarily because of reductions in travel time. As soon as suitable roads such as freeways (or lanes thereof) are declared off limits to manual driving, driverless cars will travel – safely – at much higher speeds than we do today. If you're being driven and able to do other things, does the shortest journey time still matter? You may be happier for the car to choose a longer or cheaper route.

The Road Ahead: Infrastructure

In and around most cities a lack of space precludes the building of more roads, so an increasing number of cars inevitably leads to increased congestion. We have reached a stage where most land that is available for roads has been paved. While the Romans may have introduced stone paving (with some 50,000 miles of paved roads in the Empire at its height), and tarmac was patented in 1901, it is really only the last 50-70 years that has seen modern highways and motorways cover over large

---

[201] http://urbanland.uli.org/economy-markets-trends/autonomous-vehicles-hype-potential/

chunks of land delivering increased (though often insufficient) traffic capacity and sprawling suburbs.

Making Lanes

Americans drive 6-foot-wide cars in 12-foot-wide highway lanes, largely since human driving precision isn't very accurate and a history of lanes that had to be wide enough for two horses side-by-side. This means that currently, a three-lane highway needs nearly 40 feet of pavement. With more precise automated driving eliminating human lane-weaving, lanes could be narrower. Repainting the lanes could easily divide the same width of road into four nine-foot lanes. Tighter spacing between cars would be scary at first, but we could get used to it. If we can fit more cars on roads and travel at higher speeds, we won't need to build more roads. And our lanes might last longer in the future - weight is a significant factor in road durability. Making vehicles lighter would make our roads last longer so, as well as the fuel efficiencies for car owners, the roads themselves should last longer if we can eventually remove the heavy safety equipment from future car designs.

Dynamic

Once built, roads tend to be static conduits with no flexibility. Yet in most cities with clear commuter paths to dormitory or satellite towns, demand is not constant - traffic is usually primarily uni-directional based on time of day. Those people whose journey is "against the traffic" look forward to having the road largely uncongested. Carpool and bus lanes are an attempt at dynamic use of roads, but in most cases changing the use of a particular laneway based on time is too difficult to contemplate. With driverless cars, true dynamic roads would be possible - a change of lane direction could be enforced to boost capacity to match demand based on time of day.

Smart

It is likely that our roadways will see significant developments regardless of driverless cars. Smart motorways that periodically open the hard shoulder to traffic and feature dynamic speed limits are already in limited use in the UK, and various designs are being explored for building solar panels or motion-based power generation into the road so we can harvest renewable energy from the vast area of land used for roadways. These developments don't require or rely on the growth of driverless cars but are likely to form part of future planning in the same timeframes.

Fit for Purpose?

However, any talk of future roads needs to be considered in the context of the current reality and the impediments it presents. Despite the vast sums spent over the years on creating and maintaining roads, many are not in good condition. Even if the surface is relatively serviceable, all too often those in charge of road maintenance have cut costs by skimping on ensuring that road markings and signs are kept clear and prominent. Human drivers are quite good at making out fading lines and inferring their presence based on common sense, whereas artificial intelligence "drivers" can struggle in the absence of definite markers.

"Shoddy infrastructure has become a roadblock to the development of self-driving cars, vexing engineers and adding time and cost. Poor markings and uneven signage on the 3 million miles of paved roads in the United States are forcing automakers to develop more sophisticated sensors and maps to compensate."[202]

---

[202] http://www.reuters.com/article/us-autos-autonomous-infrastructure-insig-idUSKCN0WX131

Energy Efficiency

A transportation system with a significant component of self-driving vehicles would decrease energy consumption in at least three primary ways: more efficient driving; lighter, more fuel-efficient vehicles; and efficient infrastructure. The energy policy, economic and geopolitical implications could be profound, especially when combined with the anticipated concomitant shift from ICE to Electric Vehicles.

Pollution

ICE powered cars are major contributors to pollution. They are one of the biggest contributors to CO_2 production in the developed world, and any change in the way we use cars should be considered in that light. While it's unlikely self-driving cars will be as good on a passenger mile basis as public transit, they will almost certainly offer an improvement over traditional car driving. The US has 5% of the world's population, 30% of the world's cars and 45%of the world's car-derived CO_2 emissions. Aside from any increase in the use of EV which leads to a reduction in car emissions (assuming the required electricity demand is generated in environmentally-friendly ways), improvements in the environmental performance of any remaining ICE cars will be important. Subtler changes in our behaviour could also impact - the noise and exhaust pollution from current cars encourages people to close windows and use A/C, further increasing fuel or power consumption. In a world of cleaner, quieter EV, people may be more inclined to open windows. The liberation of parking spaces discussed earlier also has a potential environmental benefit - if we planted just 1% of our paved areas which could support 273 million trees, that would absorb 1.2 billion metric tons of CO_2.

There is a long and strained history between technology, regulation and the traditionally oil-powered motor industry. Technology advances imposed by regulation led to the very positive result of a 1986 car producing 89% less emissions than a 1974 model.[203] As an example, it would take 50 new cars to produce the same emissions per kilometre as a vehicle made in 1970.[204] Yet manufacturers have resisted Government pressure to improve their environmental impacts - in 2001 GM took legal action against California's ZEV regulations[205] which required automakers to begin offering a limited number of zero emission vehicles for sale or lease in the state in 2003. After 100 years of investment in oil-fueled human-driven cars, alternatives face high hurdles for consumer adoption. As noted in The Great Race: The Global Quest for the Car of the Future by Levi Tillemann, the market does not necessarily reward socially desirable innovations and does not necessarily punish those who engage in socially destructive activities - this is called a market failure. Carbon pollution has been called the greatest market failure the world has ever seen.

However good a human driver might be, they do make suboptimal choices, and those choices have an impact on fuel efficiency. Humans drivers get lost, get angry, and struggle to find parking. Driverless cars can be programmed to be efficient, calm and smooth in their driving style. An aggressive driver uses up to 33 percent more fuel than an average driver and an average driver still uses about 10 percent more fuel than the most efficient driving possible.[206] It is reasonable therefore to project that that autonomous vehicles will be capable of saving between 10-20% more fuel on average than human drivers. Even the lower end of this estimate would equate to fuel savings approaching $50 billion per year in the US alone.

---

[203] Matthew E. Kahn, 1996. "The Efficiency and Equity of Vehicle Emissions Regulation: Evidence from California's Random Audits," Eastern Economic Journal, Eastern Economic Association, vol. 22(4), pages 457-465, Fall.

[204] http://www.seai.ie/Power_of_One/Getting_Around/HCIYC/Air_Pollution/

[205] http://articles.latimes.com/2001/feb/24/business/fi-29699

[206] https://www.fueleconomy.gov/feg/driveHabits.jsp

Better Driving

The expensive and expansive networks of Motorways/Highways that criss-cross most developed countries are designed to allow for safe higher speed travel. How? By removing the potential for distractions, such as intersections, slow moving vehicles and pedestrians. But human reaction times waste a significant amount of the potential carrying capacity of these thoroughfares. Driverless cars could drive more efficiently in the same road space, and save fuel doing it. Autonomous cars can "flock" or form a "platoon", driving close behind one another to reduce drag and benefit from improved aerodynamics for the close-following cars. This drafting concept alone could save 30% of car fuel usage.[207] But platooning is not without its challenges as our roads and junctions weren't designed with it in mind. It might have to be implemented using a dedicated lane as the outer lane that you "join" if your car is so-equipped - having it on the inside lane would lead to difficulties for cars trying to exit across a platoon.

It's not just on highways that simple improvements in car movements and reactions can increase existing road capacity. When waiting at a stop light, all automated vehicles can easily synchronize their actions: As the stop light turns to green, all waiting cars can start moving immediately; they don't need to wait until the car in front has visibly moved out of the way. In cities, this will make a large difference and thus increase the capacity of existing roads. Shorter headways between vehicles at traffic signals (and shorter start-up times) mean that more AVs could more effectively utilize green time at signals, considerably improving intersection capacities. Even in towns, raising the average speed of traffic from just 10 mph to 15 mph could increase the fuel economy of each vehicle by around 20% and the FHWA estimates that 25 percent of congestion is attributable to traffic incidents, around half of which are crashes.

---

[207] http://blog.rmi.org/blog_2013_01_25_Driving_Miss_Hazy_Driverless_Cars

Cumulatively, these advances could dramatically decrease congestion without any new roads.

In a detailed review of the potential emissions impacts of self-driving cars entitled "Help or hindrance? The travel, energy and carbon impacts of highly automated vehicles", Wadud et al[208] examined the energy consumption and emissions aspects of driverless cars. They concluded that automation can substantially reduce energy consumption and carbon emissions but that these benefits could be nullified by greater travel due to autonomous vehicles. A breakdown of the components contributing to energy consumption (both reductions and increases) is shown here:

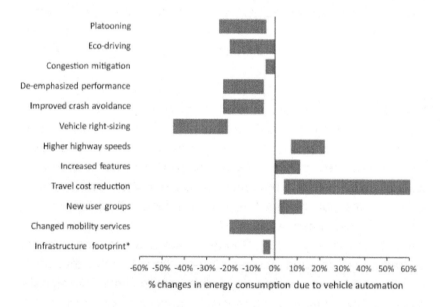

% changes in energy consumption due to vehicle automation

---

208 Transportation Research Part A: Policy and Practice

Gas Stations & Maintenance

As we examine the use of energy, it's timely to consider the role of energy stations in a future world. A periodic feature of virtually every roadside is the gas station or service area. According to the U.S. Census Bureau in 2012,[209] the US had 114,474 filling stations, with an annual turnover of $554.2 billion, with 856,538 employees receiving a combined payroll of $15.5 billion. Again, this part of the auto ecosystem is a major economic force. Human drivers stop frequently on journeys to buy fuel, food and supplies. While humans will still likely want to eat during their journeys, their stopping and purchase patterns may change hugely as driverless cars make more of the decisions, either with or without their owners' inputs.

With the ability to drive anywhere on its own, an automated vehicle could take itself to gas stations or for regular service and repair, provided that those services are set up to cater for autonomous vehicles. Already, Honda has demonstrated how a car can pay for gas itself.[210] Self-maintenance diagnosis can save time and enable the car to ensure it is in optimal condition at all times. Driverless cars' efficient driving style will also minimize the abuse of the vehicle so that minimum servicing or spare parts will be required. As a result, cars will experience fewer breakdowns and have a longer engine life while being more cost-effective and reliable. The incremental fuel economy benefits that can be obtained by proper care of a vehicle shouldn't be ignored: replacing a clogged air filter can improve a vehicle's fuel efficiency by as much as 10 percent, with tuning able to offer an additional 4 percent. Tires kept inflated to the

---

209
https://factfinder.census.gov/faces/tableservices/jsf/pages/productview.xhtml?src=bkmk
210 http://www.prnewswire.com/news-releases/honda-and-visa-demonstrate-in-vehicle-payments-with-gilbarco-and-ips-group-at-2017-ces-300386576.html

recommended pressure can save about 3.3 percent. These savings alone would total billions of dollars every year.

Law and Order

As the car became increasingly central to daily life in the 20th century and created many positive outcomes, it has also attracted its fair share of criminal attention. In 2016, stolen cars and theft from locked cars accounted for over 21% of all SFPD crime incidents.[211] How many other types of criminality rely on cars? If driverless cars radically reduce the amount of parking, theft from parked cars will no longer be a major crime category. Aside from the reduction in the number of crime victims, police time could be substantially freed up for detecting other crimes, as well as reductions in expensive court time. Driverless cars could therefore lead to efficiencies in the justice system.

The most dramatic and dangerous aspect of car crime is the high-speed pursuit, or car chase. Though popular in action movies, in real streets, these pose a huge risk to life and limb. However, in a future of driverless cars, there would be no getaway cars, high speed car chases or car jackings. Though some commentators do fear a future where driverless cars could be stopped by thieves too easily[212] (given its programmed desire not to inflict any injury) and the occupant would be powerless to drive away. However, this overlooks the likelihood that the driverless cars would be recording and even directly broadcasting video of any perpetrators. On the subject of recording and broadcasting video, as discussed in Chapter 3 driverless cars will by necessity have cameras - will police and law enforcement authorities have access to these feeds or the 'black boxes' that store them? Police could also seek to request all footage from driverless cars known to be near a crime scene,

---

[211] https://cloud.google.com/bigquery/public-data/sfpd-reports
[212] https://motherboard.vice.com/en_us/article/why-self-driving-cars-could-be-a-dream-come-true-for-car-thieves

much as they do with static CCTV sources today. But driverless cars would likely offer improved video sources over CCTV - as they record 360-degree HD video whenever they move. As Ben Evans of Andreessen Horowitz compares it, *"The police could control trains. Guard the station and your man's trapped. Cars took that away. Autonomy brings it back. Driverless cars are a moving panopticon."*[213]

More mundane than high speed chases and serious crimes, much of modern policing is organized around traffic patrols. Those are much less necessary when there are no human-driven cars likely to break traffic regulations. What is the local suburban cop who normally staffs a speed trap supposed to do? And what happens to the budget of the town when it no longer collects speeding and parking ticket revenues or court fees for traffic tickets? It might be harder for police to interdict drugs, for example, because traffic violations won't occur and thus the contraband in cars will not be found serendipitously. Today, around 4% of traffic stops lead to searches according to Bureau of Justice Statistics (BJS).[214] The widespread arrival of driverless cars would impact on the employment of police and also on how people interact with law enforcement. According to the BJS surveys, in 2011, 26.3 million people were involuntarily stopped by the police for traffic related matters. An additional 5.4 million people had other contacts with the police because of traffic accidents. In total, more than half of all contacts with the police are related to vehicles. What will that mean for the numbers of law enforcement officers? The Justice Department shows about 1.2 million people were employed by local, county and state police forces.[215] The visible public presence of police also serves as a deterrent to crime, so reductions in police forces would reduce this visible deterrent and potentially

---

[213] http://ben-evans.com/benedictevans/2017/3/20/cars-and-second-order-consequences
[214] http://www.bjs.gov/content/pub/pdf/pbtss11.pdf
[215] http://www.newsweek.com/driverless-cars-will-put-half-our-cops-out-work-314612

increase criminal activity. One upside to less police activity brought about by driverless cars would be a potential reduction in police deaths. According to FBI statistics for the period 2004 to 2013, some 368 were killed in automobile incidents, 58 on motorbikes and 101 struck by vehicles.[216]

Safer Emergencies & Less Ambulance Chasers

As part of its development programme, Google's engineers have filed for a patent[217] describing how its self-driving cars might yield the road to emergency vehicles, like police cars, automatically. The patent application describes sensors inside the car recognizing flashing emergency lights, as well as techniques to avoid false positives, and moving to the side of the road before the emergency vehicle passes. This capability might help not only to provide a speedier passage for emergency vehicles but also serve to reduce accidents associated with drivers panicking to get out of the way of a speeding emergency response vehicle only to crash themselves.

Personal injury attorneys though will see a significant decrease in demand for their services. Vehicle collisions, which accounted for 35 percent of all civil trials in 2005[218], will be all but eliminated with automated vehicles. Around 76,000 attorneys in the U.S. specialize in personal injury and make up approximately 6 percent of the country's population of lawyers.[219]

216

https://ucr.fbi.gov/leoka/2013/tables/table_63_leos_ak_circumst ance_at_scene_of_incident_by_type_of_assignment_2004-2013.xls

[217] http://www.google.com/patents/US20160252905

[218] https://www.bjs.gov/content/pub/press/cbjtsc05pr.cfm

[219] http://www.cnbc.com/2017/05/03/self-driving-cars-will-disrupt-10-industries-commentary.html

The Car as a Time Machine

"Personally, I refuse to drive a car - I won't have anything to do with any kind of transportation in which I can't read."

Arthur C Clarke

We've already discussed how the driverless car may be a "space machine", generating free space in previously densely crowded urban areas and freeing up road capacity. But driverless cars may also be seen as a time machine - a generator or more accurately a *liberator* of time, that other most precious resource. However, while driverless technology can't transport us in time, it may *create* additional time utility choices for us - freeing up time previously required for safe navigation to be spent on other tasks while still allowing us to complete the desired point to point journey. While it may be a time machine in terms of creating time, as we noted in the discussion on environmental impacts, it may also create additional journeys. Currently our car usage is ultimately limited by the time we have available to drive it, as well as the need to move ourselves and items from A to B. Of the nearly 400 billion person trips undertaken by U.S. drivers in 2008, almost forty-three percent were for "personal and family-related purposes (such as shopping trips and trips for medical care).[220]" In a scenario where we can dispatch the car to do our bidding while we complete another task, what does that do to our total logistical footprint?

Media business

The media business is fundamentally about grabbing your attention. Until the introduction of the modern smartphone in 2007, the amount of people's time available to media had been static for decades, and competition was a zero-sum game. Mobile opened up new territories for settlement — territories that

---

[220] http://nhts.ornl.gov/2009/pub/stt.pdf

have now been largely claimed by Facebook, Twitter, Snapchat, Instagram, Netflix, Spotify and a handful of other major players, notably including casual gaming. Statistics show that up to 56% of people[221] play mobile games and US citizens spent 1.15 billion[222] hours playing mobile games monthly in 2016. We are once again approaching an era of zero-sum competition as mobile penetration reaches saturation, but that era will be short-lived as the estimated 75 billion hours Americans spend commuting will gradually be up for grabs. Today's media giants will all make a play for this new supply of attention, but the jostling will make space for new upstarts or for an older player to reboot themselves.

Seventy-five billion hours is an extremely difficult number to conceptualize but, in practical terms, it represents about twice the amount of time Americans already spend on Facebook, an attention-based company worth around $350 billion. When autonomous vehicles become available at scale, the car will transform from just a mode of transportation into a new-age entertainment hub, with captive consumers surrounded by its technology for an average of at least five hours a week.[223] There will be a growing need for connectivity in automated cars as passengers need to stay entertained or engaged, and this may be the spur for the deployment of 5G mobile technologies.

Video Killed the Radio Star

The death of radio has long been predicted and exaggerated as newer media such as TV, podcast and streaming grow. Despite this, more Americans listen to AM/FM radio each week than use Facebook. Nearly 60% of the population listens to the radio daily

---

[221] https://www.statista.com/statistics/234649/percentage-of-us-population-that-play-mobile-games/

[222] http://www.vertoanalytics.com/consumers-spend-1-billion-hours-month-playing-mobile-games/

[223] http://newsroom.aaa.com/2015/04/new-study-reveals-much-motorists-drive/

and nearly 85% of the American people report listening to the radio at least once a week. Tellingly though, 44% of all radio listening is in cars.[224] Traditional radio might face its sternest test yet, having faced down the onslaught of 8 track, then cassette, then CD, then satellite to prevail as a central source in even the most advanced cars. The appeal of radio in cars is based largely on the driver's current inability to engage in any richer media activities. While many may still choose the simplicity of audio-only content, doubtless many more will use the extra time for screen-based activities. Radio stations may also face a new challenge if driverless cars manage to reduce congestion - how to fill their morning and evening shows without traffic reports!

What would you do with the "new" time in the car? Learn, talk, sleep, play, work, watch? In amongst all the industries and employers we can easily identify as at risk from driverless cars, one major area that may stand to benefit is the video production sector. The 2017 budgets[225] of "new" media players like Netflix ($6 billion) and Amazon ($4.5 billion) for original content are bigger than the traditional networks. With the additional viewing time that driverless cars could create, there will be an increased demand for additional content, which means that the 660,000 jobs contributed to the economy by the motion picture and tv industry (as of 2013[226]) may see significant upside, a positive note considering the job losses predicted in other sectors because of driverless cars.

Advertising

This is another example of the wider impacts of driverless cars. Should predictions of a switch from personal to fleet ownership

---

[224] https://qz.com/195349/the-remarkable-resilience-of-old-fashioned-radio-in-the-us/

[225] https://www.fool.com/investing/2017/04/18/amazons-content-budget-is-catching-up-with-netflix.aspx

[226] http://www.mpaa.org/wp-content/uploads/2015/02/MPAA-Industry-Economic-Contribution-Factsheet.pdf

come to fruition, given such a radical purchase criteria change in a world where riders are not buyers of cars and where car marketing is not about personal choice, the marketing departments of every car maker could be wiped out or radically changed. The auto industry has long been one of the largest spenders on advertising. Think about how many ads you see or hear about cars, car financing, car insurance, car accessories and car dealers. What happens to the advertising and marketing industry if they lose the spend of the auto industry, car maintenance sector and insurers, or see it hugely reduced?

However, advertising is an industry that typically embraces change and seeks to exploit new media opportunities. I'm sure that the emergence of driverless cars may seem like a huge opportunity for the advertising sector. Although the efficacy of bill boards may be diminished as people no longer look out of their car windows while travelling, the promise of additional screen time must be very appealing as a whole new audience is opened up. Alternatively, will mobile billboards become cost effective if you remove the requirement to pay drivers? Could out of home (OOH) advertising become more targeted with moving adverts adopting their display messages to their exact location? But consumers may not react positively to brands who clog up newly free-moving roads with mobile advertising hoardings. Or perhaps a new form of advertising might be the provision of free or reduced-price travel for riders willing to endure adverts or visit certain establishments. Might a shopping mall that collects you from and delivers you back to your residence for free triumph over venues that expect you to make your own way at your own expense? Already, Uber has started offering a service (Uber Central) for businesses wishing to give their customers free rides. More sinister, will advertisers seek to influence the navigation choice of your driverless car to bring you closer to their establishment without you knowing they've paid for that privilege? Will "Route chosen by Brand X" replace warnings of product placement on TV?

Insurance

Most countries have some requirement for motor insurance. In the US, automotive insurance covering liability for injuries and property damage is compulsory in most states. It dates back to Massachusetts in 1925 when the first law on mandatory insurance was passed. Since then, all states except Virginia, New Hampshire and Arizona have followed suit. In Virginia, residents must pay the state a $500 annual fee per vehicle if they choose not to buy insurance. New Hampshire requires the driver to be financially responsible: to compensate anyone injured as a result of their driving and holds them financially responsible for property damage. Few people would be able to do that without an insurance policy.

The US Automobile insurance sector in 2013 had premium income of $207 billion. Personal auto insurance accounts for 47 percent of global premiums, according to Aon.[227] Other large insurers such as Allianz are trying to assess the impact of automation on their biggest non-life insurance market. In Europe, motor insurance is the main non-life insurance business line with annual premium income of about 120 billion euros ($135 billion), according to data by Insurance Europe.[228] Concern in the insurance industry about the impact of driverless cars has been building. According to the Wall Street Journal in 2015, Travelers first began cautioning investors about driverless cars in 2013, and Cincinnati Financial began adding its warning to securities filings in April 2014.[229]

---

[227] http://thoughtleadership.aonbenfield.com/documents/20160911-ab-analytics-gimo.pdf
[228]
http://www.insuranceeurope.eu/sites/default/files/attachments/European%20motor%20insurance%20markets.pdf
[229] https://www.wsj.com/articles/will-the-driverless-car-upend-insurance-1425428891

Accessible autonomy will undoubtedly impact auto insurance significantly. For starters, fewer accidents will result in fewer claims and less in losses for insurance carriers. There is already evidence that technology can reduce crashes: David Zuby, EVP and Chief Research Officer at the Insurance Institute for Highway Safety stated, *"Vehicles equipped with front crash prevention technology have a 7-15% lower claim frequency under property damage liability coverage"*.[230] The NHTSA investigation and report into a fatal accident involving Tesla's Autopilot driver assistance technologies concluded[231] that crash rates involving Tesla cars have dropped by almost 40 percent since the wide introduction of Autopilot. If driverless cars deliver on their promise of virtually eliminating collisions, mandatory driver insurance may be dropped as all liability switches to the car's creator?

The UK authorities planning for driverless cars have decided that insurance will be required for when the car is in driverless mode. According to the Vehicle Technology and Aviation Bill[232], accident victims can claim compensation if a collision occurs when the cars are in automatic mode, with their insurers able to recover their costs from the vehicle makers. The legislation specifies that a vehicle's owner becomes liable if they have made unauthorised changes to the car's software or fail to install a required software update.

230

https://www.kpmg.com/US/en/IssuesAndInsights/ArticlesPublications/Documents/automobile-insurance-in-the-era-of-autonomous-vehicles-survey-results-june-2015.pdf

231 https://static.nhtsa.gov/odi/inv/2016/INCLA-PE16007-7876.PDF

232 https://www.publications.parliament.uk/pa/bills/cbill/2016-2017/0143/cbill_2016-20170143_en_2.htm

Beyond the Black Box

For insurers, establishing the facts about a crash and therefore being able to apportion liability is of crucial importance. Already, most cars manufactured and sold since 2013 come with event data recorders, sometimes known as "black boxes." These devices are computers that record and store crash data in the event of an accident. Under regulations adopted by the NHTSA,[233] the event data recorders must record 15 data inputs. They include engine rpm, steering, the length and severity of the crash, and the braking during the crash. This data is used by some insurance companies to assess claims in forensic detail, sometimes offering premium discounts to drivers who agree to the use of this information. However, access to this data is subject to 4th amendment review[234] and the current legal position remains unclear. This will need to be resolved in a driverless cars context as the black box will be the only source of data about how a driverless car was operating. It is also likely that driverless cars will be mandated to include technology that can automatically notify emergency services in the event of an accident, though if the car is unoccupied at the time, it may also be able to inform the emergency services that it has no human driver in need of medical assistance. Automatic notification technology will be compulsory on all new vehicles sold in Europe from April 2018 under the European Union's eCall initiative.[235]

Healthcare System

According to the CDC, analysis of National Hospital Ambulatory Care Survey (NHAMCS) data indicates that, in 2010–2011, there were approximately 3.9 million ER visits for motor vehicle

---

[233] https://www.law.cornell.edu/cfr/text/49/563.7
[234] https://www.washingtonpost.com/news/volokh-conspiracy/wp/2017/03/30/the-fourth-amendment-and-access-to-automobile-black-boxes/?utm_term=.b7a760f03741
[235] https://ec.europa.eu/digital-single-market/en/news/ecall-all-new-cars-april-2018

traffic injuries annually, which accounted for 10.1% of all injury-related ER visits.[236] Imaging was ordered or provided at 70.2% of ER visits for motor vehicle traffic injuries, which was higher than for other injury-related ER visits (55.9%), making these among the more expensive categories of ER visits. On a simplistic basis, ERs will lose millions of patients if driverless cars reduce car crashes. But there are many other downstream industries and professions that face significant negative impacts. There may also be massive reductions in prescriptions, for e.g. pain killers, thus reducing revenues for drug companies and dispensing pharmacies. Fewer sufferers of chronic pain may lead to reductions in pain medication addictions (with, according to the National Institute on Drug Abuse,[237] an estimated 2.1 million people in the United States suffering from substance use disorders related to prescription opioid pain relievers in 2012). Other potential 'losers' include reconstructive surgeons, rehab and occupational therapists and even dentists - car crashes are the second most common cause of broken teeth. It's worth an unsettling thought that those in the ambulance-chasing legal and private medical sectors may not be pleased to see the end of car crashes. But it may be that people find other ways to injure or harm themselves when freed from driving? Perhaps people will drink more if released from any concern about drink driving limits, leading to increases in liver issues.

Transplants

On a final note for this section, a reduction in car crashes and resultant injuries is not good news for everyone, as noted in Chapter 4, as a downside to improved safety. Organ donation and transplants are another area likely to be impacted. Motor vehicle accidents are the largest contributor to organ donations after natural-cause deaths. Currently, 1 in 5 organ donations

---

[236] https://www.cdc.gov/nchs/products/databriefs/db185.htm
[237] https://www.drugabuse.gov/about-nida/legislative-activities/testimony-to-congress/2016/americas-addiction-to-opioids-heroin-prescription-drug-abuse

comes from the victim of a vehicular accident according to the U.S. Department of Health & Human Services.[238] That's why Departments of Motor Vehicles routinely enquire of drivers whether they want to be donors. More than 123,000 people in the U.S. are currently in need of an organ, and 18 people die each day waiting.[239] A reduction in road fatalities will reduce organ donations and some of those awaiting organs will die, where as they would have been saved in the era before driverless cars, albeit at the cost of a driver or passenger's life.

The New Passengers

Google (now Waymo) announced that the world's first fully-self driven car ride took place on October 20, 2015.[240] Steve Mahan (shown below) rode alone in one of the prototype vehicles, cruising through Austin's suburbs. The human side of this technology story? Steve is legally blind.

---

[238] http://optn.transplant.hrsa.gov/latestData/rptData.asp
[239] http://fortune.com/2014/08/15/if-driverless-cars-save-lives-where-will-we-get-organs/
[240] https://medium.com/waymo/scenes-from-the-street-5bb77046d7ce#.i0scjibw5

Proponents of driverless cars make much of the fact that the technology could enable mobility for large groups of society currently unable to get around by personal conveyance, unaided. The old, young and disabled could use driverless cars, reducing social isolation and improving access to services. With an ageing population in countries like the US (there are over 40 million Americans over the age of 65, and that demographic is growing at a 50% faster rate than the nation's overall population) and Japan, the demand for driverless cars may not come from the younger generations we spoke of earlier as champions of ride-sharing but from an older population reaching the limits of their ability to drive themselves and with it the independence it brings - we take travel for granted until we can't, until we are immobilised. Self-driving cars that do not need human drivers or monitors may substantially increase mobility for those who cannot (legally) drive themselves because of youth, age, disability, or incapacitation. Nine percent of adults identify as blind or report "trouble seeing, even when wearing glasses or contact lenses." Nearly eleven percent of Americans are between ten and seventeen years old, and nearly thirteen percent are sixty-five or older. More than thirty-one percent of the total population (and thirteen percent of those sixteen or older) does not have a driver's license.[241] Many ageing drivers attempt to cope with their limitations through self-regulation, avoiding heavy traffic, unfamiliar roads, night-time driving, and poor weather, while others stop driving altogether, resulting in relinquishing their independence along with their car keys. It might be that aging baby boomers, raised with a love of cars and used to the independence they bring but faced with diminishing driving abilities, would embrace driverless cars as the best of the options available to them.[242]

---

[241] https://cyberlaw.stanford.edu/files/publication/files/BWS-2012-ManagingAutonomousTransportationDemand.pdf

[242] https://mobile.nytimes.com/2017/03/23/automobiles/wheels/self-driving-cars-elderly.html

Disability Benefits

In the United States, approximately one in every five people, or more than 57 million, has a disability. This includes the more than 3.8 million veterans with a service-connected disability. An estimated 65 million people worldwide have epilepsy, which often requires people to give up driving. The most recent government transport survey indicated that six million individuals with a disability have difficulty getting the transportation they need.[243] When a disability limits transportation options, this can result in reduced economic opportunities, isolation that exacerbates medical conditions or leads to depression, and a diminished quality of life. Mitigating transportation-related obstacles for individuals with disabilities would save $19 billion annually in healthcare expenditures from missed medical appointments.[244]

And while it may seem like an unqualified positive to bring access to groups who don't currently have it, it does of course once again raise the spectre of increased traffic - if you give access to a large segment who previously didn't have it, will it lead to an overall greater amount of VMT? Alongside any social positives for the new passengers, a significant increase in motor vehicle travel could pose myriad challenges for policymakers, including changes in rural and urban land use, shifts in congestion, increases in certain emissions, decreases in mass transit ridership, and increases in maintenance costs for roads and bridges.

---

[243] http://secureenergy.org/wp-content/uploads/2017/01/Self-Driving-Cars-The-Impact-on-People-with-Disabilities_FINAL.pdf

[244] http://www.rehasource.com/articles/detail/5

Family Time?

The phrase soccer mom broadly refers to a North American middle-class suburban woman who spends a significant amount of her time transporting her school-age children to their youth sporting events or other activities, not necessarily soccer.

Wikipedia

I would expect to see some research soon into the potential social impact of driverless cars on the family unit. Due to the hyper-scheduled free time of kids these days, busy parents are frequently called upon to provide a taxi service to their kids, giving rise to creation of an entire social group of so-called "soccer-moms". Will there be a detrimental family impact if kids can just hop in driverless cars should parents opt not to make time to shuttle them around between activities? The lost bonding time previously offered by enforced togetherness in cars as parents drove may not be good for families.

Finance

Bankers mightn't immediately strike you as one of the groups most interested in cars that drive themselves. But as we said at the outset, the emergence of driverless cars is about trillions of dollars, which is most certainly enough to grab the attention of the financial sector. With big change in the world of automobiles, comes big change in the world of financing them. According to Techcrunch, we face one of the most monumental displacements of wealth the world economy has ever seen. Auto loan balances in the U.S. total more than $1.06 trillion right now. That number doesn't even include the enormous leasing market[245]. Indeed, 86 percent of new car sales in the U.S. are financed. Without individual financing products, car sales don't happen. Financing props up the entire auto industry. The

---

[245] https://techcrunch.com/2016/07/13/the-future-of-car-ownership-that-no-one-is-talking-about/

change away from multiyear car finance commitments may free capital up for use in other areas of the economy. Releasing people from the cost of owning their own car could prompt a consumer spending boom totalling hundreds of billions of dollars. Although not directly related, the transition to electric vehicles is parallel big news. According to Citigroup, the average US family saved $1150 a year when oil prices dropped by a dollar a gallon. If half of all passenger miles were switched from gasoline to electricity, the US could reduce its trade deficit by $100bn and eliminate dependence on foreign oil.

A "better economy" is seldom for everyone. It's not just banks facing disruption with changes to the model of individual car ownership spelling the end of some portion of car loans as a source of revenue. Government and municipalities face removal of the massive revenue stream of parking/speeding infractions and also potentially devastating reductions in tax on car sales, gasoline taxes depending on how ownership and VMT play out. It seems reasonable to assume that new sources of revenue will have to be found, even if the authorities can see a fall in costs related to administering and regulating motoring.

Retail

As an area already hit hard by the rise of technology in the form of online shopping, what will happen to retailing in the world of driverless cars? What remaining strengths retail has are often linked to the car. What of weekly shopping? Will consumers who currently do their weekly grocery shop send a car to pick it up for them using some future Instacart-style service? Will shoppers seek to return to city centres if driverless cars make them more pedestrian friendly, at the expense of out of town malls? Perhaps the growth of just in time deliveries (via drones[246] or robots), anticipatory shipping[247] and re-order technologies such

---

[246] https://www.amazon.com/Amazon-Prime-Air/b?node=8037720011
[247] https://patents.google.com/patent/US8615473B2/en

as Amazon Dash[248] will change the nature of shopping patterns regardless of driverless cars? Obvious changes to the relative importance of gas stations in a world of driverless cars (and likely a world of more electric vehicles) will be accompanied by changes in the sales for products that sell in significant volumes as impulse or attached purchases. For context, remember that most gas stations make much more margin on non-gasoline products than they do fueling cars.

I touched on some potential positives for retailers already - consumers will have more disposable incomes as transportation costs decrease (transportation is a major cost, especially for lower income people and families). If there are no more DUI offenses, will restaurants and bars sell more alcohol? Perhaps retail locations will offer free rides to whisk you to and from their clutches? What's preventing them now, the cost of a driver, will be gone. In 2011, members of Google's driverless cars team filed for a patent (granted in 2014) to control offering free or discounted rides:

"The present invention relates generally to arranging for free or discounted transportation to an advertiser's business location. More specifically, aspects of the invention involve automatically comparing the cost of transportation and the potential profit from a completed transaction using real-time analysis. For example, the system may consider various factors including a consumer's current location, the consumer's most likely route and form of transportation (such as train, personal car, taxi, rental car, or shared vehicle), the consumer's daily agenda, the price competing advertisers are willing to pay for the customer to be delivered to alternate locations, and other costs. In this regard, the customer's obstacles to entering a business location are reduced while routing and cost calculations are automatically handled based on the demand for the advertiser's goods and potential profit margins."

Source: Patent US8630897 B1[249]

---

[248] https://www.amazon.com/ddb/learn-more
[249] https://www.google.com/patents/US8630897

Transportation will therefore become more tightly integrated and packaged into many services—dinner includes the ride, hotel includes local transport. The perception of the city centre and its amenities may change. Congestion and parking are barriers to people choosing to go shopping in high streets and main streets - but with driverless cars nobody will be put off by being unable to find and fund parking. Could driverless cars bring people back into the city centre and change the urban dynamic?

Commercial Vehicles

The focus of this book is on the potential impacts of self-driving cars, but it is also important to consider the potential impacts if you extend the same technologies and capabilities to the other big road user, commercial vehicles.

Driverless Trucks

The United States economy depends on trucks to deliver nearly 70 percent of all freight transported annually,[250] accounting for $671 billion worth of manufactured and retail goods transported by truck, with an estimated 15.5 million trucks operating. Add $295 billion in truck trade with Canada and $195.6 billion in truck trade with Mexico. The trucking companies, warehouses and logistics sector in the U.S. employ an estimated 8.9 million people in trucking-related jobs; nearly 3.5 million are truck drivers.

Relative to cars, trucks are statistically quite safe. Commercial trucks are involved in 2.4% of all road incidents with more than 75% of truck driving accidents being due to the driver of the passenger vehicle.[251] That still means that one person is injured or killed in a truck accident every 16 minutes. According to the

---

250

https://ops.fhwa.dot.gov/freight/freight_analysis/nat_freight_stats/docs/13factsfigures/pdfs/fff2013_highres.pdf
[251] https://www.truckinfo.net/trucking/stats.htm

National Academies of Sciences, Engineering and Medicine, there are around 4,000 fatal accidents in the US each year involving trucks or buses. Between 10% and 20% of these are linked to driver fatigue. And due to the additional mass of trucks, nearly 98% of the time, the drivers of the other vehicle are killed in a truck accident. At the same time, more truck drivers were killed on the job (835), than workers in any other occupation in the U.S, making truck driving officially the most hazardous occupation in the United States.[252]

The pressure for autonomous trucks is likely to be cost-driven more so than safety-focused. Morgan Stanley conservatively estimates that the freight industry could save as much as $168bn annually by harnessing autonomous technology – $70bn of which would come from reducing staff. (The rest is made up of $35bn from fuel efficiency, $27bn from productivity and $36bn from accidents).[253] Most of the same technologies discussed in Chapter 3 can also apply to the larger vehicles used in the trucking industry. While the benefit of reducing the construction weight is not the same as for cars, the promise of increasing fuel economy from more efficient driving and platooning could directly impact the bottom line for trucking companies, who typically work on very tight margins. MIT Technology Review editor Kevin Bullis[254] estimates that four-meter inter-truck spacings could reduce fuel consumption by 10 to 15 percent, and road-train platoons facilitating adaptive braking, potentially enable further fuel savings.

For good reason, human drivers in most jurisdictions are legally obliged not to drive for more than 11 hours in a day, and to take 8 hours rest. A driverless truck will be able to operate continuously, 24/7 if required, with only short intervals to refuel.

---

[252] http://www.bls.gov/news.release/pdf/cfoi.pdf

[253] https://www.morganstanley.com/articles/autonomous-cars-the-future-is-now

[254] Bullis, Kevin (2011) How Vehicle Automation will Cut Fuel Consumption. MIT's Technology 2 Review. October 24.

Gas stations, highway diners, rest stops, motels and other businesses catering to drivers will struggle to survive without them or with less of them. Moves towards driverless trucks may initially adopt a more auto-pilot like approach from airliners. Although largely flown by computer, pilots are still present and especially important at certain times in the journey. In freight operations, workers would likely still need to load and unload cargo.

Otto (now a division of Uber)

"We want to get the technology to the point where it's safe to let the driver rest and sleep in his cabin and we can drive for him, exit to exit"

Lior Ron, co-founder, Otto

Google has long held the PR spotlight in developing driverless technology; however, with the emergence of Otto[255] and Elon Musk's announcement of a Tesla Semi,[256] driverless trucks are coming to the forefront of the autonomous vehicle conversation. Heavily-funded start-up Peloton[257] is also active in this space. Otto was acquired by Uber for $680m in August 2016, just months after it was founded by alumni from some of Silicon Valley's leading companies. Otto doesn't make its own trucks - it instead offers kits to retrofit existing lorries. The initial focus for Otto is to enable driverless trucks on highways rather than around towns. Implementing self-driving technology on highways is technically much easier than on other roads or city streets. One of Otto's main goals will be to reduce road accidents involving drivers who work long hours. Otto's hardware works on any truck with an automatic transmission, and the retrofit includes LiDAR detection units on the cab and trailer, a radar on

---

[255] https://blog.ot.to/introducing-otto-the-startup-rethinking-commercial-trucking-cfdc502ef452#.hoxoqeyyn
[256] https://www.tesla.com/blog/master-plan-part-deux
[257] http://peloton-tech.com/

the bumper, and a high-precision camera positioned above the windshield.

Driverless trucks may be here sooner than cars, because the industry desperately needs them. Despite the concerns over the fate of trucking jobs and those dependent on them, the trucking industry also faces a chronic shortage of drivers. The American Trucking Association estimates the shortfall at 48,000 drivers, and says it could hit 175,000 by 2024.[258] Truck driving is a tough job – the hours are long and lonely, the pay is low and the lifestyle is sedentary.[259] But truck driving is one of the last widespread jobs that doesn't require a college diploma.

How Real Are Driverless Trucks?

As mentioned, driverless trucks may well hit the roads before driverless cars are in widespread use. Otto recently completed an autonomous delivery of 50,000 bottles of beer.[260] Toyota and Scania have begun the first full-scale autonomous truck platooning in Singapore where the two companies are testing a fleet of trucks composed of three autonomous vehicles following a human-driven one.[261] In June 2017, Waymo announced that it was beginning testing of their driverless technology on trucks.[262] Daimler, which owns the truck brand Freightliner, is also testing autonomous big rigs. In an interview with a German newspaper

---

[258] http://www.trucking.org/ATA%20Docs/News%20and%20Information/Reports%20Trends%20and%20Statistics/10%206%2015%20ATAs%20Driver%20Shortage%20Report%202015.pdf

[259] https://www.theguardian.com/technology/2016/jun/17/self-driving-trucks-impact-on-drivers-jobs-us

[260] https://www.uber.com/info/atg/truck/

[261] https://www.mot.gov.sg/News-Centre/News/2017/Singapore-to-start-truck-platooning-trials/

[262] http://www.reuters.com/article/us-waymo-selfdriving-truck-idUSKBN18T04V

in 2015, board member Wolfgang Bernhard predicted that production of such trucks is only "two, three years away."[263]

From Farm to Highway

Enabled by a lack of regulation on private land, simplified by a lack of concerns around unexpected obstacles or ingressors, made attractive by increased efficiency and necessitated by declining rural workforce, self-driving technology has been an increasing part of farm life for years.

Leading supplier John Deere currently has about 200,000 self-driving tractors on farms around the world. John Deere estimates there's at least a 10 percent increase in productivity[264] when farmers use self-driving machines which rapidly repays the cost of outfitting a new tractor with top-of-the-line auto-steering, navigation and guidance tech that could cost upwards of $20,000. Although more open and less predictable than fields, highways offer the next most controlled environment likely to see driverless technology. Further evidence of commercial use of driverless technology in more controlled environments than the open road comes from Rio Tinto, a mining giant, which is already using 53 self-driving big trucks across three of its sites in Australia.[265]

It's instructive that farming is once again at the forefront of revolutionary technical change. Where would we be if we had banned mechanized agriculture on the grounds that most Americans worked in farming when tractors and harvesters were introduced in the early 20th century? We often discuss the displacement of jobs by artificial intelligence and robots in the abstract, as something that we'll have to eventually tackle in the

---

[263] http://blog.caranddriver.com/autonomys-roadkill-the-path-to-driverless-cars-will-be-strewn-with-the-carcasses-of-big-industry/

[264] https://motherboard.vice.com/en_us/article/self-driving-cars-are-coming-but-self-driving-tractors-are-already-here-ai-artificial-intelligence

[265] https://qz.com/874589/rio-tinto-is-using-self-driving-416-ton-trucks-to-haul-raw-materials-around-australia/

far distant future. But the recent successful demonstration of the self-driving truck shows that we can't afford to put off the conversation on how we're going to adapt to this new reality. We'll talk more about this and other challenges posed by these changes in the next Chapter.

Impacts on other forms of Transport

If you revolutionise the primary means of individual transport to the extent we're discussing here, it's inevitable it will have repercussions for the adjacent modes of transport. If you can potentially sleep in a level 5 driverless car, will overnight trips become preferable to short flights? Would driverless car travel from San Francisco to LA in a perfectly-driven electric vehicle be less environmentally damaging than a flight and less hassle than queuing for airport security and waiting for your bag at the other end? Public-transportation policy makers will need to consider the economics of AVs and consumer attitudes toward AVs in their investment plans. Their long-term planning must consider the possibility that the favorable economics of AVs might lead consumers not only to give up their own vehicles but also to shun conventional mass transit in favor of robo-taxis.

This phenomenon could be particularly pronounced in megacities in emerging markets, where public-transit capacity can't keep up with rising demand. Policies that would incentivise drivers to switch to AVs—such as requiring expensive permits for conventional personal vehicles—could substantially quicken attempts in those cities to prioritise daily commutes and errands by other modes such as walking, bicycling, and ridesharing. Will driverless cars cherry-pick off public transport - with low income bus users suffering the consequences of even lower municipal investment in shared services?

Self-Driving Buses

Although there is much debate about the potential impact of driverless cars on transit/public transport, with the potential for affordable driverless cars to substitute for transit with the attendant environmental concerns, there are several firms working on self-driving buses. These would offer the potential cost savings from removing the labour element of operating expenses, but maintain the environmental and congestion efficiencies offered by larger vehicles.

A city in the Netherlands is home to early testing of a Mercedes Benz self-driving bus.[266] Its Future Bus vehicles have been demonstrated on a 20km route that connected Amsterdam's Schiphol airport with the nearby town of Haarlem. The bus can stop at traffic lights and navigate among pedestrians. It can drive at speeds of up to 70km/h and also takes care of navigating to raised bus stops along the route, slowing down and stopping to pick passengers up, pulling to within 2 inches from the curb.

In Helsinki, there's a trial of a small fleet of buses that act as a feeder service to the city's metro system. Carrying up to 12 passengers at a limited speed of 6mph, these buses are fully driverless but can be controlled remotely by a human driver overseeing them if required. In London, there's a trial of a 4-person mini bus in the suburb of Greenwich.

266

http://media.daimler.com/marsMediaSite/en/instance/ko.xhtml?oid=127 76245

Driverless Bus in Helsinki

Driverless Bus in Greenwich, London

Cycling

In 2014 alone, more than 50,000 cyclists were injured and over 720 were killed on American roads. If the roads populated by driverless cars are safer and you know you won't get hit, will more people consider choosing to cycle? This could also have wider implications for well-being and attempts to reduce obesity. Initially, cyclists, were especially tricky for driverless cars in development to deal with; from the top, they appear like pedestrians, from the bottom, like some kind of vehicle. But recent demonstrations of the progress of driverless cars have shown how adept they now are at identifying not only cyclists but also their behaviours, including recognising hand gestures. The emergence of driverless cars may finally be the dawn of segregated cycle ways - possible because of the additional road space made available by more accurate robot-steered cars. And the multi-sensor arrays on driverless cars should put an end once and for all to the problem of drivers not seeing cyclists.

In one of their monthly public progress reports, Google highlighted the work to make their driverless cars technology work well with cyclists.[267] Among the scenarios Google describe for the benefit of cyclists safety are:

"When our sensors detect a parallel-parked car with an open door near a cyclist, our car is programmed to slow down or nudge over to give the rider enough space to move towards the center of the lane and avoid the door. We also aim to give cyclists ample buffer room when we pass, and our cars won't squeeze by when cyclists take the center of the lane, even if there's technically enough space. Whether the road is too narrow or they're making a turn, we respect this indication that cyclists want to claim their lane. Our sensors can detect a cyclist's' hand signals as an indication of an intention to make a turn or shift over. Cyclists often make hand signals far in advance of a turn, and our software is designed to remember previous signals from a rider so it can better anticipate a rider's turn down the road. Because our cars can see 360 degrees, we're more aware of cyclists on the road — even in the dark. Bikes can come in many shapes and sizes, so using machine learning we've trained our software to recognize many different types. Our software learns from the thousands of variations it has seen — from multicolored frames, big wheels, bikes with car seats, tandem bikes, conference bikes, and unicycles — enabling our car to better share the road no matter your choice of ride".

267

https://static.googleusercontent.com/media/www.google.com/en//selfdrivingcar/files/reports/report-0616.pdf

Conclusion

All the issues considered in this chapter add up to a lot of change. And that's likely only a portion of the change ahead. The 2nd and 3rd order consequences are virtually impossible to predict, though no less important because of that. Any technology on the scale of driverless cars will bring change that few predict or envisage. Driverless cars are a perfect definition of a so-called "Wicked Problem" - *a system of highly interdependent systems with the property that actions taken to improve one aspect of the system may produce unexpected reactions and unwelcome side effects*. The lack of certainty or immediacy of some of the changes shouldn't tempt us into underestimating their inevitability or scale. Those whose lives will be impacted by driverless cars either positively or negatively would be well advised to plan now and identify what actions they should take to maximise their own position. That said, it's far from clear how the many challenges ahead will affect the timing and scale of the changes. We'll explore the key challenges in the next chapter.

Chapter 6 - Challenges

"The problems created by the prevalent way of thinking cannot be solved by the same way of thinking"

Ervin Laszlo

Before any of the seismic socio-economic changes just described can happen, there remain many challenges to the widespread deployment of driverless cars. If, how, and when these challenges are overcome will be the decisive factor in answering the big questions of timing and the extent of the impacts, both positive and negative. The sheer magnitude of a full transition from human-driven vehicles to autonomous vehicles requires the detailed consideration of a vast array of potential issues, many of which will require complex and creative solutions that may also prove very costly. Among the most important issues are system performance, cybersecurity, job loss and an appropriate regulatory framework to handle the rapidly-evolving bundle of technologies.

I have little doubt that the technical challenges outlined below can and will be overcome. Given the amount of resources dedicated to the sector, it's a matter of time, probably measured in years more so than decades. The human-related elements are actually the more complex - just because you can automate something doesn't necessarily mean you should. Technological breakthroughs may be impressive but are not an end in themselves - the impacts they have are what matters. There will be opposing and strong views on both sides. Those in favour of driverless cars should not be swept up on a wave of techno-optimism that ignores the very real barriers between the present and the utopian future free from crashes, congestion and parking. Those who are skeptical about driverless cars (for whatever true motivation) frequently point to the difficult challenges. And there are many. But I contend that solving these requires a mixture not only of cutting edge technology but more importantly also a willingness to re-think fundamental social norms. The societal benefits of driverless cars cannot and will not come if we confine our thinking to the way things have always been, or fail to consider long term infrastructural investments.

Let's say, for example, that painting a green line down the side of a road helped a robo car. Imagine my hypothetical green line is needed on every single road. That would be a daunting undertaking and used by those against driverless cars as an example of why they're impossible. But on reflection, it's no more daunting than global infrastructure projects we've already successfully achieved. Again, I point to the prize on offer when faced with "it can't be done" arguments. For better or worse, we've erected millions of traffic lights. We've already largely completed infrastructure projects like electrification, telegraph and cable TV. We've seen massive rail and road building projects the world over which brought us freedom to move goods and people but at great human and environmental cost. We've built fixed and then mobile telephony infrastructures covering much of the planet - and we've deployed satellites to cover the rest. We've converted thousands of miles of railways to electric at great cost. So I just don't buy arguments that, for infrastructural reasons at least, we can't do this, *if we want to*.

What Still Doesn't Work

The billions of dollars that the world's largest companies have already poured into driverless cars technology development in recent years has yielded impressive progress. What was a pipe dream just 10 years ago is now a credible near future. But significant challenges remain to finalise the technology to the point where it's good enough to roam among us, whatever good enough is determined to be.

Right now, the technology isn't good enough particularly in the area of perception of what it "sees". Using the technologies described in Chapter 3, driverless cars can create a centimetre-perfect representation of the world around them. In most conditions, they can identify, calculate and navigate safely, even in the highly uncertain world of humans. In most conditions is an important caveat. Just as humans struggle in some conditions like heavy rain or snow, so too do driverless cars despite their multitude of sensors. Less than ideal situations like construction zones present a level of uncertainty that is currently difficult to manage, while aberrations like potholes or even puddles can unsettle a driverless car - a car whose "mental" model mistakes a pedestrian for her reflection in a puddle or window can result in undesirable outcomes.

In November 2015, in widely reported comments, an electronics researcher for Volkswagen, said at the Connected Car Expo event in Los Angeles that even a tumbleweed in the road can bring a driverless car to a halt.[268] The point is valid in so far as an unknown object represents a challenge to a driverless car where normally none would exist for a human. I agree that we must plan for the unusual but we must also keep some perspective. Is it really any harm if a car stops for a tumbleweed? As long as the cars all stop, it's better than the number of accidents caused by drivers avoiding more real obstacles today. More likely though, the computer vision technology will soon evolve to the point where it can identify tumbleweeds and deal appropriately with them. These challenges can either be presented in a sensationalist negative way or as a more matter-of-fact challenge to solve.

---

[268] https://www.ft.com/content/e698c396-8d61-11e5-8be4-3506bf20cc2b

Stop the Lights!

Another often quoted challenge for driverless cars is identifying traffic lights. Uber garnered headlines when their short-lived driverless car testing in San Francisco in December 2016, resulted in footage being shared of their car failing to stop at a red light.[269]

Traffic light detection poses quite a challenge for a driverless car. While humans are quite adept at identifying traffic lights and their state (if not always excellent at acting legally in accordance with their state), computers can struggle to pick out traffic lights and discern their colour, especially in difficult conditions, e.g. strong sunshine behind the light. Driverless car makers have put a lot of effort into solving this seemingly simple problem. There is also the risk of a computer being confused by signs like this, which they could mistake for an actual traffic signal:

Could a driverless car mistake these signs for a traffic signal?

However, driverless cars are being taught through deep learning to identify this and similar signs so as not to confuse them with traffic lights. The best solution to date is for driverless car manufacturers to create a prior map of traffic signals, enabling the driverless cars and its perception systems to anticipate the locations of traffic lights and improve detection of the light

---

[269] http://fortune.com/2017/02/26/uber-self-driving-car-red-lights/

state.[270] Thus the vehicle can predict when it should expect traffic lights and concentrate its search. Prior knowledge can also allow it to take conservative action, such as braking gradually and asking a human (if present), when it is unable to observe any lights. Given that there are usually multiple equivalent lights visible at an intersection, it is important that the mapping includes all sets of lights. To obtain certainty that driverless cars can "see" traffic lights, there are a few options. Pre-mapping the location of lights is a fairly reliable option but hard to maintain, and doesn't address the risk of the car being unable to determine the state of the light even if it can find the light cluster. There are already trials in some cities of smart lights that broadcast their status via a radio signal. Audi have demonstrated this system with the status of the light, including the time it will take to change, displayed on the dashboard. Some more extreme solutions show that it would be possible to remove traffic lights at many junctions using Vehicle-2-Vehicle (V2V) communications.[271]

To ensure driverless cars can always "see" traffic light, we may need to change traffic lights - not a trivial task worldwide. Refusing to consider it is an example of trying to fit to an existing world paradigm. Ideally, you'd replace the traffic light, a one-hundred-year-old technology, with a device that also transmits its status in a way not open to interpretation or obfuscation. Daunting? Perhaps. Strategically possible? Yes. And not an unthinkable amount of money compared to the cost to society of cars.

270

https://static.googleusercontent.com/media/research.google.com/en//pubs/archive/37259.pdf
[271] http://www.computerworld.com/article/3045942/car-tech/mit-hopes-to-eliminate-traffic-lights.html

An Audi's dashboard shows the current status of the traffic
signal and remaining seconds until it changes.[272]
Image courtesy, Audi.

We may have to face up to the fact that Intersection control
protocols were designed for people and perhaps not be
surprised that we need to consider if we should redesign for their
new non-human users. One Russian designer has proposed
new traffic light designs to suit both robots and humans.[273] Many
research projects, such as this one at the University of Texas,[274]
are underway to consider how intersections could be optimised
in the future, and almost all rely on removing human control. I
think the difficulty that driverless cars can face in identifying
traffic lights as a barrier to their progress is a good illustrative
example of how we can approach integrating driverless cars into
our world. We can either attempt to make driverless cars work
like humans or consider a new approach - creating a robo-
friendly system either in parallel or as a replacement. In the
meantime, the way that driverless cars see the world and

---

[272] https://www.engadget.com/2016/08/15/audi-cars-will-start-talking-to-city-
traffic-systems-this-fall/
[273] https://www.wired.com/2017/04/newfangled-traffic-light-built-
people-robots/
[274] https://www.youtube.com/watch?v=4pbAI40dK0A - 4 minute
video

respond to it will undoubtedly improve. Given that several years ago my Home Xbox could tell how many fingers I was holding up via a $100-dollar accessory called Kinect, I expect that we won't be talking about driverless car's inability to read hand signals for long. Until then, there is much we can do to facilitate the technology if we choose to - like changing traffic lights where sunshine makes it hard to discern colours, or equipping construction workers with clear signs to guide driverless cars.

A Nod and a Wink

For all the technicalities and legalities of driving, it is frequently quite a social interaction, dependent on non-verbal signals - especially in cities. Drivers make eye contact before proceeding or use hand gestures to signal to pedestrians, while larger vehicles use recorded verbal warnings before reversing or turning. In a world devoid of drivers, how might we compensate for the lack of a human controller to signal their intention to other road users? A recently granted patent (see extract below)[275] shows how one driverless car company is trying to anticipate and solve some of the issues when pedestrians and other drivers interact with driverless cars on real streets. The graphic below from the patent application shows ideas for displays on the side and front of the driverless cars to make it clear to pedestrians if the driverless cars has seen them and whether they should proceed - a substitute for what would likely today be brief eye contact and a hand gesture. Although only patent illustrations and therefore no guarantee that they will see production, it seems very likely that future driverless cars will have some means of communicating with humans.

Aspects of the disclosure relate generally to notifying a pedestrian of the intent of a self-driving vehicle. For example, the vehicle may include sensors which detect an object such as

---

275

http://pdfpiw.uspto.gov/.piw?PageNum=0&docid=09196164&IDKey=&HomeUrl=http%3A%2F%2Fpdfpiw.uspto.gov%2F

a pedestrian attempting or about to cross the roadway in front of the vehicle. The vehicle's computer may then determine the correct way to respond to the pedestrian. For example, the computer may determine that the vehicle should stop or slow down, yield, or stop if it is safe to do so. The vehicle may then provide a notification to the pedestrian of what the vehicle is going to or is currently doing. For example, the vehicle may include a physical signaling device, an electronic sign or lights, a speaker for providing audible notifications, etc.

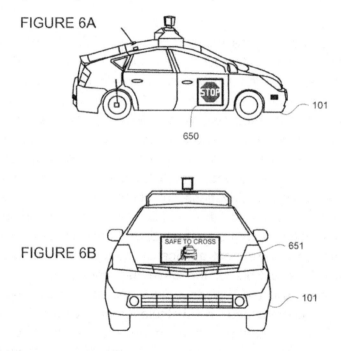

FIGURE 6A

FIGURE 6B

Without augmenting or replacing the social cues and nonverbal communication of driving with clear visual signs, it will be hard for driverless cars to gain public trust. Again, there are precedents where we've already adapted to specific challenges - such as the addition of audible warnings when trucks are reversing or turning; turn signals have been mandated on all cars for decades to indicate the driver's intentions for turning or changing lanes. Could displays become similarly standard for driverless cars?

Negative Interactions

Public safety is the key concern for any robot that must interact with humans. From mall security robots to take-out delivering robots (shown below), the first waves of robots are leaving the confines of purely closed environments and mixing with humans who have varying degrees of readiness for their new mechanical companions. These machines are by design programmed to yield to humans and take great care not to harm them. This is reassuring for most people, but for others it represents an opportunity.

A Knightscope[276] security robot patrols a Stanford Mall

---

[276] http://www.knightscope.com/

A Starship[277] robot delivers a takeout order in London

In a paper examining the potential interactions on our future streets,[278] an assistant professor in the Environmental Studies Department at the University of California, Santa Cruz uses game theory to analyze the interactions between pedestrians and autonomous vehicles, with a focus on yielding at crosswalks. Because autonomous vehicles will be risk-averse, the model suggests that pedestrians will be able to behave with impunity, and autonomous vehicles may facilitate a shift toward pedestrian-oriented urban neighborhoods. Pedestrians will soon know that they are up against vehicles that are exclusively law-abiding and risk averse. With absolute confidence that the car will stop, will humans be emboldened and look to take advantage by crossing whenever and wherever they want? If humans choose to assert this advantage, the hoped-for smooth traffic flow that will be the hallmark of driverless cars may never come true. Attempts to curtail newly-fearless pedestrians may include fences to discourage or stop illegal crossing, although

---

[277] https://www.starship.xyz/
[278] Pedestrians, Autonomous Vehicles, and Cities. Adam Millard-Ball. Journal of Planning Education and Research, October-27-2016

attempts to regulate pedestrian crossing have been largely unsuccessful, dating back to the 1920s and the origins of the term jaywalking.[279]

And it's not just the question of how pedestrians will respond to driverless cars that is a cause for concern among those charged with designing their roll-out. Volvo[280] have already announced that the first 100 vehicles they will make available for trialists will not be visibly marked as driverless cars. This is to avoid situations where human motorists might slam on their brakes or drive erratically to force the driverless cars into submission. As driving regulations are updated, it is likely they will be amended to cater for these challenges and make the intentional interference with the progress of a driverless car an offense - one which will of course be captured in HD by the driverless car's cameras.

AV Phone Home

Given the unpredictable nature of scenarios that a driverless car could ultimately find itself in, it is likely to be virtually impossible to pre-programme a suitable course of action for every instance. And while the machine learning abilities that underpin driverless car decision making will continue to improve, waiting for a completely demonstrably fool-proof system would likely delay the introduction of driverless cars by many years. To help deliver the benefits that driverless cars can bring in the majority of everyday driving scenarios, we need a solution to help the driverless cars make decisions in unfamiliar conditions. Just as we insist that learner drivers are accompanied by an experienced driver, companies are working to create similar backup advisors for driverless cars.

---

[279] https://en.wikipedia.org/wiki/Jaywalking
[280] https://www.theguardian.com/technology/2016/oct/30/volvo-self-driving-car-autonomous

In the event that a driverless car encounters a situation it cannot safely navigate, it will be able to call on the services of a remote contact centre for support. The operator in the call centre can temporarily access all the car's sensor data and make a decision about how best to proceed. New instructions can then be sent to the car - and the driverless car's software can learn from its experience, and then share that experience with all other driverless cars. For example, if the car was confused by an unmapped construction zone temporarily requiring cars to "illegally" cross solid lines to navigate an obstacle, the remote operator could "reassure" the driverless car that it was ok to do so. This is clearly an area of interest for driverless cars manufacturers. For example, Google has a patent[281] for augmented trajectories for autonomous vehicles, Toyota has a patent[282] for remote operation of autonomous vehicle in unexpected environment, and Nissan[283] has cooperated with NASA to use the remote guidance software adapted from the Mars Rover.

Obstacles - Literal and Imagined

While researching the topic of driverless cars, I've seen countless articles on why driverless cars "simply won't work". The better-written articles provide scenarios and justifications for their conclusions, but many seem more intent on trying to appear smart and find reasons it might struggle to be deployed in current situations rather than trying to constructively consider what it would take to deploy it successfully.

A similar analysis a century ago on the prospects for the human driver car would have concluded that paved roads didn't exist, nobody knew how to drive (a much more mechanical task back then than now), we'd need petrol stations all over the world and

---

[281] https://www.google.com/patents/US9008890
[282] https://www.google.com/patents/US20160139594
[283] https://www.wired.com/2017/01/nissans-self-driving-teleoperation/

we'd need to dedicate massive amounts of our cities to provide parking. Guess what, as unreasonable as all that seems with hindsight, we managed it. The roll-out of cars wasn't predicated on keeping stables and blacksmiths - they had to be replaced with car parks and mechanics, and so it turned out.

Concerns about system reliability top many lists of misgivings about driverless cars. These are understandable and naturally worrying, as is the case in any automation situation. But given the levels of reliability we have seen achieved in other sectors, I believe we can expect driverless cars to reach a high degree of reliability - in fact, I hope our regulators insist on it! The most common metric for assessing the reliability of systems is the mean time between failure (MTBF). To put system failures in context, a 50 years study of commercial airliners[284], found that there was one fatal system failure every 2 million flights, roughly 100 times better than planes in the 1950s, despite flying further, faster and for longer than planes then. In order to deliver safety benefits (by being better than current human drivers), driverless cars would need to have a MTBF > 3 million vehicle hours leading to a fatal crash and no worse than a MTBF of > 65,000 vehicle hours for a crash resulting in injuries[285]. There is no reason to doubt that we can achieve similar levels of system safety for driverless cars, though to be clear it does represent orders of magnitude improvements over the current performance displayed in driverless car testing. The manufacturers of driverless cars are all engineering for reliability, as cars are a far more hostile environment than the static, vibration-free, temperature controlled data centers that advanced technologies are more familiar with. Thankfully, the consequences of a failure in a car relative to a plane are likely less drastic, and as we've

---

[284] https://asndata.aviation-safety.net/industry-reports/Boeing-Statistical-Summary-1959-2013.pdf

[285]

http://itscalifornia.org/Content/AnnualMeetings/2013/PRESENTATIONS/Wed%20Tech%20Session%2010%20-%20%20Automation4ITS-CA.pdf Steven E. Shladover, University of California, Berkeley October 2, 2013

just discussed above, it is highly possible that a car will be able to slow or stop and seek help from a remote contact centre.

Another frequently mooted challenge is the condition of roads.[286] Between their multitude of sensors, GPS and detailed map data, driverless cars can now cope much better with obscured, weathered, or inaccurate road edges or lane markings than they could at the start of their development. But it remains preferable for them to have good quality markings, and I, for one, would certainly prefer that the computer vision abilities of the car were scanning for any danger rather than exerting effort on simply trying to figure out where the road was supposed to be. We know that trains aren't very good at running without tracks. But if we want trains, we put tracks down and maintain them. Similarly, we know that cars need roads. Just as humans find it more tiring to drive on poor quality roads, we should fix or replace defective infrastructure to ensure the safe running of cars - and this should be true for human and robot drivers alike.

Ethics

A vehicle driven by a computer using advanced sensors on public roads opens up the possibility of many insurance, liability and ethics issues. Much of the debate to date around driverless cars has gravitated towards the ethical issues raised. Even with near-perfect autonomous driving, there may be instances where a crash is unavoidable. What should happen in those circumstances? What value system should be applied to choose the preferred outcome, where there is no "good" outcome? This is not an area that gets much attention for human drivers, but in the absence of a human, how and why decisions are made suddenly become more important.

---

[286] http://www.forbes.com/sites/neilhowe/2016/09/15/driverless-cars-unsafe-at-any-speed/

For example, if an animal jumps in front of the driverless car, does the system determine to hit the animal or veer off the road in an attempt to avoid the collision? Although physics, reactions and instincts in the heat of the moment may make the outcome unpredictable, most human drivers would say with varying levels of regret that it's preferable to hit the animal rather than risk potentially worse injury to the human by veering off the road. Authorities have tried to educate motorists not to risk a worse outcome with advertising campaigns and road signs.

Signs Educating motorists not to follow their instincts and veer to avoid animals

There are 1.3 million deer-related crashes in the US each year according to State Farm Insurance.[287] While deer collisions are an example of unexpected incursions onto the road to which drivers have to react, driverless cars can be programmed to respond with more certainty. They won't close their eyes and hope for the best - they can be designed to identify deer and not to reactively veer, and will have faster reactions and better car control under duress.

---

[287] https://newsroom.statefarm.com/download/234883/allstates2015-16deerstats-finalpdf.pdf

But how might the decision change if the animal is actually another car, a large truck, a motorcyclist, bicyclist, baby stroller or pedestrian? What if swerving to avoid the initial obstacle means certainly striking another vehicle, cyclist or pedestrian? When faced with such an instant decision, human drivers typically are not held at fault if they survive, regardless of whether their decision was in hindsight judged the best. We understand it was not premeditated. However, driverless cars may be held to a different scale of ethics. Humans will react to the situation they find themselves in, based on instinct. For driverless cars, their decision-making algorithms need to be taught how they should try to react in a given situation. A Google patent[288] describes how the driverless cars system makes risk-cost analysis in situations where it may consider gaining additional inputs to make a decision:

Consider a possible active-sensing action where an autonomous vehicle can switch lanes to, e.g., allow its camera(s) or other sensors to obtain more information regarding a traffic light. The autonomous car may determine that it could get a clearer or less ambiguous view of the traffic light by changing lanes, so that it is not blocked by a large SUV, is closer to the light, etc. Based on historical and/or learnt data regarding the potential information gain when such an action is taken, the autonomous car may determine an information-improvement value, which indicates how much information it expects to learn by changing lanes. Further, the autonomous car may determine a risk cost for changing lanes, which may take into account risks such as running off the road, hitting a pedestrian (e.g., 0.1% chance of hitting a pedestrian in the lane closest to the curb versus a 0.07% chance in the lane closest to the middle of the road), having an accident with another car, annoying passenger(s) in the autonomous car and/or other cars resulting by changing lanes, and so on. A combination of the information-improvement

---

[288] https://patents.google.com/patent/US9176500B1/

expectation and the risk cost may then be used to determine whether to switch lanes.

Other philosophical questions also need consideration - like to what degree should driverless cars in these impossible positions prioritize minimizing injuries to their occupants, versus other crash-involved parties? And should owners be allowed to adjust such settings? Or should users be able to choose a brand of driverless car that transparently places a higher value on attempting to protect its occupants over other parties in all situations? Say your driverless car ends up in a no-win situation where it will hit either a cyclist wearing a helmet or one with no protection. Objectively, the cyclist with no helmet is likely to suffer worse injuries. But choosing to hit the more responsible cyclist seems like a perverse decision.

Speaking in September 2016,[289] Bill Ford, the great-grandson of Henry Ford and Executive Chairman of Ford, called on the auto industry to work with academics, ethicists and public institutions to address ethical issues emerging in a world where robot cars will make life-and-death decisions.

Germany for example, is gearing up to lay down the ethical foundations for self-driving cars, banning systems from making decisions that could harm one group of people over another:[290]

(1) "It is clear that property damage takes always precedence of personal injury.

(2) "There must be no classification of people, for example, on the size, age and the like."

(3) "If something happens, the manufacturer is liable"

---

[289] http://www.bloomberg.com/news/articles/2016-09-13/robot-car-ethics-need-urgent-review-in-society-bill-ford-says

[290] https://www.inverse.com/article/20716-germany-outlines-three-laws-of-robotics-for-self-driving-cars

The third rule may seem to suggest that the manufacturer cannot depend on the driver stepping in during an emergency. A black box will show whether the machine or driver was in charge at the time of the accident.

Trolleyology

In philosophy circles, there's an ethical question to explore this phenomenon, known as the trolley problem. It challenges that if you had to push one large person in front of a moving trolley to save a group of people on the tracks, would you? This abstract thought exercise has been widely applied in discussion about how we should design the programming for self-driving cars: what should it choose to do in a trolley-style situation where not everybody can be saved but relative value choices need to be made?

In an interesting public exploration of the trolley problem in the context of driverless cars, MIT have created a website[291] offering users the chance to choose their preferred outcome in a variety of scenarios. The MIT reworking of the trolley problem replaces the trolley with a driverless car experiencing brake failure. The experiment depicts 13 variations of the "trolley problem", asking users to decide who should perish, which involves agonising priority choices: more deaths against fewer, humans over animals, elderly compared to young, professionals against criminals, law abiding people over jaywalkers, and larger people against athletes. I strongly recommend you try it yourself: http://moralmachine.mit.edu/ and see how your choices compare with others who have completed the experiment. Apparently, the most common outcome is that people prefer utilitarian outcomes which places the highest value on the fewest total number of lives lost. One study's[292] participants disapprove of enforcing

---

[291] http://moralmachine.mit.edu/

[292]

https://www.researchgate.net/publication/301293464 The Social Dilemma of Autonomous Vehicles

utilitarian regulations for AVs and stated they would be less willing to buy such an AV. Accordingly, any Government decision regulating for mandatory utilitarian algorithms may paradoxically increase casualties by postponing the adoption of a safer technology by an unaccepting public. However, despite the results of an abstract thought experiment, it is not so clear cut when the person taking the survey is the one in the firing line - a study in Science Magazine[293] showed that nearly 60% of people were likely to purchase a driverless car that always attempted to prioritise the driver's life. Or as Patrick Lin of Stanford summarises it: "No one wants a car that looks after the greater good. They want a car that looks after them."[294]

While utilitarianism promotes the best outcome for the largest number of people (even if that's not you), an alternative school of thought is known as Deontology. This suggests that there are certain absolute values such as the notion that intentional killing is always wrong. In relation to the Trolley problem, this means that even if shifting the trolley will save five lives, we shouldn't do it because we would be actively killing one.

In their paper on Implementable Ethics for Autonomous Vehicles,[295] Gerdes & Thornton contend that the behavior of the vehicle and its control algorithms will ultimately be judged not by statistics or test track performance but by the standards and ethics of the society in which it operates. This places a considerable responsibility on the programmers of automated vehicles to ensure their control algorithms collectively produce actions that are legally and ethically acceptable to humans.

---

[293] http://science.sciencemag.org/content/352/6293/1573

[294] https://www.wired.com/2016/06/self-driving-cars-will-power-kill-wont-conscience/

[295] Autonomes Fahren, https://link.springer.com/chapter/10.1007/978-3-662-48847-8_5/fulltext.html

Taking the idea of prioritizing human life and the most vulnerable road users and phrasing the resulting hierarchy in the spirit of Asimov's laws gives:

1. An automated vehicle should not collide with a pedestrian or cyclist.
2. An automated vehicle should not collide with another vehicle, except where avoiding such a collision would conflict with the First Law.
3. An automated vehicle should not collide with any other object in the environment, except where avoiding such a collision would conflict with the First or Second Law.

In addition to protecting human life, automated vehicles must also follow the appropriate traffic laws and rules of the roads on which they are driving. It seems reasonable to value human life more highly than adherence to traffic code so one possibility is to simply continue adding deontological rules such as: 1. An automated vehicle must obey traffic laws, except where obeying such laws would conflict with the first three laws. Such an approach would enable the vehicles to break traffic laws in the interest of human life when presented with a dilemma situation, an allowance that would most likely be acceptable to society. Moving forward, Asimov's laws raise another point worth considering. The Second Law requiring the robot to obey human commands cannot override the First Law. Thus, the need to protect human life outweighs the priority given to human commands. All autonomous vehicles with which the authors are familiar have an emergency stop switch or "big red button" that returns control to the driver when desired. The existence of such a switch implies that human authority ultimately overrules the autonomous system since the driver can take control at any time. Placing the ultimate authority with the driver clearly conflicts with the priority given to obeying human commands in Asimov's laws. This raises an interesting question: Is it ethical for an autonomous vehicle to return control to the human driver if the vehicle predicts that a collision with the potential for damage or injury is imminent?

Human Choices

The context for deciding on robot ethics is their ability to make decisions compared to what a human would do in the same situation. It's said that in the moments before an inevitable crash, for those involved, time slows. For a robocar, relative to humans, everything is in slow motion. It can meticulously review the situation in milliseconds and make rational decisions.

The notion that human drivers always act responsibly, ethically or even consistently when behind the wheel is a blatantly false assumption. Driving under the influence of alcohol or drugs is a crime in all US States, yet Federal statistics show that alcohol was a primary factor in crashes that killed over 10,000 people in 2013 - 31% of vehicle related deaths[296]. Given that trolley situations are incredibly rare, you could argue that the ethics question is not that important. What is more important is that driverless cars can likely avoid the 41% of motor vehicle crashes that the CDC estimates[297] were caused by human recognition errors.

So before we allow driverless cars development to get too distracted with solving the trolley problem, let's consider how humans respond. I've never heard of a real-life situation where a human had to make a trolley-style choice, and I certainly wasn't quizzed on my ethical leanings before being given a driving license. If such an event did happen, we're assuming that a human would be able to go through a complex sequence of steps in a fraction of a second:

- Accurately assess and understand the situation
- Be aware of the braking capabilities and handling of the vehicle in the precise circumstances (tire condition, brake wear and road adhesion)
- Calculate whether the car can avoid either outcome

---

[296] http://www-nrd.nhtsa.dot.gov/Pubs/812102.pdf
[297] http://www-nrd.nhtsa.dot.gov/pubs/812115.pdf

- Make a moral decision

Whatever "choice" the driver makes will probably not have been a choice at all, but simply a panicked reaction, based largely on instinct and fear. And there's little guarantee that their evaluation of the situation will be mechanically and physically correct. You won't get the same result from humans in every situation, by intent, inattention or incompetence. It's impossible to predict with certainty what a human would do in each situation. Even with the best will in the world, they may not be able to react. They may not make the utilitarian choice they would have in a laboratory. They may make no choice - frozen into inaction by fear. So programming cars for the best possible outcome, even if unfavourable, adds a degree of certainty we don't currently have.

The driverless cars trolley problem discussions portend many forthcoming debates about ethics in the time of Artificial Intelligence and how we will hold machines to different standards than we do humans. We don't endlessly debate the trolley problem for human drivers, nor is it part of any driver test. Patrick Lin, a philosopher at California Polytechnic State University, San Luis Obispo and a legal scholar at Stanford University notes that *"Even if a machine makes the exact same decision as a human being, I think we'll see a legal challenge."*[298]

For all the debate about how to treat ethics in relation to driverless cars, it's also noteworthy that today we commonly put our safety in the hands of a driver who may be forced to make a life or death decision every time we get into a taxi. We don't know in advance if the driver is a utilitarianist. We also conveniently ignore the studies that show a likelihood for human

---

[298] https://www.wired.com/2016/06/self-driving-cars-will-power-kill-wont-conscience/

drivers in crashes to turn away from impacts, thereby exposing their passengers to likely greater harm than themselves.

Concluding the Debate

A quick review of driverless cars commentary to date reveals much discussion about the trolley problem. I don't see this as an insurmountable issue. It's incredibly rare and unlikely and there may well be no clear ideal agreed outcome. But if we move to driverless cars, what we will have is a lower overall death toll than we do today. Some decisions made by the new systems will be wrong, as doubtless some are wrong or just not made today by humans.

As the developer of driverless cars with the most experience on public roads, it's worth noting Google's response to trolleyology: *"The main thing to keep in mind is that we have yet to encounter one of these problems. "In all of our journeys, we have never been in a situation where you have to pick between the baby stroller or the grandmother."*[299] And they have encountered a woman in a wheelchair chasing a duck with a broom![300]

I think it would be far more morally troubling if we delay the introduction of driverless cars while we try to solve an academic scenario that will impact far fewer lives than the number that have been lost to preventable, real incidents since you started reading this Chapter, let alone this book. The decisions we make about how we want driverless cars to behave are important. But given the rarity of the life or death situations, I don't think it should become a barrier to their further development and deployment. With an admittedly utilitarian perspective, the number of lives that can be saved by driverless cars far outweighs the numbers that will be involved in trolley-type

---

[299] https://www.theguardian.com/technology/2016/aug/22/self-driving-cars-moral-dilemmas

[300] http://wardsauto.com/autonomous-vehicles/google-self-driving-car-passes-woman-wheelchair-chasing-duck-test

situations. Where these situations might arise, it's potentially because a driver wasn't paying attention, which won't be the case with driverless cars. These discussions are by nature somewhat abstract and speculative - there is no guarantee that the predicted outcome will happen - a car may "intend" to protect its occupants but who knows what will happen....I think that the trolley problem poses interesting questions and merits discussion, but if we allow the debate to continue for too long, thereby delaying driverless cars, we are guilty of deluding ourselves that a "correct" answer exists and indulging philosophers at the expense of saving lives. I'll conclude this section on ethics with a diagram that I think neatly summarises the trolley problem:

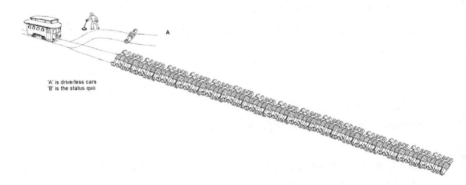

Image courtesy Caleb Watney (https://twitter.com/CalebWatney)

Transition

A new kind of vehicle has taken to the roads, and people aren't sure what to make of it. Is it safe? Can it cope with other road users? Will it require a radical overhaul of the transport infrastructure? The questions that are being asked today about self-driving cars were raised a century ago when the first motor cars roared onto the roads

The Economist [301]

We've been here before. Transitioning from one major, ingrained form of mass transport to another that requires substantially different rules for other road users and its environs happened about 100 years ago. In today's terms, getting from a point in time where all vehicles are driven by humans, to a point in time where all vehicles are automated, given the scale and size of our cities today, is set to be far more complicated than the horse to car transition.

In his book, Fighting Traffic: The Dawn of the Motor Age in the American City,[302] Peter Norton explored the transition from streets for horses and people to streets for cars. *"Today we learn that streets are for cars. That's 100 percent opposed to the dominant view a century ago/ It's a different mental model of what a street is for. Of course, the social change required to revolutionize transportation under the current rule of the car will be formidable. Habits do change, though, and so do societies. A lot of assumptions we treat as laws of nature are inventions. A lot of mental models we think can't change, can change. The proof is that they've changed in the past."*

---

[301] https://www.1843magazine.com/technology/driving-lessons
[302] Fighting Traffic: The Dawn of the Motor Age in the American City, Peter Norton

How long might the transition take? It won't happen overnight. The so-called "meteoric" rise of Facebook took 8.5 years to reach a billion users. The fastest-adopted technologies in the world are still measured in years, perhaps decades to reach mass penetration. The chart below shows the relative adoption curve for major technologies in US households. Remember that few technologies require the levels of change that driverless cars do. But few offer benefits or threats on the same scale either, so although it's often observed that new technologies are gaining widespread acceptance more quickly than ever, I don't believe that driverless cars fit into the same category as more affordable convenience items.

Image courtesy New York Times[303]

The transition phase to driverless cars will be a difficult time - while they are promoted on their benefits in reducing congestion and accidents, it's much harder to gauge how much those reductions will offer in a mixed environment with semi-autonomy and human drivers. The inevitable coexistence, at least initially, of self-driving vehicles with their human-operated counterparts will certainly pose quandaries. What is the correct perspective - is it a question of us learning to drive with them, or them learning to drive with us? Most of the emphasis so far has been on the latter with an assumption that human drivers will be unwilling to alter their behaviour to better accommodate their new fellow travellers.

---

[303] Nicholas Felton, NYT, 2008

The UK Department for Transport[304] predicted a decline in "network performance" once one in four cars become driverless saying that driverless cars could initially lead to longer delays on the UK's major roads. However, if driverless vehicles eventually make up between 50% and 75% of cars, DfT researchers say they will reduce congestion.

McKinsey have modelled several scenarios (see chart below) showing how long it might take for driverless cars to reach a significant share of the market, based on several factors, from regulations and consumer acceptance, to the performance of the technology itself. While it's speculative, it is a useful thought exercise to show that even in an impossibly positive scenario, it's still a decades-long process. As it's focused on market share of driverless cars, what this model doesn't show is a scenario whereby human and driverless cars are separated, with perhaps a gradual shift in the balance between them. I think this is one of the more likely scenarios to play out - with a gradual shift in favour of driverless cars - first fleets of driverless cars operated in contained areas, then contained lanes, then zones dedicated to driverless cars (to the exclusion of human drivers), with human drivers eventually being marginalised to devoted lanes.

---

[304] https://www.gov.uk/government/publications/driverless-vehicles-impacts-on-traffic-flow

How many new cars may be fully autonomous by 2030?

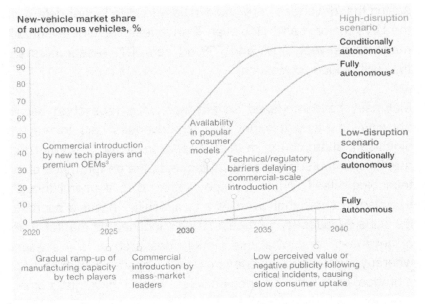

New-vehicle market share of autonomous vehicles, %

High-disruption scenario

Conditionally autonomous[1]

Fully autonomous[2]

Availability in popular consumer models

Commercial introduction by new tech players and premium OEMs[3]

Technical/regulatory barriers delaying commercial-scale introduction

Low-disruption scenario

Conditionally autonomous

Fully autonomous

(years axis: 2020, 2025, 2030, 2035, 2040)

Gradual ramp-up of manufacturing capacity by tech players

Commercial introduction by mass-market leaders

Low perceived value or negative publicity following critical incidents, causing slow consumer uptake

Factors in disruption scenarios	High disruption	Low disruption
Regulatory challenges	Fast	Gradual
Safe, reliable technical solutions	Comprehensive	Incomplete
Consumer acceptance, willingness to pay	Enthusiastic	Limited

[1]Conditionally autonomous car: the driver may take occasional control.
[2]Fully autonomous car: the vehicle is in full control.
[3]Original-equipment manufacturers.

McKinsey&Company

Image Courtesy McKinsey[305]

[305] http://www.mckinsey.com/industries/automotive-and-assembly/our-insights/disruptive-trends-that-will-transform-the-auto-industry

(Un)Employment

"The American economy is moving into a new era. It is an era that will be defined by a fundamental shift in the relationship between workers and machines"

Martin Ford, Rise of the Robots and the Threat of a Jobless Future[306]

The coming hard wave of technologies and driverless cars signal just the beginning of humans transitioning from using tools to being fully replaced by them. Make no mistake that radical economic change underpins many other societal issues. Mass unemployment leads to social unrest and radicalisation. We've seen the very real devastation that the end of industries can cause to communities: Coal country that has gone from prosperous to hopeless was a high-profile feature of the controversial 2016 US Presidential election campaign.

In 2008, the US government made a specific policy decision to rescue some of America's automotive heavyweights with the largest government intervention in industry in a generation, because of its significance to US employment, technology and economic growth. The automotive industry has been—and continues to be—a critical component of the U.S. economy, directly employing 1.7 million people (across manufacturers, suppliers, and dealers) and providing $500 billion in annual payroll, as well as accounting for approximately 3 to 3.5% percent of GDP.[307] Though already significantly automated, motor car manufacturing still requires much labor. Directly and indirectly, it employs a significant share of the labor force of the countries where it is well established.

---

[306] Rise of the Robots: Technology and the Threat of a Jobless Future Hardcover – 2015

[307] https://www.selectusa.gov/automotive-industry-united-states

Just as the Railways heralded the demise of the horse-drawn carriage era for long distance passenger travel, affecting various occupations from innkeepers to veterinarians, when driverless vehicles are ready to take to the roads, some 200,000 taxi drivers and 3.4 million truck drivers will be at risk. according to the U.S. Bureau of Labor Statistics (BLS)[308] there were about 665,000 jobs for bus drivers in the U.S. as well as more than 230,000 taxi and chauffeur jobs in 2014. Since the initially steep upfront costs of driverless vehicles can be offset by lower labor costs, the freight, transit, and taxi industries could be early adopters of driverless technologies, affecting the country's millions of bus, taxi, and truck drivers — mostly men with high school level (or less) education completed; a demographic that has not fared well in the recent recession or the larger digital revolution. Virtually all of these jobs will be eliminated within 10-15 years of the arrival of driverless vehicles, and this list is by no means exhaustive.

Looking at the bigger picture, some 14 million US jobs today are tied directly or indirectly to producing and servicing automobiles, building and maintaining roads, supplying fuel and governing infrastructure. 20% of the nation's retail sales are automobiles. The BLS lists that 915,000 people are employed in motor vehicles and parts manufacturing.[309]

---

[308] http://www.bls.gov/ooh/transportation-and-material-moving/taxi-drivers-and-chauffeurs.htm
[309] http://www.bls.gov/iag/tgs/iagauto.htm

For the love of driving

*"The car as we know it is on the way out. To a large extent, I
deplore its passing, for as a basically old-fashioned machine, it
enshrines a basically old-fashioned idea: freedom. In terms of
pollution, noise and human life, the price of that freedom may be
high, but perhaps the car, by the very muddle and confusion it
causes, may be holding back the remorseless spread of the
regimented, electronic society"*

J.G. Ballard, Drive, 1971

The reality of day-to-day driving rarely reflects or resembles the
conditions portrayed in car adverts and is more likely a stressful
time inching through traffic and dealing with other angry
motorists. But there are millions of people who love their cars
and love driving. If there comes a time that human driving is
severely restricted in favour of driverless cars, such a move will
likely face significant opposition.

Driving is not just a means to get from A to B. For many people,
it is an enjoyable means, it represents their own space, their
control, their personality and on the open road, a feeling of
freedom. Not everyone may want a driverless car, despite or
perhaps because of the risks of driving. Guaranteed safe driving
may seem too bland for some people. Oliver Blume, CEO of
Porsche says that people want "to drive a Porsche by
oneself"[310]. Porsche has no plans to develop driverless cars,
unlike most other carmakers who are embracing the
autonomous driving revolution, its chief executive said. The
typical American male devotes more than 1600 hours a year to
his car. More than 250 hours are devoted to the myriad small
tasks associated with car ownership: washing it, taking it to the
garage, filling it with fuel, looking for the keys, de-icing, finding a

---

[310] http://www.roadandtrack.com/new-cars/future-cars/news/a28053/no-self-driving-porsches/

parking space. He has to work about 100 hours every year to earn the money to pay the extra interest because he has a house with a garage.

There is also a complete culture behind the modification of vehicles for racing, aesthetics, or to suit personal interests. There will always be auto enthusiasts who will keep their car because of the amount of time and heart put into the changes. The feeling of taking a nice car out for a drive on a nice sunny day on fun roads can never be replaced. A modified car shows a part of a person's character. If a car is shared among multiple people, it is harder for someone to want to put work into modifying a vehicle. There is no doubt that the implementation of autonomous vehicles will hurt the culture and economy around personal car modification.

"The one thing that unites all human beings, regardless of age, gender, religion, economic status, or ethnic background, is that, deep down inside, we all believe that we are above-average drivers."
Dave Barry, Dave Barry Turns Fifty

"Have you ever noticed that anybody driving slower than you is an idiot, and anyone going faster than you is a maniac?"
George Carlin

Driving is an emotive subject for many. Will car enthusiasts end up sharing the road happily with fleets of autonomous cars? Or will human driving be relegated to dedicated tracks to drive for fun? Undoubtedly more people will participate in vehicle racing (cars, off road, motorcycles) to replace their emotional connection to driving. Though some more entrenched car proponents will feel it is, the driverless car does not represent a war on human driven cars or a war on freedom of choice. It is not a zero-sum game where humans must lose for the robots to win. It is about creating a technology that is better than humans at driving safely. This may require that we forgo individual freedoms for the greater good whilst still achieving as much individual freedom as possible. We will still be able to get from point to point anytime. But even if arguments about safety, efficiency or environmental benefits are compelling on paper, hyper-logical engineering views may not reflect the emotional reality when we're faced with the prospect of robots taking our place. It will be interesting to see the language used in this debate - Some will see positives in "delegating" control to the car, some will perhaps talk of "relinquishing", while others will consider it "losing" control.

Stopping the Robots?

Negatively affected stakeholders—including professional drivers, insurers, and personal-injury and traffic litigation lawyers—may exert significant pressure on public-policy makers to protect their interests. Authorities may need to develop mitigation strategies to soften the blow on the stakeholders that suffer the greatest disruption. But we should be vigilant in the coming debates for vested interests disguised as aggrieved parties. I would caution we shouldn't underestimate how far certain parties might be willing to go to protect the status quo. Those who wanted to impede or even sabotage the perception of driverless cars could cause accidents, use social media to spread scare stories, support petrol heads who oppose driverless cars on the grounds of love of driving, lobby congress to delay/block/make changes difficult and cut prices on regular cars to make them more attractive.

When people talk about a right to drive, I'm not sure they've got the correct terminology. It is perhaps more about confusing norms with rights. It's normal in most countries to be able to drive but we don't necessarily have a right to it. And in most territories, it requires a license to drive and insurance cover. The very need to have a license precludes it from being a right - it is an entitlement that you must earn. And that license is usually dependent on exercising a degree of responsibility. When reading articles on the topic of driverless cars, I've seen numerous opposition comments on topics to the effect of - *"I love driving my car, end of!"*. I've tried to think of parallels - something we've come to take for granted but then circumstances change and it is questioned. People loved to smoke but it's been decided as a society that smoking isn't healthy, so you now must go to designated areas to smoke. You can't generally shoot a gun on the street, but you can go to a shooting range if you enjoy firearms. The same might come for driving, with human drivers confined to tracks.

To date, robots have existed primarily in tightly controlled areas, where human interaction or the potential for human interaction is minimal/tightly controlled - such as in factories, or warehouses. In those instances where robots venture out, it tends to be in dedicated areas such as tunnels or lanes, again devoid of humans. As they venture visibly further into our lives and although protecting us from harm, become a threat to employment or perceived freedom, pushing us out of the way, how will we react?

Privacy & Security

Privacy is already a hotly debated topic and will likely only become more so as technology pervades more of our lives. As mentioned under the section on Law and Order in Chapter 5, driverless cars are essentially mobile sensor and data recorders. They boast powerful cameras and highly advanced systems that analyse the world around them in minute detail. Insurers and security services may want to see this data saved and made available, while privacy advocates will want to ensure it used only for the purposes of navigation and is transient in nature. In ride-sharing and on-demand scenarios, there is already little privacy - Uber have a record of all my journeys, knowing when and where I am going, and could easily deduce patterns and perhaps even intentions and relationships. With driverless cars, the levels of detail will only increase. But before you start to worry, it's worth remembering that the majority of people already carry an advanced, camera-equipped device replete with multiple sensors with them everywhere they go. Your mobile network already knows huge amounts about your movements and location so I don't see driverless cars as being significantly different from that point of view. But privacy in the context of driverless cars is different - why? Because it's not a list of embarrassing web sites...it's your real-world information. It's physical not virtual.

On the Inside

Future cars are likely to have multiple sensors inside the car, as well as those pointed at the outside world. There are plenty of benefits in a car's knowing how many passengers it has, where they are, and what they're doing. In case of emergency — a sensor failure, for instance — the car will know how long it will take for a driver to reach the wheel. If a kid in the back seat slips out of their seatbelt while mom and dad are taking a nap (the privilege of owning a self-driving car), they can be warned. In a collision scenario, the car could steer so that it prioritises being struck in an unoccupied quarter. Airbag deployment, too, could be adjusted to the size or position of a passenger. I expect that some or all of these internal sensors will have a privacy over-ride but many taxis today have CCTV fitted, primarily for the safety of the driver, so but being under surveillance while using transport is not new. We'll return to the topic of privacy in the next Chapter where we'll look at the regulatory framework(s) for privacy in a driverless cars world.

Hacking

While privacy is a major concern for some, an even more widespread concern about the proliferation of technology in cars is the threat of hacking. Nobody wants to think of a malicious or even just mischievous force taking control of their car via hacking. In a public service announcement issued together with the Department of Transportation and the NHTSA, the FBI released a warning[311] to drivers about the threat of over-the-internet attacks on cars and trucks:

"Modern motor vehicles often include new connected vehicle technologies that aim to provide benefits such as added safety features, improved fuel economy, and greater overall convenience. Aftermarket devices are also providing consumers with new features to monitor the status of their vehicles. However, with this increased connectivity, it is important that consumers and manufacturers maintain awareness of potential cyber security threats."

In an attempt to address concerns about potential vulnerabilities to hacking, Waymo have clarified that their cars will remain unplugged from the internet most of the time to prevent them from being hacked "Our cars communicate with the outside world only when they need to, so there isn't a continuous line that's able to be hacked, going into the car," John Krafcik told the Financial Times.[312] "When we say that our cars are autonomous, it's not just that there's not a human driver, but also that there is not a continuous cloud connection to the car," he said, adding that cyber security was "something that we take very very seriously". The US Federal Policy on Automated Vehicles[313] includes guidance on cybersecurity that we'll discuss in Chapter 7.

---

[311] http://www.ic3.gov/media/2016/160317.aspx

[312] https://www.ft.com/content/8eff8fbe-d6f0-11e6-944b-e7eb37a6aa8e

[313] https://www.transportation.gov/briefing-room/federal-automated-vehicles-policy-september-2016

Developing Countries

"If cities in the developing world go through the same cycle that we have in the past 50 years, we have a problem"

Bruno Moser[314]

Although the push for driverless cars is being led from the upmarket valley towns south of around San Francisco, the car is a global phenomenon. The latest WHO data for cars totals 1.77 billion in 173 countries around the world[315]. Those designing and testing driverless cars need to be mindful too of the very different needs of the developing world when it comes to the terrain and baseline infrastructures involved.

Today, transport accounts for nearly a quarter of energy-related global greenhouse gas emissions. The lack of road safety also costs up to 5 percent of countries' GDP, mostly affecting the poorest ones.[316] Most developing countries are still far from being as car-centric as the developed world. City travel is still mostly composed of walking, bicycling and public transport, much more in line with Marchetti's constant. It is probably preferable if these cities do not replicate the urban mistakes of others, as to multiply them on the scale of Mexico City or Rio would not be feasible. The driverless car might help save developing countries from ever having to replicate the car-centric infrastructure that has emerged in most western cities. This leapfrogging has already happened with telephone systems: Developing countries that lacked land-line telephone and broadband connectivity, such as India, made the leap directly to mobile systems rather than build out their land-line infrastructures. With an annual toll of 150,000[317] deaths, over

---

[314] https://www.theguardian.com/cities/2015/apr/28/end-of-the-car-age-how-cities-outgrew-the-automobile
[315] http://apps.who.int/gho/data/node.main.A995
[316] http://www.worldbank.org/en/news/feature/2016/05/05/transforming-the-worlds-mobility---its-time-for-action
[317] http://www.bbc.com/news/magazine-37362728

10% of all the road deaths in the world are in India. Given the population densities in some of these megacities, the relatively young populations and the lack of a historical model of car ownership, there may just be an opportunity for shared self-driving cars to avert a generation of carnage and pollution spreading further around the globe.

Framing the Future

"The world as we have created it is a process of our thinking. It cannot be changed without changing our thinking"

Albert Einstein

Just as we don't know for certain the timeline for truly driverless cars, we also don't know which will prove to be the biggest barriers. Will it the intense lobbying by people or industries identified as potential losers, ethical dilemmas or will cybersecurity and privacy issues make driverless cars grind to a halt faster than an obstacle detected by their LiDAR? Cars need to navigate the complex world of city streets, passing inches away from fragile, litigious human beings. Will privacy concerns be outweighed by the prerogatives of climate change, individual safety and crime reduction?

John Jordan, a Professor at Penn State[318] sees parallels in the past: *"About 125 years ago, when the internal combustion engine supplanted equine power for personal mobility, there was much talk regarding 'horseless carriages', defining the future in terms of the past. We are at much the same juncture today. Much of the conversation starts with what we know human drivers do: 'How will self-driving cars avoid bicyclists? How will self-driving cars merge in construction zones? How will self-driving cars make left turns across oncoming traffic with solar*

---

[318] http://earlyindications.blogspot.ie/2016/08/early-indications-august-2016-next-car.html

glare?' All of these questions must be answered, of course, but I believe it's not too early to ask what we want of the next car."

Sociologist and economist Thorstein Veblen introduced the concept of Technological Determinism[319] in the 1920s, which proposed that a society's technology determines the development of its social structure and cultural values. There seems little doubt that the technology for driverless cars will overcome its technological challenges at some point and offer genuinely new alternatives for transport, and all that entails and affects. How we approach the attendant challenges will determine its ultimate impact more than the technology itself, though the development of the capabilities and the ultimate decisions to deploy it will be shaped to a great degree by two constituencies who may or may not be very closely aligned: the regulators and the public.

---

[319] http://communicationtheory.org/technological-determinism/

Chapter 7 - Regulation and Acceptance

"Salus populi suprema lex esto"
(The health of the people should be the supreme law)

Cicero

Who decides if and when autonomous cars should be allowed on our roads? What are the criteria that should be applied? Who will have the final say - will it be regulators or will public opinion prevail? As the driverless cars manufacturers battle to resolve the technological challenges, they will do so against a backdrop of increasing regulation and public scrutiny. Although not currently a major concern for most people, the regulatory environment for driverless cars should be of interest - the decisions made at Federal and State levels will impact safety and economic investments.

Normally invisible regulators will have the power to determine the next trillion-dollar industry, and perhaps pick some of the winners and losers, shaping many aspects of our society for decades to come. If they speed approvals, they will be accused of playing fast and loose with lives, bowing to cavalier corporations. If they don't, they will be accused of obstruction and old fashioned favouritism. And many of their decisions will directly and indirectly impact on areas dauntingly far beyond their normal remit - policy makers operate on a four or five-year popularity cycle, which can make it harder to implement strategic initiatives that involve short term pain.

The existing regulatory bodies will face many challenges in the coming years as technology accelerates and boundaries blur. They have a difficult path to navigate - between technology providers keen to benefit from the technology, and groups opposed to the technology for various reasons; they face opposing forces and rapidly evolving capabilities challenging entrenched and trenchant views. Are the current regulators equipped to deal adequately with this emerging technology? Can they somehow balance the short-term challenges and the strategic perspective?

The Emergence of the Driving Regulator

As noted in Chapter 2, when the automobile pervaded society, it quickly generated opposition. Some feared it as a danger to life and limb because of dangerous driving or the many accidents that occurred from horses panicking when confronted by these vehicles. The implementation of a novel transportation technology gave rise to concerns about the danger of defective implementation. Governments in the US and other countries sought to deal with the defective implementation issue by registering cars and drivers and regulating driving, especially with regard to speed.

In the US, motor vehicles interests opposed the imposition of special automobile speed limits, arguing that motor vehicles should be subject to the same rules as horse-drawn vehicles that the only requirement on roads should be that the driver maintain a speed that was reasonable and proper with respect to the road and traffic conditions. This effort was successful until the turn of the century when the obvious disparities between the speed of horse drawn vehicles and automobiles soon prompted several states to impose speed limits on the operation of motor vehicles.

The regulation of speed and further provisions such as signalling and lighting were analogues of the rules intended to address similar concerns resulting from the widespread use of bicycle technology. The automobile rules were in fact based on the bicycle statutes. Adopting rules prescribing equipment for automobiles and defining a few basic standards for their operation was not the full extent of official efforts to protect citizen from the mass implementation of this new technology. In an initiative that went beyond what they had required of cyclists, governments adopted laws that were intended to ensure a measure of competence in the use of automobile technology.

Rhode Island passed the first driver's license law in 1908 - all US states have required drivers to be licensed since 1954. Many countries are signatories to the Vienna Convention on Road Traffic. This requires that 'every moving vehicle or combination of vehicles shall have a driver' and that 'every driver shall at all times, be able to control his vehicle'. Some have taken this to be a barrier to the introduction of automated vehicles.

Today, U.S. automakers self-certify that they are meeting U.S. vehicle standards. In Europe, vehicles must obtain "type approval" from a government before an automaker can release a new model for sale in the EU. Human drivers must pass a test administered by the DMV or equivalent local agency. Each manufacturer's vehicles are generally tested and certified as being road worthy and then regularly checked by national testing schemes. However, drivers are rarely retested, simply able to renew their license every ten years in most countries, at least until the age of 70 or so, where shorter validity licenses are issued, with medical certification required for renewal.

Regulations for Driverless Cars

"I am not an advocate for frequent changes in laws and Constitutions. But laws and institutions must go hand in hand with the progress of the human mind. As that becomes more developed, more enlightened, as new discoveries are made, new truths discovered and manners and opinions change, with the change of circumstances, institutions must advance also to keep pace with the times. We might as well require a man to wear still the coat which fitted him when a boy as civilized society to remain ever under the regimen of their barbarous ancestors."

Thomas Jefferson

Self-driving cars sound pretty much like a custom-made list of things that worry regulators: autonomous robots with lethal force, disruptive new technology, mechanized unemployment, and large corporations putting millions of cameras all over the world. It is almost inevitable that their arrival will be met with significant resistance, mistrust, and potentially even hostility.

The NHTSA is the US regulator charged with ensuring the safety of the nation's road and travellers. Founded in the 1960s, the second 50 years of its existence will be very different to its first 50 as its challenges moves from mechanical engineering to artificial intelligence. Its mission is to "save lives, prevent injuries, reduce vehicle-related crashes," it welcomes autonomous technology with open arms - The US DOT prefaced its policy on automated vehicles with this unashamedly positive attitude: *"Recognizing this great potential, this Policy sets out an ambitious approach to accelerate the [...]revolution"*.

There isn't a legal system in the world equipped to deal with self-driving cars and the wave of technologies enabled by robots and Artificial Intelligence. Few countries have legislation relating to robots. In fact, most legal systems date back closer to the invention of the wheel than the microprocessor, as demonstrated by the continued use of Latin in legal circles. Regulators will have to walk a tight balance between being seen to foster progress without taking too many risks. They will face heavy pressures from entrenched incumbents with powerful influence, stakeholders and lobbying budgets. They will sometimes have to offset potential and unproven gains against short term losses or pain to particular sectors. They also will find themselves in the unenviable position of keeping some of the world's most innovative yet revenue-hungry companies from taking too many risks. And all of this will happen under the microscope of social media commentary, and against the backdrop of litigation that previous technological advances did not endure.

The purpose of a regulator for transport is to enable as many people to get where they need/want to go as safely, speedily and cheaply as possible with the least environmental impact. It is not to favour any mode over another. The primary concern of regulators regarding driverless cars will be safety. This must take priority over questions of congestion, environmental impact, ownership or employment. It is not for regulators to decide if people wish to still own their cars or will prefer to use rideshare services - that is for the market to determine.

There are two key steps for regulators tackling the question of driverless car safety: first, a method to assess the safety of autonomous vehicles, and, more challengingly, what level of safety would be required before autonomous vehicles are deemed acceptable for availability on a limited and/or general basis. Essentially, the immediate need will be to determine a driving test equivalent for driverless cars and decide what is a passing grade. There are no tests of skill that can judge how safe a vehicle is in all circumstances —there are just too many conditions and scenarios to account for them all. Current (human) driving tests don't prove how good people are at driving—they only serve to demonstrate if the human can satisfy a designated examiner that they have a suitable level of skill on that day, in those circumstances, as a basis to decide they are acceptable to let loose on public roads. Testing humans is relatively easy yet still largely arbitrary - another human decides how well you comply with a fairly narrow set of regulations in fairly standard conditions, lacking much scientific precision, with an assumption that you will continue to adhere to those regulations and be able to adapt to whatever conditions you encounter.

Things are different when it comes to machines driving and how we test them for safety, and to what standard they (and their manufacturers) are held accountable. To demonstrate safety with statistical confidence based on current test fleets would take decades. We will likely start by trying to decide what constitutes "safe enough" - do we expect the driverless cars to work flawlessly or simply break fewer laws and get into fewer accidents than human drivers do? Is society ready to let robots make life or death decisions?

Regulators tackling the issue of driverless cars will have to start somewhere. Mark Rosenkind, NHTSA administrator noted: *"Everybody asks, 'When are they going to be ready?' I keep saying they're not coming; they are here now. Without federal instructions, "people are just going to keep putting stuff out on the road with no guidance on how do we do this the right way."* Comparing the opinion of domain experts, it's clear that regulators will be receiving widely varying advice as they craft their legislation:

Rand Corporation's Center for Decision Making: *It seems sensible that autonomous vehicles should be allowed on America's roads when they are judged safer than the average human driver, allowing more lives to be saved and sooner while still ensuring they don't create new risks. But, there is even an argument to be made that autonomous vehicles should be allowed even if they're not as safe as average human drivers if developers can use early deployment as a way to rapidly improve the vehicles. They might become at least as good as the average human faster than they would otherwise be, and thus save more lives overall.*[320]

Princeton University Professor Alain Kornhauser & Gill Pratt, CEO of the Toyota Research Institute, note that we will hold robots to very different standards than humans. There's no way we as a society would accept self-driving cars that cause the same number of fatalities as humans: *"Society tolerates a lot of human error, but we expect machines to be much better than us."*

Philip Koopman, associate professor of electrical and computer engineering at Carnegie Mellon University, says there's so much uncertainty around the technology that you might need close to

---

a billion miles of test-driving data to ensure safety on roads populated with both human and machine-driven cars. *"There's a possibility at least some companies are just going to put the technology out there and roll the dice. My fear is this will really happen, and it will be bad technology."*[321]

Federal Regulation

"In the 50 years of the U.S. department of transportation there has never been a moment like this, a moment where we can build a culture of safety as a new transportation technology emerges. We are witnessing a revolution in auto technology that has the potential to save thousands of lives. In order to achieve that potential, we need to establish guidelines that clearly outline how we expect automated vehicles to function – not only safely, but more safely – on our roads. The DoT believes that automated vehicles hold enormous potential benefits for safety, mobility and sustainability."

Anthony Foxx, Secretary of Transport, U.S. Department of Transportation[322]

Driverless technology poses a fundamental, even existential, challenge to driving regulators - it aims to remove the very thing they regulate most heavily - the human driver. In May 2013, the NHTSA issued a preliminary statement[323] regarding automated vehicles. Their guidelines were initial suggestions for discussion, as they looked to create the basis for future laws as companies sought to press ahead with testing on public roads, essentially forcing the issue of regulatory advancement. The starting point was to require special driver's license endorsements for anyone operating an autonomous or semi-autonomous car requiring, that the driver take lessons and tests on the capabilities and limits of the autonomous vehicle, as well as how to take over

---

[321] http://www.consumerreports.org/autonomous-driving/with-autonomous-cars-how-safe-is-safe-enough/

[322] https://one.nhtsa.gov/nhtsa/av/av-policy.html

[323]

https://www.nhtsa.gov/staticfiles/rulemaking/pdf/Automated_Vehicles_Policy.pdf

control in an emergency. Other recommendations include state limitations on where and in what types of conditions autonomous cars can operate on public roads, requirements that the cars operate for a certain number of miles on private roads before use on public roads, and a system to record and report any failures or accidents of autonomous cars. The document concluded with a realisation that further research and updates would be required; *"As innovation in this area continues and the maturity of self-driving technology increases, we will reconsider our present position on this issue"*. In 2016 the Department of Transportation and the NHTSA, released an updated policy statement concerning automated vehicles which stated, *"it is becoming clear that existing NHTSA authority is likely insufficient to meet the needs of the time."*

In an unusual move for a sitting President, then President Barack Obama released an op-ed about driverless cars.[324] Regardless of your views on driverless cars, they seem to have had attention at the highest levels of Government:

"Of course, American innovation is driving bigger changes, too: In the seven-and-a-half years of my presidency, self-driving cars have gone from sci-fi fantasy to an emerging reality with the potential to transform the way we live. Right now, too many people die on our roads – 35,200 last year alone – with 94 percent of those the result of human error or choice. Automated vehicles have the potential to save tens of thousands of lives each year. And right now, for too many senior citizens and Americans with disabilities, driving isn't an option. Automated vehicles could change their lives. Safer, more accessible driving. Less congested, less polluted roads. That's what harnessing technology for good can look like. But we must get it right. Americans deserve to know they'll be safe today even as we

---

[324] http://www.post-gazette.com/opinion/Op-Ed/2016/09/19/Barack-Obama-Self-driving-yes-but-also-safe/stories/201609200027

develop and deploy the technologies of tomorrow. That's why my administration is rolling out new rules of the road for automated vehicles – guidance that the manufacturers developing self-driving cars should follow to keep us safe. And we're asking them to sign a 15-point safety checklist showing not just the government, but every interested American, how they're doing it. We're also giving guidance to states on how to wisely regulate these new technologies, so that when a self-driving car crosses from Ohio into Pennsylvania, its passengers can be confident that other vehicles will be just as responsibly deployed and just as safe. Regulation can go too far. Government sometimes gets it wrong when it comes to rapidly changing technologies. That's why this new policy is flexible and designed to evolve with new advances. There are always those who argue that government should stay out of free enterprise entirely, but I think most Americans would agree we still need rules to keep our air and water clean, and our food and medicine safe. That's the general principle here. What's more, the quickest way to slam the brakes on innovation is for the public to lose confidence in the safety of new technologies.

Both government and industry have a responsibility to make sure that doesn't happen. And make no mistake: If a self-driving car isn't safe, we have the authority to pull it off the road. We won't hesitate to protect the American public's safety.

Even as we focus on the safety of automated vehicles, we know that this technology, as with any new technology, has the potential to create new jobs and render other jobs obsolete. So it's critical that we also provide new resources and job training to prepare every American for the good-paying jobs of tomorrow."

Can a Machine be a Driver?

With current legislation, one of the biggest challenges for driverless cars is the definition of a driver. Not surprisingly, laws have been crafted to describe humans in control. New York's vehicle code[325] directs that "no person shall operate a motor vehicle without having at least one hand or, in the case of a physically handicapped person, at least one prosthetic device or aid on the steering mechanism at all times when the motor vehicle is in motion." None of the driverless cars technologies have a "hand" - all simply send commands to actuators that direct the car.

Google wrote to the NHTSA requesting clarification of the law and its application to driverless cars. In their response[326], the NHTSA indicated that it will *"interpret driver' in the context of Google's described motor vehicle design as referring to the [self-driving system] and not to any of the vehicle occupants. We agree with Google its [self-driving car] will not have a 'driver' in the traditional sense that vehicles have had drivers during the last more than one hundred years.".* Although the clarification regarding the definition of "driver" answers one question, there are remaining statutes that mandate braking systems activated by foot control inside the vehicle. Google told the NHTSA that human controls could be a danger, if passengers attempt to override the car's own judgements and driving decisions: *"the company expresses concern that providing human occupants of the vehicle with mechanisms to control things like steering, acceleration, braking, or turn signals, or providing human occupants with information about vehicle operation controlled entirely by the Self Driving System (SDS), could be detrimental to safety because the human occupants could attempt to override the SDS's decisions."*

---

[325] http://www.popsci.com/cars/article/2013-09/google-self-driving-car#page-4

[326] https://isearch.nhtsa.gov/files/Google%20--%20compiled%20response%20to%2012%20Nov%20%2015%20interp%20request%20--%204%20Feb%2016%20final.htm

Lobbying

Not surprisingly given the stakes and the conflicting interests, several powerful lobbying groups have been formed by interested parties. The Self-Driving Coalition for Safer Streets (SDCSS) includes proponents of the technology comprised of major names with an interest in the area such as Ford, Google, Lyft, Uber and Volvo as well as interest groups such as Mothers Against Drunk Driving, National Federation of the Blind, United Spinal Association, the R Street Institute, and Mobility 4 All. It is headed up by a former administrator of the NHTSA. The Global Automakers industry group (which represent the U.S. divisions of 12 motor vehicle manufacturers) is urging a more cautious approach and used a public hearing to caution the NHTSA to slow down while crafting regulations for autonomous driving tech, wary that the regulator is moving too quickly and tying itself to "arbitrary, self-imposed deadlines" instead of allowing "robust and thoughtful" analysis.[327]

State by State

In the period 2015/2016, sparked by enthusiasm and a sense of local opportunity from driverless cars - or simply fear of missing out (FOMO) - more than 20 US states have introduced over 50 pieces of regulations seeking to address the legal framework for driverless cars. The growing patchwork of state laws is of increasing concern to companies trying to develop driverless cars, giving rise to fears about how it would be possible to test across state boundaries. "The worst possible scenario for the growth of autonomous vehicles is an inconsistent and conflicting patchwork of local, municipal and county laws that will hamper efforts to bring autonomous vehicle technology to market," said Joseph Okpaku, Lyft's director of public policy. "Regulations are necessary, but regulatory restraint and consistency is equally as

---

[327] Paul Scullion, safety manager at the Association of Global Automakers

important if we are going to allow this industry to reach its full potential."[328]

Here are some examples from 4 states showing the varying approaches and thinking currently evolving:

California has led the way, with the most companies testing driverless cars in the Golden State. As of April 2017, DMV has issued Autonomous Vehicle Testing Permits to 30 separate entities[329]. The DMV also require that the driverless car manufacturers submit system disengagement reports and accident reports. Although disengagement reports (where the human supervisor had to assume control back from the driverless car system) are seen by some as onerous, the Californian authorities believe it to be an important transparency tool towards improving the technology and building public trust in it. But I would argue that capturing this sort of data could also have significant on-going benefits for urban design. Imagine, if in urban areas, all vehicles were required to report whenever their sensors detected a collision or near-miss incident. This data could be analyzed to better identify dangerous areas and recommend suitable improvements in road layout, signage etc. While we don't require driving schools to note and report on every learner driver's mistakes - which may be a missed learning opportunity - with driverless cars, we can capture and learn from each incident, adding to the collective knowledge and experience of the system.

New York's Upstate Transportation Association (UTA) and Independent Drivers Guild (IDG) are both pressing for bans on autonomous vehicles in the state, out of concern that they'll ultimately cost thousands of transportation jobs. The IDG believes that it only needs to preserve existing laws to guarantee

---

[328] http://www.mercurynews.com/2016/09/02/driving-regulation-how-lyft-works-to-shape-ride-hailing-legislation/

[329] https://www.dmv.ca.gov/portal/dmv/detail/vr/autonomous/testing

a ban, but the UTA is considerably more aggressive - it wants a 50-year ban on self-driving cars.[330]

Michigan, historic home to the auto industry, has introduced legislation to reclaim its crown as the centre of the industry. While the state has tried to create a progressive/permissive framework that allows autonomous technology on public roads, including testing of platoons and on-demand fleets of autonomous vehicles, there's a protectionist element (also seen in Tennessee), where the wording reserves the right to operate on-demand robo-fleets for "motor vehicle manufacturers", which would disqualify technology companies such as Uber and Waymo who are not manufacturers, to the benefit of incumbent auto manufacturers[331].

Finally, in Chicago, two aldermen have proposed banning driverless car testing from their streets. In a press release[332] announcing the stance, Aldermen Ed Burke and Anthony Beale described it as "pre-emptive strike" after Uber's announcement it was beginning a pilot of self-driving cars in Pittsburgh. "We do not want the streets of Chicago to be used as an experiment that will no doubt come with its share of risks, especially for pedestrians. No technology is one-hundred percent safe." The aldermen did not offer any explanation for how they propose to protect pedestrians from the risks of human driven cars - 46 people died in Chicago in 2015, up 31% on the previous year. If they are motivated solely by safety concerns, proposing a ban on a technology designed to reduce this without any better suggestion seems unhelpful.

It's also worth noting that while those charged with regulating for road safety may be busy considering the implications of

---

[330] http://money.cnn.com/2017/01/10/technology/new-york-self-driving-cars-ridesharing/index.html
[331] https://www.wired.com/2016/05/detroit-wants-go-spot-self-driving-tech-big-automakers/
[332] http://imgur.com/a/gNXJj

driverless cars, there may be a disconnect to their colleagues in the urban planning departments - even though by most estimates fully autonomous cars could be ready for the road within the next decade, only 6% of the country's most populous cities have accounted for them in their long-term plans, according to a study from the National League of Cities.[333] Regulation that stops short of considering and providing for the ramifications of enabling and allowing driverless cars would be an incomplete response from the authorities. Simply regulating for safety will make it harder to reap the benefits of driverless cars beyond crash reduction and could delay the uptake of driverless cars if and when they are considered safe enough.

The International Picture

Thanks to international agreements (like the 1949 Convention[334]), you can travel to most countries in the world and drive (temporarily at least) as your driver's license will be recognized. The cross-border implications of driverless cars remain to be seen. Driverless cars software will need to be "aware" of local regulations and practices. Certain jurisdictions may opt to enforce laws in different ways, or rules may be substantially different across borders, just as today those disembarking the Eurostar or Car Ferry between the UK and France need to adapt to driving on the opposite side of the road and shift between signs in MPH and KPH. Without local knowledge, a driverless car from the UK might consider the speed limits in the rest of Europe very generous! In a signal of support for testing of driverless cars and preparation for their arrival, an amendment to the UN Convention on Road Traffic,

---

[333] http://fortune.com/2015/12/02/somerville-driverless-car/

[334]

https://en.wikipedia.org/wiki/International_Driving_Permit#The_1949_convention

which came into force on 23 March 2016,[335] allows control of the vehicle to be transferred to the car in real world usage, provided that these systems can be overridden or disabled by the driver.

The UK government is developing a light touch approach to the testing and development of these technologies using a Code of Practice. The current Highway Codes, for example, states that you should have both hands on the wheel where possible[336] (I guess it's not possible if there's no steering wheel...). Likewise, Rule 126[337] which refers to a two second gap for minimum distance between vehicles would need to be amended to allow for autonomous platooning. From a regulatory and lobbying point of view, it's instructive to see who responded to the UK Government consultations[338] on driverless cars:

---

[335] http://www.unece.org/info/media/presscurrent-press-h/transport/2016/unece-paves-the-way-for-automated-driving-by-updating-un-international-convention/doc.html

[336] http://www.highwaycode.info/rule/160

[337] http://www.highwaycode.info/rule/126

[338]

https://www.gov.uk/government/uploads/system/uploads/attachment_data/file/581577/pathway-to-driverless-cars-consultation-response.pdf

Type of Organisation	Number of Responses
Insurance Bodies	16
Law Firms	14
Road Safety Groups	7
Transport Groups	7
Manufacturers	5
Automotive Membership Groups	5
Police Groups	4
Driver Training Bodies	4
Local Authorities	3
Technology Firms	2
Unions	2
Motorcycling Groups	2
Cycling Groups	2
Services Firms	2

Regulation & Revenue

Police officers in the US issue about 112,000 tickets a day on average, to 41 million drivers generating $17,024,000 a day[339]

Many of the current regulations around driving are among the worst observed and enforced statutes in existence. Nearly 50 per cent of UK drivers admit breaking traffic laws, with around half of them doing so deliberately.[340] Not only will self-driving vehicles likely be much safer than humans, they also will adhere to traffic rules and regulations, although those rules and regulations may be quite different than the ones in effect today. A driverless cars world that obeyed all laws, except perhaps in emergencies, would wipe billions from public coffers. Technology has already impacted revenues with apps designed to make it easier for people to comply with regulation - Even the seemingly small advance such as the ability to pay for parking meters via an App a led to a $6 million decrease in ticket revenue in Washington, D.C., in one year.[341]

This could very well revolutionize traffic regulation and management. While State and local governments, for example, would lose the revenue from traffic fines, their payrolls might also shrink as demand for highway patrol officers plummets and court time is freed up from having to deal with traffic offenses. Authorities may still seek to replace the lost revenue—perhaps with infrastructure usage fees? Traffic citations make a very significant contribution to local governments. The city of Chicago installed red-light and speeding cameras in 2003 and according to the Chicago Sun-Times, the Windy City has raked in about $600

---

[339] http://www.statisticbrain.com/driving-citation-statistics/

[340] http://www.telegraph.co.uk/news/uknews/road-and-rail-transport/11566026/How-is-your-driving-Half-of-drivers-admit-breaking-traffic-laws.html

[341] https://www.brookings.edu/wp-content/uploads/2016/06/desouza.pdf

million in fines from the automated systems.[342] Of course the regulatory imperative should be safety, not revenue. But the simple fact is that some administrations may have come to depend on traffic transgressions as a source of revenue. Time will tell if the savings from driverless cars, in terms of reduced policing and emergency services costs, will outweigh the lost revenues from fines. Or perhaps the monies previously paid in penalties will help the local economy in the form of disposable income.

New Areas of Regulation

Aside from the crucial regulatory decisions required for the operational roll-out of driverless cars, there are numerous other legal and administrative frameworks that will be important, some far removed from traditional motoring. Chapter 6 highlighted the challenging areas of privacy and cyber security as they relate to driverless cars. Defining regulations around these will require an entirely new skillset for agencies used to dealing with mechanical issues.

SDC will generate and collect more data than any other mass market machine yet invented. Although our smartphones are full of sensors that can track and record location, online activity, sound, movement and even video, these pale by comparison with the 4TB of data that a self-driving car collects each day by necessity. It is required for its safe operation, but what happens to the data, who owns it and who has access to it in what circumstances are crucial questions. Even before driverless cars become a reality, the number of connected cars and the number of sensors they contain is growing rapidly each year. While the data collected can be of great value to the car manufacturers, increased connectivity also means an increase in attack vectors

---

[342] http://chicago.suntimes.com/news/7/71/1345175/judge-declares-red-light-speed-cam-tickets-void-city-violated-due-process

for hackers and increases in concern about the ownership and potential additional uses for the data.

Two US senators have already introduced a (brilliantly named) bill to address motoring cybersecurity issues: Security and Privacy in Your Car (SPY Car) Act of 2017.[343] The proposed Act nominates the NHTSA and the Federal Trade Commission (FTC) as the guardians of motoring cyber security. The Act details measures such as a requirement to isolate critical systems (i.e. the ones that are required for the operation of the vehicle) from other systems - reflecting how aircraft systems are configured, where, for example, flight control networks are physically isolated from in-flight entertainment systems - and also requires technologies to identify and report hacking or intrusion attempts.

The FTC and NHTSA are still formulating their positions but have raised several questions to be addressed at a joint public workshop,[344] including:

- What data do vehicles with wireless interfaces collect, store, and transmit, and how is that data used and shared?
- What are vehicle manufacturers' privacy and security policies and how are those policies communicated to consumers?
- What choices are consumers given about how their data is collected, stored, and used?
- What are the roles of the FTC, NHTSA, and other federal agencies with regard to the privacy and security issues raised by connected vehicles?
- What self-regulatory standards apply to privacy and security issues relating to connected vehicles?

---

[343] https://www.congress.gov/bill/115th-congress/senate-bill/680

[344] https://www.ftc.gov/system/files/attachments/press-releases/ftc-nhtsa-conduct-workshop-june-28-privacy-security-issues-related-connected-automated-vehicles/notice_connected_cars_workshop_with_nhtsa_1.pdf

Privacy & Security

Privacy is an issue that various industry groups are also proactively addressing, in a desire to help their members (car makers who aren't necessarily experts in consumer data issues) and to help instil public trust. In the U.S., the Alliance of Automobile Manufacturers and Global Automakers has published a set of privacy protection 'principles'.[345]

The dedicated section on Privacy and Security in the Federal Guidelines[346] sets out the following principles:

The DOT and NHTSA strongly believe in protecting individuals' right to privacy. Highly Automated Vehicle (HAV) manufacturers and other entities, either individually or as an industry, should take steps to protect consumer privacy. Manufacturers' privacy policies and practices should ensure:

A. *Transparency: provide consumers with accessible, clear, meaningful data privacy and security notices/agreements which should incorporate the baseline protections outlined in the White House Consumer Privacy Bill of Rights and explain how Entities collect, use, share, secure, audit, and destroy data generated by, or retrieved from, their vehicles;*
B. *Choice: offer vehicle owners choices regarding the collection, use, sharing, retention, and deconstruction of data, including geolocation, biometric, and driver behavior data that could be reasonably linkable to them personally (i.e., personal data);*
C. *Respect for Context: use data collected from production HAVs only in ways that are consistent with the purposes*

---

[345] https://autoalliance.org/connected-cars/automotive-privacy-2/principles/
[346] https://www.nhtsa.gov/technology-innovation/automated-vehicles

for which the data originally was collected (as explained in applicable data privacy notice/agreements);

D. *Minimization, De-Identification and Retention: collect and retain only for as long as necessary the minimum amount of personal data required to achieve legitimate business purposes, and take steps to de-identify sensitive data where practical, in accordance with applicable data privacy notices/agreements and principles;*

E. *Data Security: implement measures to protect data that are commensurate with the harm that would result from loss or unauthorized disclosure of the data;*

F. *Integrity and Access: implement measures to maintain the accuracy of personal data and permit vehicle operators and owners to review and correct such information when it is collected in a way that directly or reasonably links the data to a specific vehicle or person;*

G. *Accountability: take reasonable steps, through such activities as evaluation and auditing of privacy and data protections in its approach and practices, to ensure that the entities that collect or receive consumers' data comply with applicable data privacy and security agreements/notices.*

Vehicle Cybersecurity Manufacturers and other entities should follow a robust product development process based on a systems-engineering approach to minimize risks to safety, including those due to cybersecurity threats and vulnerabilities. This process should include systematic and ongoing safety risk assessment for the HAV system, the overall vehicle design into which it is being integrated, and when applicable, the broader transportation ecosystem. The identification, protection, detection, response, and recovery functions should be used to enable risk management decisions, address risks and threats, and enable quick response to and learning from cybersecurity events. While this is an evolving area and more research is necessary before proposing a regulatory standard, entities are encouraged to design their HAV systems following established best practices for cyber physical vehicle systems. In particular, entities should consider and incorporate guidance, best practices, and design principles published by National Institute for Standards and Technology (NIST), NHTSA, SAE International, the Alliance of Automobile Manufacturers, the Association of Global Automakers, the Automotive Information Sharing and Analysis Center (ISAC) and other relevant organizations.

As with safety data, industry sharing on cybersecurity is important. Each industry member should not have to experience the same cyber vulnerabilities in order to learn from them. That is the purpose of the Auto-ISAC, to promote group learning. To that end entities should report any and all discovered vulnerabilities from field incidents, internal testing, or external security research to the Auto-ISAC as soon as possible, regardless of membership. Entities involved with HAVs should consider adopting a vulnerability disclosure policy.

This final provision on data sharing is very interesting - the agencies are suggesting that cybersecurity data and accident data be shared with them and between other manufacturers. In recommending this approach, regulators have borrowed from the Federal Aviation Administration model where airline data is shared via an independent system. Sharing would represent a significant shift for automakers and tech companies, who usually fiercely protect their proprietary information and aren't likely to be enamoured with sharing data at a time where knowledge may still yield competitive advantage in this nascent industry.

Some automakers believe that industry self-regulation in line with the Federal proposal is preferable to individual local motoring authorities regulating the area. For example, in their response to California DMV proposals, Volvo Car Group stated:[347]

---

[347] https://www.dmv.ca.gov/portal/wcm/connect/58a64bed-2bf3-449f-a270-822c208bb7f0/Volvo.pdf?MOD=AJPERES

Cybersecurity is a constantly evolving global field and it is impossible for regulation to keep up. VCG is a part of the Automobile Information Sharing and Analysis Center (ISAC) which serves as the central organization for analysis and sharing of cyber threats. This global collaboration with other automakers and suppliers has drafted the Automotive Cybersecurity Best Practices[348]. These best practices will be updated continuously and therefore much more effective at quickly resolving these global issues that involved all connected cars. VCG therefore believe that CA DMV should harmonize with these efforts and instead require certification that the AD vehicles are in line with the Automotive Cybersecurity best practices.

One further security-related question is how much responsibility makers will have to patch software vulnerabilities through updates after the car has been sold. I would suggest that regulators mandate that all driverless cars vehicles must receive all relevant safety updates free for the lifetime of the vehicle in a manner that is easy for the owner(s).

A final privacy implication of driverless cars is that for the first time in decades, the driver's license may no longer be the de-facto form of personal ID in the US. There is no obvious proof of identify document to replace it. It's clear that regulating for privacy and security is a complex area and one that requires significant additional regulatory preparation. A more detailed exploration is beyond the scope of this Chapter but for those interested, I'd recommend starting with this comprehensive article from IBM Research, Chris Poulin.[349]

---

[348] https://www.automotiveisac.com/best-practices/

[349] https://techcrunch.com/2015/10/23/connected-car-security-separating-fear-from-fact/

Public vs Private

The regulation of driverless cars is a strange mix of public and private interests. The public sector will determine if the benefits will come sooner or later, while private companies are the ones pouring billions into the development of the technology. The public sector stands to gain from improved safety and rejuvenated urban planning opportunities. And the driverless cars are travelling on roads created and paid for from the public purse that will likely require consequential additional investments. With the increasing complexity of ventures such as self-driving cars and delivery drones, we are venturing into pretty unknown territories and it's unclear who if anyone is qualified to legislate for these approaching realities. You have private companies that are in some ways more powerful than governments and less constrained. The more than $200 billion cash reserves of Apple is unprecedented in corporate history. Google has over $64 billion in cash. This is in stark contrast to the debt-laden position of most governments, that constrains their abilities to take risks. With intense lobbying, there have already been examples of Regulatory Capture (where regulators protect the industry they regulate, instead of the public). The attempts to limit testing of self-driving cars to existing auto manufacturers in some states is a clear attempt to reduce competition from new entrants.

Regulators and policy makers have much to ponder in the coming years. Faced with conflicting interests, it will likely be impossible to satisfy all parties and not easy to make decisions for the greater good where benefits may not materialise for an extended period, or come at great cost to individuals or particular constituencies. Any temptation to leave the eventual result to market forces is unlikely to yield the optimal societal outcome. The negative externalities associated with individual driving have demanded a heavy social and environmental toll but any reversal of the status quo towards a position of public good may not result without prescriptive interventions. Previous regulatory attempts to counter market failures, such as incentives for purchasing electric cars, have met with limited success, proving that consumer demand can outweigh desired outcomes. The next few years may be the most important in automotive regulation history, as federal and state authorities work out their response to the impending arrival of autonomous vehicles. Regulators must try to tackle the safety, operational and privacy/cybersecurity questions blocking the technology's way; as its creators lobby and play states off against each other seeking to overcome, circumvent, or potentially ignore the obstacles in their bid for public acceptance and commercial success.

Perception

Even the most supportive, progressive and permissive regulatory frameworks imaginable won't be enough to guarantee success for driverless cars if the public do not adopt and adapt. So far, there has been a lot of biased media comments from those trying to manipulate public opinion. Despite what you might think after reading just a few of the statements from proponents of the technology, majoring on the great positives in terms of lives saved by reducing/eliminating crashes, there's no proof yet that it's going to be all plain sailing. Yet the naysayers like to point to extreme edge cases as justification for slowing the rollout, even if it potentially costs lives in the meantime. It's going to be hard for the public to form a fact-based opinion of this new technology and to objectively determine if and when they want to share the streets with it. I hope this volume helps to inform a rational evaluation of this momentous technology.

As the technological, operational and regulatory issues around driverless cars get resolved, the costs drop and the implications become clearer, the most important remaining factor in their success or failure will be the public's perception of them. We will almost certainly hold robots to higher standards than human drivers. While many techno-enthusiasts will contend that the driverless car doesn't have to be perfect—it only has to be better than the human driver - in practice, people will have vastly less tolerance for a system or machine that kills people than they do for deaths that occur as the result of human action or inaction.

Just Asking

"The adult public's taste is not necessarily ready to accept the logical solutions to their requirements if the solution implies too vast a departure from what they have been conditioned into accepting as the norm."

Raymond Lowey[350]

People think in the frame of reference they're familiar with. But when presented with a completely radical alternative, what happens? The old saying that "if you'd asked people what they wanted, they'd have said faster horses" is particularly apt once again. Humans are always sceptical about new technologies of which they have little experience. That scepticism usually diminishes with usage, however. Once again, if we refer back to the transition from horse to motor car, there was widespread negativity towards the new machines. Over time, humans came to trust the motor car and to a large extent the other road users who drove them, despite the negative impacts.

As Steve Jobs famously said of market research, *"A lot of times people don't know what they want"*. I'm similarly wary of surveys directly asking people about the future when they don't yet have enough information to make an informed decision. I'm not convinced that surveys are the best way to gauge an opinion on something people haven't thought about, experienced or have any real frame of reference for. It's too easy to skew the results the way the survey's sponsor wants. I've seen reports of surveys both wildly positive and wildly negative towards driverless cars. That's hardly surprising when questions can be framed as "Do you think driverless cars reducing deaths by 90% is a good

---

[350] http://www.raymondloewy.com/about.html

thing", or "Are you afraid to get in a driverless car that may be programmed to kill you?", and both results can be presented as reliably indicative of sentiment towards driverless cars.

Faith in the Machines

"Anything new is guilty until proven innocent. The point of maximum ignorance about the benefits and costs of any new activity or product is before testing. If testing is not permitted and people cannot gain experience using a new technology, the result amounts to not doing anything for the first time."

Robert Graboyes

The latest technology doesn't always have a very positive perception among people outside of technology circles. While most love their smartphones, others' perceptions are soured by crashed computers, unintelligible error messages or unresponsive machines. The acceptance of driverless cars will be largely a matter of trust - do people trust robocars to be on the roads? Ironically, despite the demonstrable and consistent behaviour of robots, many people are inherently nervous of them. How do we react to the notion of planes flying overhead? I think it's fair to say we trust them. We believe that the odds of these machines harming us are very low, even if there's an autopilot in control most of the time. Our perception that flying is safe is based on empirical data. Our attitudes to driving may be different as most of us have experience of it, whereas we don't have experience of piloting a plane. That makes it harder to feel that we could do it ourselves and therefore have no need of a robot replacement - there is no perceptible personal threat to us from pilots.

A key question I believe we should consider as much as we should ask about trusting robots, is do you (and should you) trust other human drivers? Every time we go on the road in a car, we are trusting other human drivers. Yet our trust in these humans is frequently misplaced. They do not all share one set of values, comparable abilities or unified priorities. We know that a substantial proportion of them will speed, will be intoxicated or will be distracted. How many times per trip do you have to take action to avoid crashing due to another human driver's decision? Driverless cars will behave with a predictability and consistency we cannot assume of our fellow humans. For 1 million people a year, the decision to trust humans is a fatal decision.

I talked in Chapter 5 about how some people see that driverless cars are somewhat ungainly with all their sensors; there may be a phase when manufacturers choose to ensure sensors are prominently visible to reassure consumers that the cars are sufficiently high-tech and thereby help to generate trust. And although the arguments in favour of removing steering wheels and pedals from driverless cars are based on sound research, it may be a step too far for some to accept. Industrial design pioneer Raymond Loewy summed up this principle in the aphorism "Most Advanced, Yet Acceptable," or MAYA. He believed that designers should take gradual steps—delivering innovative designs and experiences that break new ground, but still containing enough of the familiar to be "acceptable" to the target audience.

Despite initial indications that driverless cars are rapidly improving in terms of safety, and a belief from their creators that they will be massively safe, there's not yet enough information to prove it definitively. Notwithstanding the impressive-sounding millions of miles of testing so far, it's equivalent to only a tiny fraction of the human-driven miles each day. The perception will start to form more quickly as more companies get involved, there's more coverage of them in the media and as the public gets a chance to ride in them through programmes like Waymo's and Uber's early access testing in Arizona and Pittsburgh. Although likely biased by self-selection of early adopters, those programmes will hopefully start to confirm if the manufacturers' assertions that riders quickly trust the cars when they can see what the car sees, are true.

Learning to Trust

"I think the hardware may be ready before society is ready."

Bill Ford, the great-grandson of Henry Ford[351]

Someone will have the very dubious distinction of being the first person to be killed by a fully autonomous driverless car. Whether it happens naturally or maybe encouraged by vested interests, it will inevitably unleash a torrent of bad publicity and calls for stricter regulations. It is vital that when these events happen, they are investigated thoroughly and lessons learned. Where there are proven failures, then just as the FAA can ground an aircraft type, I expect regulators will have the power to insist on withdrawal of faulty driverless car software. The cause for optimism, though, is that we can learn from such events and immediately share that knowledge with all the other driverless cars out there, programming them to avoid the same outcome. We can learn from accidents and changes can then be mandated to vehicles, software and procedures as required to continue to improve safety. Over the years, fatalities have decreased in air travel because of this approach. And leaving that aside, just because someone dies doesn't mean we should give up on the technology. We grieve, learn, improve and move on. The world would be a very different place if we had given up on developing every technology that had ever killed a human in its early days. By contrast, we can hope that someone in the coming years may be the last person to die at the hands of a distracted human driver.

There will be several factors crucial to creating trust in driverless cars. The need for trust is especially important given the high perceived risk. People will have a sense of uncertainty, and a genuine fear given the potential seriousness of an outcome in the event of a failure - it's not comparable to the technological

---

[351] https://www.ft.com/content/97a04f76-3494-11e7-99bd-13beb0903fa3

frustrations of lost hours of typing if a word processor freezes. Most people will not understand how driverless cars work and therefore cannot establish trust based on familiarity with the underlying technology and how it operates. In an effort to reassure its trial customers, Uber installed screens in the rear of its self-driving vehicles to show riders how the car was navigating and let them watch how much the car could "see".

The rider information screen showing a LiDAR view to passengers in the rear of an Uber driverless car prototype.

Media Coverage

"One thing I should mention here that frankly has been quite disturbing to me is the degree of media coverage of Autopilot crashes – which are basically almost none – relative to the scarcity of media coverage of the 1.2 million people that die every year in manual crashes. It's something that I think does not reflect well upon the media. It really doesn't. You need to tread carefully about this because if in writing some article that is negative you are effectively dissuading people from using autonomous vehicles, you are killing people"

Elon Musk, CEO, Tesla

Media coverage is under the spotlight worldwide as never before after allegations of fake news, echo bubbles and social media complicity in spreading misleading information. It is against this backdrop that the emergence of driverless cars is taking place. What I've seen so far regarding driverless cars has often been sensationalist (both negative and positive) rather than genuinely analytical or even just informative. I don't think the fact that the robocars (which are by all accounts still years away from use) needed occasional intervention is worthy of a headline like the BBC used: "Google's self-drive cars had to be stopped from crashing" as they reported[352] in January 2016 on Google's publication of data related to disengagements. The media coverage of a fatal collision involving a Tesla in Autopilot mode in Florida gained dramatic headlines around the world. The NHTSA report that concluded "A safety-related defect trend has not been identified at this time and further examination of this issue does not appear to be warranted"[353] received far less column inches. The other 90+ fatal car crashes that day caused by human drivers received none of the same scrutiny.

---

[352] http://www.bbc.com/news/technology-35301279
[353] https://static.nhtsa.gov/odi/inv/2016/INCLA-PE16007-7876.PDF

It's important that journalists covering driverless cars don't look for easy headlines - and that applies for both sides of the debate. They need to look critically at the rose-tinted, tech-apologist view in the hundreds of gushing press releases they'll be sent, that ignore the very real practical challenges that remain beyond current technology, but also look critically at the strident views of those opposed to change. Similarly, they'll need to be aware of vested interests who cavil at every potential issue, intent on delaying or impeding the arrival of driverless cars.

Getting Ready, Carefully

"We've got a clock ticking. This technology is coming.
Ready or not, it's coming."

Anthony Foxx, U.S. Transportation Secretary, April 2016[354]

Driverless cars, in their current state of development, are best compared to learner drivers - inexperienced and error prone, but expected to be ready for the road soon enough, once they've been assessed as competent. Only in this case, we haven't decided on the driving test they'll need to pass. We do know that the existing rules of the road are not fit for purpose - because they never envisaged that technology could replace the driver. Technology frequently if not always outpaces legislation and regulation. Regulators are facing what in psychology circles would be called the Marshmallow Test[355] - a quandary of immediate gratification over a bigger future benefit.

If we allow driverless cars on the road too soon, they may actually cause preventable deaths, while the technology learns and improves. Yet, in order for them to learn, they need to operate on public roads, just as learner drivers do. If we delay

---

[354] http://www.reuters.com/investigates/special-report/autos-driverless/
[355] https://en.wikipedia.org/wiki/Stanford_marshmallow_experiment

too long, until there's more certainty over the safety levels, more preventable deaths caused by human drivers will continue to occur. Perhaps the most compelling argument is that while self-driving cars are potentially dangerous, human drivers are definitely dangerous and show no signs of improving.

In their submission to the NHTSA,[356] Apple expressed the belief that safety and progress are not conflicted under sensible regulation: *"It is vital that those developing and deploying automated vehicles follow rigorous safety principles in design and production. Such principles should not, however, inhibit companies from making consequential progress; there is no need to compromise safety or innovation."*

It's Not Just Driving

"Emerging technology requires a regulatory approach that emphasizes safety; promotes innovation and supports creativity"

Elaine Chao, U.S. Transportation Secretary, May 2017[357]

It's unlikely that regulators will get everything right first time. It is however very encouraging that the NHTSA have issued comprehensive guidelines and continue to engage with the industry and the public. It's less promising that urban planners don't seem to be sharpening their regulatory pencils with the same haste. Given the scale of the investments to date and the size of the financial prize(s) on offer, the companies pushing the driverless agenda will continue to seek the path of least regulatory resistance.

In the absence of progressive regulation, the companies developing driverless cars may choose to relocate to more permissive jurisdictions, wherever in the world that may be. Just

---

[356] https://www.scribd.com/document/333075344/Apple-Comments-on-Federal-Automated-Vehicles-Policy
[357] Remarks at Infrastructure Week, May 2017

as countries already compete to make themselves attractive destinations for high-tech investment, there will be big incentives on offer around the world, along with legislative regimes conducive to rapid development. Those eager to facilitate driverless cars will be hoping to gain substantial economic advantage from the ecosystem that will grow to support driverless cars and to profit from the new time and consumption opportunities the technology will create.

I'll leave the last word in this section to Dr. Chris Urmson, former head of Google's driverless cars project and founder of self-driving start-up, Aurora:

"What's going to happen, no matter what the law says, is people are going to get sued. But that doesn't mean the development of potentially lifesaving technology should be halted. There wasn't legal protection for the Wright brothers when they made that first plane. They made them, they went out there, and society eventually realized its value."

Chapter 8 - The Driverless Dividend

"The major breakthroughs in the advance of human knowledge, those that constitute the dominant sources of sustained growth over long periods and spread to a substantial part of the world, may be termed epochal innovations"

Simon Kuznet's Nobel lecture, 1971

The course of human civilization has been shaped by transportation for millennia. The Romans would not have expanded across Europe without the paved roadway, the Mongols could not have conquered Asia without the horse, America would not have grown inexorably without the train, and modern trade would not be possible without container ships and jet airliners. Our modes of movement empower us. Few technologies have been as economically important and transformative as the automobile. Today, automotive manufacturing accounts for almost $3 trillion of economic output. And the automobile's impact on growth, trade, innovation, military technology and the environment is for practical purposes, immeasurable. Yet, the car is something of a conundrum; it has granted us the freedom to travel short and long distances, imbued with a sense of control and relative affordability. But it also consumes inordinate amounts of our time and money, and led to the construction of sprawling cities and suburbs. And that's before you consider the huge human toll in deaths and injuries.

The new technologies moving us towards driverless cars could provide solutions to some of our most intractable social problems—the high cost of traffic crashes and transportation infrastructure, the millions of hours wasted in traffic jams, and the wasted urban space given over to parking lots, just to name a few. But if and when self-driving vehicles become a reality, the implications would also be profoundly disruptive. Driverless cars have remarkably broad implications for society, for the economy and for individuals.

When cars first came to prominence, they were called horseless carriages because not immediately recognising their disruptive and transformative potential, people characterised them in the familiar terms of the past, using the only frame of reference with which they were comfortable. Similarly, most people think of autonomous vehicles simply as driverless cars, when in fact they potentially represent a revolutionary new form of transportation. But no matter how innovative, transformative or disruptive a technology is, the reality remains that there are numerous factors standing between technical viability and widespread adoption—cost, customer acceptance, entrenched interests, regulations and more.

The Next Revolution?

"A great surge of development is defined here as the process by which a technological revolution and its paradigm propagate across the economy, leading to structural changes in production, distribution, communication and consumption, as well as to profound and qualitative changes in society. Societies are profoundly shaken and shaped by each technological revolution and in turn, the technological potential is shaped and steered as a result of intense social, political and ideological confrontations and compromises."

Carlota Perez

Since the late 18th century, there have been five successive technological revolutions:

(1) 1771 - The First Industrial Revolution
(2) 1829 - The Age of Steam and Railways
(3) 1875 - The Age of Steel and Electricity
(4) 1908 - The Age of Oil, the Automobile, and Mass Production
(5) 1971 - The Age of Information and Telecommunications

In her landmark book in about technological revolutions, Carlota Perez, visiting Professor at the London School of Economics, explored the characteristics of each revolution[358] which seem like an excellent framework to assess the promise and perils of driverless cars:

"The full deployment of the enormous wealth-creating potential brought forward by each technological revolution requires, each time, the establishment of an adequate socio-institutional framework. The existing framework, created to handle the growth based on the previous set of technologies is unsuited to the new one. In the first decades of installation, there is an increasing mismatch between the techno-economic and the socio-institutional spheres. The process of re-establishing a good match and creating conditions both for recoupling and full deployment of the new potential is complex, protracted and socially painful.

Any transformation in technology can only take place through an interactive and accompanying process of social, political and managerial change. Countries and regions vary in their capacity and their desire to make such institutional changes, depending on social and political factors, the particular historical circumstances and other social and political conflicts and ideas. The explosive upsurge of the new industries takes place within

---

[358] Technological Revolutions and Financial Capital, Carlota Perez, 2002

an environment still dominated by "old" institutions - a phase of structural adjustment. The full fruits of the technological revolutions that occur about every half century are only widely reaped with a time-lag. Two or three decades of turbulent adaptation and assimilation elapse, from the moment when the set of new technologies, products, industries and infrastructures make their first impact to the beginning of a golden age or era of good feeling based on them"

In a time of more instant gratification, it will be interesting to see if Perez's observations on the speed of change will be true this time around? Given that there is such a public health aspect, will any country try to be more aggressive in pushing forward? Creating the appropriate context for such an effort would require a risky commitment. While competitive forces, profit seeking and survival pressures may help to diffuse the changes in the economy, the wider social and institutional spheres where change is also needed are held back by strong inertia stemming from routine, ideology and vested interests. Perez also cautions that *"The sequence described involves profound changes that upset people's lives and views of the world, and motivate some to get deeply involved in taking advantage of the opportunities while others, who feel negatively affected, will strongly resist the changes".*

Time for Change?

"My prediction is that in fewer than 15 years, we will be debating whether human beings should be allowed to drive on highways. After all, we are prone to road rage; rush headlong into traffic jams; break rules; get distracted; and crash into each other."

Vivek Wadhwa, Distinguished Fellow and professor at Carnegie Mellon University[359]

---

[359] https://www.washingtonpost.com/news/innovations/wp/2014/10/14/move-over-humans-the-robocars-are-coming/

The car and all related personal transport services will change more in the next twenty years than in the previous 120. It is likely the first of many, or the most visible of many, new technologies that will have dramatic impacts over the next generation, challenging many powerfully entrenched beliefs and powers. The human driven car has had a good run. Its dominance and influence have gone unchallenged and unchecked for decades.

We may seem largely locked-in to the human-controlled car but daunting as the change may seem, the push and pull factors for change are at least worthy of consideration. But "better" technologies don't always automatically take over. Those who feel the human-driven car has outlived its usefulness, need to remember that less than ideal, or outdated reasons for retention of older technologies, can and do persist. For example, the QWERTY keyboard[360] was designed in the 1870s to slow down typists but is still in use today despite there no longer being any mechanical reason for it to remain. Will human drivers still be in use in future decades when they are similarly no longer required?

Even assuming an unlikely smooth uptake, the journey of driverless cars to market maturity will take 20 years or more to complete. But it is not too soon for the automotive industry, regulators and all players in the transportation and technology spheres to consider the implications of this revolutionary development and prepare for the changes it will unleash. Although it would be helpful to have an exact date to work with, whether driverless car availability actually takes 5, 10 or 20 years doesn't really matter - 10 years of a difference isn't a long time in the bigger picture. The interstate highway system took about 35 years to complete. Even the most rapidly adopted gadget in history, the smartphone took about 10 years to become massively ubiquitous. And at a cost that's a fraction of a

---

[360] https://www.cnet.com/uk/news/a-brief-history-of-the-qwerty-keyboard/

car, and a replacement cycle about 5 -10 times faster than cars, so it's hardly comparable. But it is worth pointing out the change-motivator that in a 10-year period, over 10 million humans will be killed by cars and more than 9 million of those will be attributable to humans driving badly.

Skepticism Is Only Human

"If at first the idea is not absurd, then there is no hope for it."
Albert Einstein

Although many of the wider public are not yet very aware of driverless cars, among those that are, there's a lot of skepticism - about how successful they'll be, about whether people will really want to use them, about whether they're safe. I've found talk of driverless cars elicits the full gamut of emotions from skepticism to disbelief to excitement to fear. For some the idea of a driverless car is still so fantastical that it struggles to get respect. But a prediction a hundred years ago that there would be between six and ten thousand planes in the air at any given moment, and double decker planes capable of ferrying 800 people, would have been seen as absurd. The first flight by the Wright brothers in 1903 lasted just 12 seconds covering a total distance of 120 feet - less than the wingspan of a Boeing 747. Just under 70 years later, the 747 could fly 400 people for 12 hours across continents. This illustrates that whatever we're familiar with becomes a seemingly fixed certainty, and paradigm shifts are hard to comprehend.

Early indications are that public opinion on self-driving cars is split. It's just not that easy for many people to imagine putting their lives, or the lives of their loved ones, into the passenger seat of an autonomous car. Acceptance and adoption will take time. But as the technology begins to prove itself in terms of safety, reliability, savings and convenience, opinion and the debate could quickly shift from, "I don't want to share the road with robots" to "I don't want to share the road with people driving their own cars."

The Disruption Dilemma

"It's difficult to make predictions, especially about the future."
Yogi Berra

Driverless cars are effectively the digitization of a very visible part of the physical world. They have emerged as the new battlefront for some of the largest companies in the world, primarily from outside the traditional auto industry. Why? The technology required is beyond most traditional car companies, at least without significant expenditure to quickly gain expertise. The voracious digital giants are reaching saturation point for many of their current digital platforms - the new prize is to embed deeper into people's lives, to create and control access to a whole new tranche of time they can monetise, which is vital to their growth ambitions.

For a technology industry that frequently worships at the altar of disruption, it would be sage to consider the impact of what they are striving for and to temper their claims so as to be mindful that driverless cars is not a simple or fool proof technology. Longer term, it may come to be recognised as a massive positive for society on balance. But in the shorter term, it will face many challenges, from hostile regulatory environments to consumer backlashes. A sensible strategy must be not to overpromise; when selling the vision its supporters need to be mindful of the human, emotional and social consequences that may get overlooked in excited technology-led rationalisations.

The desire to disrupt, regardless of the rights and wrongs of it, is not sufficient to make it happen. There are tons of barriers: financial, behavioural, political, technical, emotional among others. But there are also unprecedented incentives for us as a society to overcome the barriers. We won't succeed with rose-tinted techno-optimism, nor must we allow the barriers, selfish intransigence and vested interests to prevent us realising the benefits. Every year we find a reason not to push through the barriers, 1 million people will die needlessly. I can't think of another preventable cause of death on such a scale that we would fail to address. In this case, the technology to address it already nearly exists - posing a very real dilemma for the coming decades as the disruption extends so far beyond just replacing drivers.

The Driverless Dividend

"Remember cab drivers? Remember traffic jams? Remember when parents lived in dread that their children would die in a car accident? Death and major injury from traffic accidents will drop drastically. The automobile's other costs—decreased productivity, fuel burned in uncoordinated traffic—will be swept away"

Wall Street Journal[361]

Death by autocar for over a million people a year has been the price we've paid for freedom of mobility - for decades, there has been no viable alternative, no credible solution to the desire to move easily around urban and rural areas. It became a silent, accepted problem. But now there is a potential solution - a solution that requires relinquishing things that have come to be normal. The end game is clear - to enable more people to move about with greater freedom and affordability in greater safety at less cost to the environment. An end to road deaths and congestion, along with a decrease in crime and greater mobility for the aged and disabled. Saving over 1 million people a year from death and even more from injury, is for most people, worth paying quite a high price for. The greater good is surely a valid

---

[361] http://www.wsj.com/articles/could-self-driving-cars-spell-the-end-of-ownership-1448986572

compass as we determine our future regulations. But realistically, solving problems on the scale of congestion, pollution and mass death is unlikely to come without some cost or sacrifice.

Money & Infrastructure

Driverless technology is not only about attempts to reduce deaths and injuries - it promises other significant benefits. Morgan Stanley believe that "beyond the practical benefits, autonomous cars could contribute $1.3 trillion in annual savings to the U.S. economy alone".[362] Global savings? Somewhere in the neighborhood of $5.6 trillion. Considering the inherent inefficiencies of individual car ownership, its exorbitant cost, the sheer volume of urban space devoted to serving cars, driverless cars may also offer an opportunity to radically redesign our cities. "Even though driverless cars may be shoehorned to fit the traditional urban environment in the short term, it won't be a long-term solution for maximizing potential benefits," says Lili Du, an assistant professor of transportation engineering at Illinois Tech. It's just possible that the coming of driverless cars may break the stranglehold that the car has on cities.[363]

The 20th century was devoted to building the infrastructure to service the personal automobile across two building eras - the Great Depression and the 1950s interstate highway building. It is acknowledged that much of this crumbling infrastructure needs to be updated but perhaps the 21st century will be devoted to undoing most of it - is it time for a third era of rebuilding - reworking our environment to accommodate driverless cars, return space to people and save lives? Or do we honestly want to continue to accept 1 million deaths a year? Is it good enough to say "it's too hard, we can't stop it" because sensors can't see

[362] https://www.morganstanley.com/articles/autonomous-cars-the-future-is-now
[363] https://www.wired.com/2016/04/american-cities-nowhere-near-ready-self-driving-cars/

traffic lights in sunlight? Surely the answer in that case is to fix the sensors or fix the traffic lights. Or both. I've seen arguments that driverless cars shouldn't be funded by public monies that will benefit a few large corporations creating the technologies. This strikes me as short-sighted and flawed. Weren't roads created with public monies which inevitably created profits for car companies? In fact, many car makers grew to become some of the largest companies in the world arguably on the back of publicly funded investment in roads and infrastructure. But this infrastructure also contributes to the fact that we have less people in the world living in poverty than at any time in history. Yes, some companies will profit from the emergence of driverless cars but they are ones that have taken risks, invested heavily and have no guarantee of success.

Winners & Losers

"And it ought to be remembered that there is nothing more
difficult to take in hand, more perilous to conduct, or more
uncertain in its success, than to take the lead in the introduction
of a new order of things. Because the innovator has for enemies
all those who have done well under the old conditions, and
lukewarm defenders in those who may do well under the new.
This coolness arises partly from fear of the opponents, who have
the laws on their side, and partly from the incredulity of men,
who do not readily believe in new things until they have had a
long experience of them. Thus it happens that whenever those
who are hostile have the opportunity to attack they do it like
partisans, whilst the others defend lukewarmly, in such wise that
the prince is endangered along with them"

Machiavelli[364]

---

[364] Machiavelli, The Prince, Chapter 6

Concerns about seismic new technologies are understandable, and can be a positive influence towards ensuring a cautious approach. Unleashing such a change needs to be done without unbridled techno-optimism or progress-inhibiting Luddism. Much of the debate to date represents opposite ends of a spectrum from a utopian future of safety, no pollution and extra time, versus the dystopian tragedy of job losses, increased traffic and omnipresent surveillance. History tells us that the result will not be at either extreme of the continuum, but will require careful management over many years to ensure that the final result settles at a point the majority are happy with. It is a very large long-term project, but the outcome is not predetermined as either a utopian or dystopian one.

Driverless cars could be the biggest transformation project in history. In the US alone, there are 250 million cars and trucks, 203 million licensed drivers, 4 million miles of road and 14 million people who make their living from that ecosystem. Achieving sustainable, substantial and significant change is not going to be easy, quick or painless, just as it never has been. Think back to other large-scale changes - did the notion of putting electricity cable into every home seem that viable? Or building roads in the first place? Or rolling out a network of cell towers? The thoughts of installing traffic lights, marking lanes, and setting up petrol stations must have seemed at least as daunting as the changes that driverless vehicles will require. And just as the ecosystem that grew up to support horses, and those whose livelihoods depended on the, was replaced, there will be casualties in industries that rely on human driving.

No technology is an actor in its own right. How we choose to harness it determines the outcome, and the resulting winners and losers. Will we seek to deploy it for our immediate safety benefit? Or will we decide to prioritize regulation to control and maximise its geographic, urban or environmental impacts? The list of potential downstream effects is limitless. It is these second- and third-order upheavals − politics, policing, etc. −

where the driverless car may create profound societal change, far beyond the obvious. It is in these areas that planning to properly support those adversely affected will be harder than designing retraining courses for former professional drivers that we can easily predict as casualties of driverless technologies.

Many of the benefits of enhanced technologies accrue to society, not the individual. In fact, it can be detrimental, or perceived so, to individuals. Securing our safety can mean placing responsibility, intruding upon rights (real or perceived) and sacrificing some level of convenience. Introducing driverless cars is thus as much a human challenge as a technical one. We have many hard decisions to make and not everyone will agree on them. Critically though, driverless cars won't exist in isolation - there is also the rise of robots, home working and delivery drones that may reshape the demand for transport, or at least work-related transport to consider. There will also be contra technology forces in the future - VR might keep you at home, online shopping reduces the need to go out, but less work due to automation might create more leisure time and cultural engagement.

Like all disruptive technologies, change means there will be losers and winners. That change, however, is not likely to begin in earnest until about 2020. It will take a decade or more to ripple across America and far longer to spread throughout the world. Different parts of the world will change at different paces, as will different parts of the same countries. This will provide industries and economies time to adapt. But we would be foolish to think that we somehow have the luxury of time. We need to start thinking with a degree of urgency about how we want this transition to play out, how we will cope with it and how we try to ensure that the most positive outcome possible is what actually transpires for as most people. What role should government take to help the millions of professional truck drivers, taxi drivers, and others who stand to lose their jobs, or should these displaced workers be left to fend for themselves? Should we require the winners from this new technology—most likely some giant corporations and the public users of new services—to somehow share their gains with the losers, perhaps through some special levy on these new vehicles to finance programs to help the losers? I believe we need to evaluate both the potential good and bad of this stunning new technology. We need to balance the imperatives - save lives, save money, gain time, reduce pollution, gain space, with the undeniable and very broad drawbacks - loss of control, privacy concerns, loss of jobs. The winners will find their path significantly easier if they are mindful of the impacts, and work to ensure that "losers" are acknowledged and attempts are made to mitigate the losses.

The End of Driving?

"The next step after making driverless cars legal will be making them mandatory. Today you pay higher insurance premiums to drive a zippy roadster than a dowdy minivan. Tomorrow you could well be paying a steep price for any steering wheel at all. They can have our gearshifts when they pry them from our cold dead hands, many will cry. The coming years will no doubt be a seesaw of competing calculations, in which irrefutable data vies with ingrained passion"

Time Magazine[365]

Much like the infamous prediction from IBM that only 5 computers would be required worldwide, the prediction from Karl Benz in 1886 that the global car market would be limited to about a million cars, because of a relative shortage of people skilled enough to drive has proven to be wide of the mark - the prediction was actually wrong by a factor of 1,000 as there are over 1 billion cars in the world. Unfortunately, the annual global death toll of 1 million suggests he was somewhat right about the lack of skilled chauffeurs. Now that we finally have an alternative to human drivers, will we be willing to cede control?

---

[365] http://time.com/4236980/against-human-driving/

For some, a resistance to change will be a matter of passion - those who enjoy driving will not welcome attempts to remove them from the driving seat. For others, it will be a matter of trust - a concern about the wisdom of putting robots in charge will be a controlling fear factor for even those who dislike driving themselves. For many more, it will be a question of economics - those that have no strong feeling on the joys or frustrations of driving may have very strong views on their economic dependence on the current model of ownership and operation of vehicles. The most vocal will likely be those threatened by change. For example, I can't see people who love their cars being happy at being confined to circuits as the only place for manual driving. Assessing the validity of opposition to driverless cars will be difficult as our leaders attempt to consider the merits of the arguments. Loud objections, rooted only in inertia and self-interest, should not outweigh the societal benefits to the majority. Policy makers too often struggle with uncertainty and projects that don't deliver within the lifetime of their election mandate.

Intertemporal Choices & Exponential Change

"Brilliant technologies transform the magical into the banal. An idea that seems outlandish to one generation becomes commonplace to the next. So it has been with electricity, space flight and the internet. So it is likely to prove with driverless cars."

The Financial Times[366]

---

[366] https://www.ft.com/content/e961f914-6ba3-11e6-ae5b-a7cc5dd5a28c

Intertemporal choices is an economic term describing how an individual's current decisions affect what options become available in the future. Historically, we tend to make terrible intertemporal choices - as Paul Roberts put it in his book, The Impulse Society: *"Intertemporal choices are amongst our most fraught. Time and time again, we get them wrong opting to enjoy an immediate reward (or defer an immediate cost) even when we know with utter clarity that any short-term pleasure will be dwarfed by long-term pain"*.[367] We have some very big intertemporal choices to make as driverless cars approach technological viability. Although the scale of the changes within the scope of this book is massive, it is only part of an even larger point where humans need to decide how much of their traditional roles they are going to delegate to computers. That may sound dramatic, but that is the decision point humans are approaching. Questions like the future of work after robots, climate change and driverless cars are trans-generational where the final consequences may not be seen by the generation making many of the decisions. Several excellent studies on the future of work have been compiled and I've included some in the references section.

Epochal innovations are by definition rare but there is no constraint that says several cannot come at once, or over a short period of time. Not all epochal innovations are good ideas on every level or even desirable from all perspectives, but they deserve to be assessed with a different lens than other ideas. Driverless cars represent a level of change beyond what we're familiar with. We struggle to understand change on the scale of driverless cars - it is hard for people to deal with nonlinear concepts - most people's experiences have been predominantly linear, where there's a proportional relationship between actions and outcomes. Futurist Ray Kurzweil believes: *"our intuition about the future is linear because that is the way the world*

---

[367] Paul Roberts, The Impulse Society: What's Wrong With Getting What We Want, 2014

worked for most of history. But the reality of information technology is exponential, and that makes a profound difference. If I take 30 steps linearly, I get to 30. If I take 30 steps exponentially, I get to a billion."[368] Given that the negative impacts of driverless cars (e.g. job losses, first deaths of humans due to system errors) are likely to happen before the positives are fully realised, we face the very real chance that coping with the change will exceed our ability to prepare for it - especially when the outcome of a nonlinear change is negative, tendencies like loss aversion can kick in and people can react in highly emotional ways.

Driverless cars are not the first transit technology to challenge our conceptions of time and space. The increased speed made possible by the first railroads totally changed the contemporary perception of distance between locations. The Liverpool to Manchester railway announced the demise of the horse drawn carriage for long distance passenger travel, affecting various occupations from innkeepers to veterinarians. The actual routes joined by new technology became abstractions, defined and navigated by means of timetables rather than maps. Geographic proximity became less relevant than whether or not the location was connected to and by the new transportation network.

Different people see evolving technologies differently and they fight for their vision of the technology's future. The 19th century was the heyday of rail, the 20th the car but what about the 21st? How prominent will driverless cars be when future historians come to review the 2020s? Now that the technology exists to change or reduce crashes, we will have to choose to use it. It involves big decisions to make fundamental changes. What problem is the technology solving - is it safety, creation of time, reduction of pollution, freeing of capital or all of the above? Are we consciously deciding to relinquish century old freedom for the

---

368

http://content.time.com/time/magazine/article/0,9171,2033076,00.html

greater good or are we rushing headlong into an Orwellian 1984 scenario?

In many ways, the car with its associated activities and technologies, is the most powerful product or system there has been over the last century or so. More than that, it has defined how and where we live and work. If driverless cars represent progress, they cannot turn the clock back and the individual flexibility, comfort and convenience that the car provides, yet they must somehow solve the problems that cars created. And there's the very real risk that even if driverless cars solve some problems, they may create or exacerbate others - if transport is easier, safer and cheaper, will there be more of it? Could we see improved safety but increased congestion? And if we do, is that a positive outcome?

Automation

"Live out of your imagination, not your history"

Stephen Covey

The role of machines in our world is fundamentally changing as their abilities evolve. After decades of anticipation, they are finally starting to learn on their own. They've learned to understand what we say (e.g. Amazon Alexa/Apple Siri/Google Assistant), identify people in photos (e.g. Facebook) and defeat world champions at games as complex as Go (Deep Mind). Now they're learning to drive, with all that entails outside a closed environment in the real world. After much academic debate and endless fictional scenarios, driverless cars are the first example of in-your-face intelligent, disruptive technology that will impact us all daily.

This debate is surely only the first of many we face in coming years. Disruptive technologies by definition don't respect borders or history. They lack sentiment or morals. When you think about it, we have already silently automated a huge number of tasks. It may have been as simple as having a machine record TV for us. Without automation, many of the things we take for granted would not be possible and modern society would fall apart. Already algorithms decide what offers and adverts we should see. Algorithms buy and sell shares on our behalf - in fact, up to 80% of all stock trades.[369]

But just because we can automate something doesn't mean we should. Yet it's hard to think of something that isn't automated once it's technically possible - it's very hard to put the automation genie back in the bottle, such are the cost savings it usually brings. But the human displacement seems to be increasing with each subsequent generation of technology.

The End/The Beginning

"Let us not be content to wait and see what will happen, but give us the determination to make the right things happen."

Horace Mann

For the past century, our car-centric culture has shaped infrastructure and ideals, landscape and lifestyles, ethics and enterprise. We rely heavily on the mobility that cars provide us with but the car's purpose and meaning change as the driver fades out. When the car drives itself, what we do in the cars will be different. Driverless cars will change our perception of time and space, how we commute, where we live and how we shop. The idea that our lives will be changed by what is still an imperfect, speculative technology, seems unlikely to many people. But so did the idea of mass car ownership in the 1890s. As unlikely as it seemed until recently, the driverless car will undoubtedly be possible in the coming years.

---

[369] http://www.ft.com/intl/cms/s/0/da5d033c-8e1c-11e1-bf8f-00144feab49a.html#axzz1t4qPww6r

Those who see problems are indeed seeing real and substantial challenges. But they are seeing things in the current world. They are not seeing how things could be if we take a different approach. Trying to cram such a revolutionary technology into current thinking will likely not yield an optimal outcome. If we want to harness the potential of driverless cars to its fullest, we will need to make many difficult decisions. We are facing some decisions we may be poorly equipped to take as we reach a point in our evolution where our technical capabilities challenge long-established pillars of our society and threaten social, political and economic change on an unprecedented scale. The reach of emerging technologies will make the Luddite movement of the industrial revolution seem very, very small in nature. And it's not just driverless cars - changes are coming thick and fast - from transport, to health to 3D printing, robots and virtual reality - it's the Hard Wave and we can't assess this change with a mentality of *ceteris paribus* (all else being equal).

The final push towards driverless cars is going to require a massive amount of engineering effort but, more importantly, regulatory and societal accord about acceptable levels of risk (including very sizable risks to a whole swathe of human employment). Technology, regulation, legal, commercial and political systems all move at different paces and that's not necessarily a bad thing. But when they end up too far out of sync, things can get complicated. Ultimately, this may well be a 50-year play. But that's still twice as fast as cars took to take over. Even though creating a functioning autonomous car may count among technology's greatest achievements, it is undoubtedly the human elements that are the most complex - drivers, pedestrians, the winners, the losers and policy makers.

The car has brought untold freedom, development and progress. Yet the car has stolen time, money and lives from us. If self-driving technology proves to be safe or evolves to be safer than humans, thereby saving as many lives as its supporters hope, we could eventually have a different debate: whether to allow people to drive their own cars at all. Revolutionary technical developments are taking place in the face of entrenched evolutionary social forces. Our grandchildren will probably be appalled when we tell them that once upon a time humans were allowed to pilot these 2-ton death machines. 100 years ago, you could buy heroin in a pharmacy and I suspect that in 100 years' time, the notion of a human controlling a car for daily travel may be just as ridiculous. Another way of looking at it is to consider how future generations will talk about current generation - will we be seen as the generation who had technology at their disposal to address world-changing issues and chose to delay action?

Bryan Reimer, the associate director of the New England Transportation Center at MIT, says autonomous vehicles will change everything. *"It changes how we move. It changes how packages are moved. It changes how we behave. It changes the future of old age. It changes everything. But there are going to be some difficult growing pains along the way. They're policy, they're societal." "Now the real core question becomes: Do we move and continue down a society built upon vehicle ownership, or do we move to one that is based upon ridesharing? But that's against the basic culture that has existed in this country for decades."*[370]

As I've spent more time examining driverless cars, it's become clear to me that the driverless future will have huge impacts on our daily lives, our economy and, maybe even on the very power and wealth structures of the world. The adoption of driverless cars, as it almost inevitably happens in the coming decade(s) will change everything in almost every sphere - choices for consumers, the nature of work, the value of property, the fortunes of companies and, ultimately, the fate of cities and even nations. But it's not a simple decision. Transportation choices

---

[370] http://www.wbur.org/bostonomix/2016/04/29/traffic-future-driverless-cars

are never purely rational ones. Habit, myth, culture, inertia, and lifestyle can and do trump logic, practicality and efficiency in transportation. There's no certainty that a rational decision to remove humans from driving will happen. Can it happen? Absolutely. Will it happen? That's uncertain - probably, eventually, it will. But should it happen? There are plenty of reasons it couldn't work but there are more than a million reasons a year why it must.

Reading & References

Books:

I've included links here to Books I found useful in my research:

Amazon

Amazon

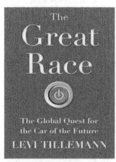

Amazon

Amazon

Amazon

Amazon

Amazon

Amazon

Amazon

Amazon

Amazon

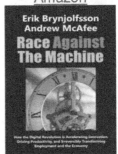

Amazon

Amazon

Amazon

Amazon

Amazon

Amazon

Amazon

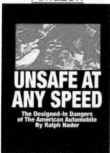

Amazon

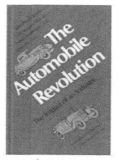

Amazon

Amazon

Amazon

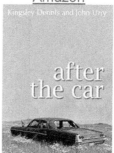

Amazon

Amazon

Amazon

Articles:

These are some additional articles on the topic of Driverless Cars that I'm including for reference, for anyone who wants to read more background material on any topic.

General Driverless Car Articles & Reports

http://www.forbes.com/sites/joannmuller/2013/01/25/will-google-kill-the-auto-industry/

http://cityminded.org/how-will-driverless-cars-affect-our-cities-6526\

http://arstechnica.co.uk/cars/2015/11/tesla-will-restrict-self-driving-autopilot-mode-to-stop-people-doing-crazy-things/

http://www.strategyand.pwc.com/media/file/Connected-car-report-2016.pdf

http://www.sae.org/misc/pdfs/automated_driving.pdf

https://www.bbhub.io/dotorg/sites/2/2017/05/TamingtheAutonomousVehicleSpreadsPDFreleaseMay3rev2.pdf

http://www.vtpi.org/avip.pdf

Apple Letter to DMV, April 2017
https://www.dmv.ca.gov/portal/wcm/connect/15fa2d8e-8732-43c3-9e39-e71ec5e8f9a8/Apple.pdf?MOD=AJPERES

Chapter 2 - The Machine that Changed the World

http://www.slate.com/articles/life/walking/2012/04/why_don_t_americans_walk_more_the_crisis_of_pedestrianism_.html

http://www.techworld.com/personal-tech/huge-impact-driverless-cars-will-have-on-parking-urban-landscapes-3637704/

http://www.digitaltrends.com/cars/traffic-drives-reduced-urban-auto-usage/#ixzz43fDqVfPV

http://www.bbc.com/news/business-35242514

Chapter 3 - Driverless Cars - Really?

Google announce Car:
https://googleblog.blogspot.ie/2010/10/what-were-driving-at.html

http://www.makeuseof.com/tag/how-self-driving-cars-work-the-nuts-and-bolts-behind-googles-autonomous-car-program/

https://techcrunch.com/2017/02/12/wtf-is-lidar/

http://velodynelidar.com/hdl-64e.html

https://www.bloomberg.com/news/articles/2017-05-04/another-group-of-google-veterans-starts-a-self-driving-technology-company

http://www.wsj.com/articles/google-tries-to-make-its-cars-drive-more-like-humans-1443463523

Skill Atrophy:
http://cacm.acm.org/magazines/2016/5/201592-the-challenges-of-partially-automated-driving/fulltext

http://news.stanford.edu/2016/12/06/taking-back-control-autonomous-car-affects-human-steering-behavior/review/

https://arxiv.org/pdf/1704.07911.pdf

https://blogs.nvidia.com/blog/2017/04/27/how-nvidias-neural-net-makes-decisions/

https://www.technologyreview.com/s/601567/tesla-tests-self-driving-functions-with-secret-updates-to-its-customers-cars/

http://www.engadget.com/2016/01/11/ford-is-testing-autonomous-cars-in-the-snow/
http://www.engadget.com/2015/11/13/ford-first-self-driving-mcity-michigan/

https://www.dmv.ca.gov/portal/dmv/detail/vr/autonomous/diseng agement_report_2016

If you want to understand more about the technicalities of SDC Computer Vision, there's a massively detailed review of computer vision. https://arxiv.org/pdf/1704.05519.pdf

Chapter 4 - Safety

Cost of crashes:
http://www.rmiia.org/auto/traffic_safety/Cost_of_crashes.asp
http://www.who.int/mediacentre/factsheets/fs358/en/
http://www.ncbi.nlm.nih.gov/pmc/articles/PMC2610566/

http://www.nytimes.com/2016/05/23/science/its-no-accident-advocates-want-to-speak-of-car-crashes-instead.html?_r=0

Chapter 5 - All Change

http://www.wsj.com/articles/could-self-driving-cars-spell-the-end-of-ownership-1448986572

http://www.bloomberg.com/news/articles/2016-09-11/self-driving-cars-to-cut-u-s-insurance-premiums-40-aon-says

http://www.wsj.com/articles/will-the-driverless-car-upend-insurance-1425428891

https://www.wsj.com/articles/driverless-cars-threaten-to-crash-insurers-earnings-1469542958

http://www.datakind.org/projects/creating-safer-streets-through-data-science/

https://twitter.com/BenedictEvans/status/721484633351696384?replies_view=true&cursor=ARAUhOE6Awo

https://techcrunch.com/2015/10/30/ride-sharing-will-give-us-back-our-cities/

http://dupress.deloitte.com/dup-us-en/focus/future-of-mobility/roadmap-for-future-of-urban-mobility.html?id=us:2el:3pr:prwhatnext:eng:cons:091516

https://www.planning.org/planning/2015/may/autonomouscars.htm

http://www.uspirg.org/news/usp/new-report-shows-mounting-evidence-millennials%E2%80%99-shift-away-driving

http://www.slate.com/articles/business/the_juice/2014/07/driving_vs_flying_which_is_more_harmful_to_the_environment.html

Chapter 6 - Challenges

http://www.wsj.com/articles/driverless-cars-to-fuel-suburban-sprawl-1466395201

https://www.washingtonpost.com/news/energy-environment/wp/2016/06/23/save-the-driver-or-save-the-crowd-scientists-wonder-how-driverless-cars-will-choose/?utm_term=.4d4d2f0dad4c

http://philosophicaldisquisitions.blogspot.ie/2017/04/the-ethics-of-crash-optimisation.html

https://www.wired.com/2017/03/make-us-safer-robocars-will-sometimes-kill/

http://www.wired.com/2016/06/self-driving-cars-will-power-kill-wont-conscience/?mbid=nl_6916

Tumbleweeds example coverage:
http://www.ft.com/intl/cms/s/0/e698c396-8d61-11e5-8be4-3506bf20cc2b.html?siteedition=uk#axzz3rtZYwi9N

http://www.express.co.uk/life-style/cars/620296/self-driving-cars-could-be-stopped-by-tumbleweed-technology-problems

Employment: https://techcrunch.com/2016/08/18/dropping-off-drivers/

https://www.wired.com/2017/01/nissans-self-driving-teleoperation/

https://www.bloomberg.com/news/articles/2017-04-17/will-autonomous-driving-kill-the-sports-car

http://www.wired.com/2016/03/self-driving-cars-wont-work-change-roads-attitudes/?mbid=nl_31516

http://www.nlc.org/article/new-autonomous-vehicle-guide-helps-cities-prepare-for-a-driverless-future

http://www.nctr.usf.edu/wp-content/uploads/2016/11/Implications-for-Public-Transit-of-Emerging-Technologies-11-1-16.pdf

http://globalpolicysolutions.org/wp-content/uploads/2017/03/Stick-Shift-Autonomous-Vehicles.pdf

https://www.technologyreview.com/s/607841/a-single-autonomous-car-has-a-huge-impact-on-alleviating-traffic/

Chapter 7 - Regulation & Acceptance

https://www.transportation.gov/AV/federal-automated-vehicles-policy-september-2016

https://www.scientificamerican.com/article/when-it-comes-to-safety-autonomous-cars-are-still-teen-drivers1/#

http://www.newsweek.com/when-will-we-know-self-driving-cars-are-safe-501270

http://www.huffingtonpost.com/entry/how-safe-are-self-driving-cars_us_5908ba48e4b03b105b44bc6b?ncid=engmodushpmg00000004

http://www.reuters.com/article/us-germany-autos-self-driving-idUSKBN1881HY

http://techcrunch.com/2016/01/28/security-and-privacy-standards-are-critical-to-the-success-of-connected-cars/

https://techcrunch.com/2016/11/06/why-the-department-of-transportations-self-driving-car-guidelines-arent-enough/

https://electrek.co/2016/10/19/elon-musk-says-the-media-is-killing-people-when-writing-negative-articles-about-self-driving-cars/

http://readwrite.com/2017/05/07/responsible-autonomous-car-regulations-tl1/

https://www.enotrans.org/wp-content/uploads/2015/09/AV-paper.pdf

http://www.lexology.com/library/detail.aspx?g=43194ac7-9d44-46f5-9e4c-9c759f8e3641

https://www.bloomberg.com/amp/news/articles/2017-05-16/waymo-s-next-challenge-making-driverless-passengers-feels-safe

http://newsroom.aaa.com/2017/03/americans-feel-unsafe-sharing-road-fully-self-driving-cars/

https://www.fastcompany.com/40419374/the-future-of-autonomous-vehicles-relies-on-middle-america

Negative articles include:
http://www.computerworld.com/article/2599426/emerging-technology/did-you-know-googles-self-driving-cars-cant-handle-99-of-roads-in-the-us.html

https://www.technologyreview.com/s/530276/hidden-obstacles-for-googles-self-driving-cars/

https://www.theguardian.com/commentisfree/2016/dec/15/the-guardian-view-on-self-driving-cars-apply-the-brakes

https://www.nytimes.com/2016/12/19/opinion/google-wants-driverless-cars-but-do-we.html?_r=0

Blogs:

A selection of blogs on the topic of Driverless cars:

http://penguindreams.org/blog/self-driving-cars-will-not-solve-the-transportation-problem/#

http://utilware.com/autonomous.html

http://ideas.4brad.com/rodney-brooks-pedestrian-interaction-andrew-ng-infrastructure-and-both-human-attitudes

https://medium.com/@alexrubalcava/a-roadmap-for-a-world-without-drivers-573aede0c968

http://www.newgeography.com/content/005024-preparing-impact-driverless-cars

http://blog.piekniewski.info/2017/05/11/a-car-safety-myths-and-facts/

https://medium.com/@christianhern/self-driving-cars-as-the-new-toolbar-8c8a47a3c598

https://backchannel.com/self-driving-cars-will-improve-our-cities-if-they-dont-ruin-them-2dc920345618#.4va0brsyg

Videos:

A selection of Videos on the topic of Driverless cars:

Video of Tesla Auto pilot -
https://thescene.com/watch/arstechnica/cars-technica-hands-on-with-tesla-s-autopilot

https://youtu.be/tiwVMrTLUWg **(15 Minute TED Talk by Chris Urmson of Google, 2015)**

Made in the USA
Middletown, DE
02 February 2021